THE BOOKS OF

JAMES &
fIRST
AND
SECOND
PETER

fAITH, SUffERING,
AND KNOWLEDGE

AMG *Publishers*
CHATTANOOGA, TENNESSEE

TWENTY-FIRST CENTURY
BIBLICAL COMMENTARY SERIES

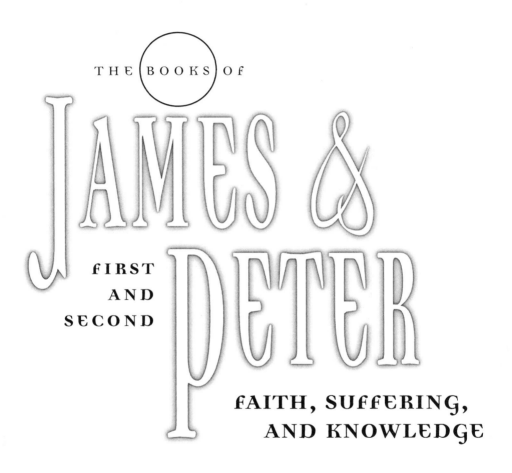

THE BOOKS OF

JAMES &

FIRST
AND
SECOND

PETER

FAITH, SUFFERING,
AND KNOWLEDGE

WILLIAM
BAKER

GENERAL EDITORS

MAL COUCH & ED HINDSON

Copyright © 2004 by Tyndale Theological Seminary
Published by AMG Publishers
6815 Shallowford Road
Chattanooga, TN 37421

ISBN 0-89957-816-0

Cover Design by Market Street Design
Interior Design and Typesetting by Warren Baker
Edited and Proofread by Warren Baker, Patrick Belvill, and Weller Editorial Services, Chippewa Lake, MI

Printed in the United States of America
08 07 06 05 04 –R– 7 6 5 4 3 2

Twenty-First Century Biblical Commentary Series

Mal Couch, Th.D., and Ed Hindson, D.Phil.

The New Testament has guided the Christian Church for over two thousand years. This one testament is made up of twenty-seven books, penned by godly men through the inspiration of the Holy Spirit. It tells us of the life of Jesus Christ, His atoning death for our sins, His miraculous resurrection, His ascension back to heaven, and the promise of His second coming. It also tells the story of the birth and growth of the Church and the people and principles that shaped it in its earliest days. The New Testament concludes with the book of Revelation pointing ahead to the glorious return of Jesus Christ.

Without the New Testament, the message of the Bible would be incomplete. The Old Testament emphasizes the promise of a coming Messiah. It constantly points us ahead to the One who is coming to be the King of Israel and the Savior of the world. But the Old Testament ends with this event still unfulfilled. All of its ceremonies, pictures, types, and prophecies are left awaiting the arrival of the "Lamb of God who takes away the sin of the world!" (John 1:29).

The message of the New Testament represents the timeless truth of God. As each generation seeks to apply that truth to its specific context, an up-to-date commentary needs to be created just for them. The editors and authors of the Twenty-First Century Biblical Commentary Series have endeavored to do just that. This team of scholars represents conservative, evangelical, and dispensational scholarship at its best. The individual authors may differ on minor points of interpretation, but all are convinced that the Old and New Testaments teach a dispensational framework for biblical history. They also hold to a pretribulational and premillennial understanding of biblical prophecy.

The French scholar René Pache reminded each succeeding generation, "If the power of the Holy Spirit is to be made manifest anew among us, it is of primary importance that His message should regain its due place. Then we shall be able to put the enemy to flight by the sword of the Spirit which is the Word of God."

The letters of Peter and James reflect the heart of apostolic Christianity. They defend the faith, warn the faithful, and encourage the flock of God. In an era when the relevance of the Christian faith is often questioned, these powerful letters continue to speak loudly to our own times. These two giants of the apostolic church, Peter and James, have something to say to our generation that we dare not miss.

Michael Green argues: "So long as sin needs to be exposed, so long as man needs to be reminded that persistent wrongdoing ends in ruin, that lust is self-defeating, that intellectualism devoid of love is a barren thing, and that Christian theology has no right to outrun the faith once delivered to the saints, these Epistles will remain uncomfortably, burningly relevant."

Contents

The Book of James—Working Faith

The Book of First Peter—Godly Suffering

I. The Resources for Suffering

II. The Relationships for Suffering

III. The Attitudes for Suffering

The Book of Second Peter–Effective Knowledge of God

THE BOOK OF JAMES

Working Faith

CHAPTER 1

Background of James

Bible students often avoid the book of James because they think it is too difficult to interpret. But a second look at this little epistle cuts through the controversy and reveals a blessed portion of the written Word of God. James puts feet to the Christian walk, urging the child of God to focus on living out what he or she believes. In a sense, James deals with the "primitive" aspects of New Testament faith. Although the book does contain some doctrinal teaching, James does not deal with heavy doctrinal issues. Rather, he deals in a straightforward manner with temptation, anger, immorality, the tongue, prejudice, partiality, hypocritical teachers, jealously, lust, humility, trusting God, conviction of sin, self-justification, confession of sin, and more. One cannot read James without experiencing a strong tug of conviction.

James and the Canon of Scripture

Because on the surface James seemed to contradict Paul's doctrine of justification by faith, and because the book appeared to be so "Jewish" in nature, it was not universally endorsed by the early church. I am not saying that it was rejected across all church lines, because it was not. However, there was much discussion about the book until around A.D. 397 and the Third Council of Carthage, when it was generally accepted as inspired and a part of the New Testament.

James may be the most Jewish book in the New Testament, even above Matthew, Hebrews, and the book of Revelation. Some have said that, minus the few references to the Lord Jesus, the book might appear to be part of the Old Testament canon. This cannot be said of any other writing in the New Testament. The Christianity of James is not so much its subject matter as it is its spirit. "It is an interpretation of the Old Testament law and the Sermon on the Mount in the light of the Christian gospel."[1]

The noncanonical book The Shepherd of Hermas seems to quote James 4:7 and 5:1-4. James is also alluded to in The Epistle of Barnabas and Testaments of the Twelve Patriarchs, and in the early writings of the church fathers Clement of Rome, Polycarp, Origen, Cyril of Jerusalem, Athanasius, Jerome, and Augustine.

Who Wrote James?

The internal and external evidence is strong that the book of James was authored by the half-brother of Jesus. This seems to be affirmed by the Jewish historian Josephus (*Antiquities* 20.9), from the book of Acts (15:13-21; 21:17-25), from Galatians (1:19; 2:9-10), and from what is known of the problems of the Christian Jews in the dispersion from Jerusalem.

Four New Testament men have the name James. (1) the son of Alphaeus (Matt. 10:3), possibly known also as the Less or the Little (Mark 15:40), (2) the son of Zebedee (Matt. 4:21), (3) the father of the apostle Judas, not Iscariot (Luke 6:16), (4) and the Lord's brother (Matt. 13:55; Gal. 1:19).

The first two are more than likely discounted. The last two were apostles. Since the book of James begins with, "James, a bond-servant of God and of the Lord Jesus Christ," which one would this be pointing to? The early church probably knew for certain, and it would be most likely that they accepted the epistle realizing that the author was related to Christ.

Since James the son of Zebedee was martyred under the reign of Herod Agrippa I, no later than A.D. 44, and since the content makes it unlikely that he would have authored such a letter before that date, the apostle is ruled out as the author of James. All evidence then focuses on Jesus' half brother James. Jesus and James shared the same mother but not the same father (Matt. 13:55). James was probably the one who sought to speak with Christ in Galilee (Matt. 12:46), was with Him at Capernaum (John 2:12), tried to persuade the Lord to go up to the Feast of Tabernacles (John 7:3), was early an unbeliever (John 7:5), and remained with his mother in Jerusalem after the crucifixion.[2]

Jesus appeared to this James after the resurrection (1 Cor. 15:7). This James was in the company who was waiting for the coming of the Holy Spirit (Acts 1:14) and helped select Matthias to take the place of Judas (vv. 15-25).

Occasion and Date

Most evangelical scholars place the date of the book at around A.D. 45, just before the Jerusalem Council (Acts 15; A.D. 48-49). The issue before this meeting was the admission of Gentiles into the church and the practical implications of doing so. This makes sense, because the subject of Gentile believers is not brought up in James's epistle. And again, there is the Judaic tone throughout the book, emphasizing the Law, though not with the hyper-legalistic interpretation taught by the Pharisees. In fact, the Law is retitled by the apostle "the royal law" (2:8) and the "law of liberty" (1:25; 2:12). Obviously James saw the Law differently under the bright light of grace declared so clearly in the gospel itself.

In this epistle, James writes that he is addressing "the twelve tribes who are dispersed abroad" (1:1). He was speaking to believing Jews who were part of the early Diaspora throughout the Mediterranean region. The gospel had traveled quickly out of Jerusalem by the many Jewish pilgrims who were there for Passover when the Lord Jesus had been crucified and come forth from the grave. The news of this event traveled fast to the synagogues throughout the Roman world, and many Jews realized that Jesus was their promised King and Savior. It appears that James's audience had been believers for some time.

Characteristics

Certain things about the book of James stand in sharp contrast to other New Testament letters. (1) Nearly every verse is an imperative. The author does not mince words about the need for Christian living. (2) The work has a decisive tone of authority, yet it does not bully the readers. In fact, James often calls the recipients "brethren." (3) Hard doctrinal issues are not part of the book. There is no teaching on redemption or the resurrection of Christ, though Christian sanctification is strong in the epistle. (4) The letter is eminently practical about the Christian walk. (5) The epistle is impersonal in that no one specific believer is referred to. (6) More is written about nature in this work than in most other letters. (7) Less is written about Christ directly, but the book contains principles similar to those in the Sermon on the Mount. (8) Some have compared James's letter with the wisdom literature of the Old Testament because of its emphasis on spiritual living. (9) The Greek of James is of a high quality, comparing favorably with Hebrews and 1 Peter, and it has a high percentage of words peculiar to itself among New Testament writings.[3]

Important Words and Concepts

James repeats certain words and ideas often. Most expressions have practical implications in view. James applies spirituality and law in the proper way to living the Christian life. He proves that this dispensation of grace, or the church age, is not antinomian, or without rules and authority. While the church is not *under* the sway of the Mosaic Law as a system, that legal code and its eternal moral expression still stands as a test and a guide for living. Yet it is not in conflict with carrying out the Christian walk by the principles of grace. The following words give insight into this Christian experience.

- *Endurance, patience*
- *An effectual doer, doers of the word, doer of the law*
- *Faith without works is dead*
- *Brother, brethren*
- *Hear, hearer*
- *The law*

    the whole law

    the perfect law

    the royal law

    the law of liberty

    the doer of the law

The Quoting of the Law by James

Early church history described James as "old camel knees" because of his prayer life and his deep piety. As a godly Jew, he honored the Law of Moses and did his best to obey it. Yet, there is no indication that he ever placed the Law over grace. Instead, he used it to demonstrate the demands of morality expressed in it. Dispensationalists certainly understand this. While believers today are not under Law as a system, many moral and spiritual lessons can be learned from its commands and instructions. Besides referring indirectly to the Law in many passages, James also quotes it directly in three verses:

Love your neighbor as yourself (2:8 cf. Lev. 19:18).

Do not commit adultery (2:11 cf. Ex. 20:14).

Do not commit murder (2:11 cf. Ex. 20:13).

Besides the Law, James also alludes to many other Old Testament passages. He speaks of care for widows and orphans (1:27 cf. Deut. 14:29; Job 31:16–17), Abraham's offering up of Isaac (2:21 cf. Gen. 22:9–12), Abraham's belief in God and his justification (2:23 cf. Gen. 15:6), Rahab the harlot and her faith (2:25 cf. Josh. 2:4–15), the poison of the tongue (3:8 cf. Ps. 140:3), the seed whose fruit is righteousness (3:18 cf. Prov. 11:18), drawing near to God (4:8 cf. 2 Chr. 15:2), the need for humility (4:10 cf. Job 5:11), God as the Lawgiver and Judge (4:11 cf. Isa. 33:22), and finally, the patience and endurance of Job (5:11 cf. Job 1:21–22; 42:10–17). James, with the eye of an artist, weaves Old Testament truth skillfully into the fabric of New Testament principles.

The Commands for Christian Living

Since James is the book of *doing* the Christian life, the book is full of imperatives. James wants believers in Christ to be living what he is adhering to. He puts it this way: "Prove yourselves doers of the word, and not merely hearers who delude themselves" (James 1:22), and "faith without works is dead" (2:26). James is not arguing for a form of works sanctification; rather, he is putting forth a dynamic belief and trust that can be tested by actions. Lest one think this is a cover for legalism, James makes it clear that grace living can be accomplished by spiritual humility. He quotes Psalm 138:6, God "gives a greater grace. Therefore [the Scripture] says, 'God is opposed to the proud, but gives grace to the humble'" (4:6). Relying on Him makes it possible to live a victorious life. The commands of James are these:

James 1

- *Consider it all joy.*
- *Let endurance have its perfect result.*
- *Ask God if you lack wisdom.*
- *Ask in faith.*
- *Let the double-minded not expect anything from the Lord.*
- *Let the humble have glory; let the rich have humiliation.*
- *Let the tempted not say he is tempted of God.*
- *Do not be deceived about your temptation.*
- *Be quick to hear; slow to speak; slow to anger.*
- *Receive the word implanted.*
- *Prove yourselves doers of the word, and not mere hearers.*

James 2

- *Do not show favoritism.*
- *Listen, God chose the poor of this world to be rich in faith.*
- *So speak and so act [what you believe].*

James 3

- *Let not many become teachers...*
- *Behold, the ships . . .*
- *Behold, how great a forest is set aflame by such a small fire!*
- *Do not be arrogant.*

James 4

- *Do not think the Scripture speaks to no purpose.*
- *Submit therefore to God.*
- *Resist the devil.*
- *Draw near to God.*
- *Cleanse your hands.*
- *Purify your hearts.*
- *Be miserable [in looking at your sins].*
- *Mourn and weep [over your sins].*
- *Let your laughter be turned into mourning, and your joy to gloom.*
- *Humble yourselves in the presence of God.*
- *Do not speak against one another.*
- *Come now and do not say, "Today or tomorrow" we shall do such and such.*
- *You ought to say, "If the Lord wills."*

James 5

- *You rich, howl for your miseries that are coming upon you.*
- *Behold, the pay you withheld from the laborers...*
- *Be patient until the coming of the Lord.*
- *Be patient, strengthen your hearts.*
- *Do not complain against each other.*
- *Count those blessed who endure.*
- *Do not swear, either by heaven or by earth.*
- *Let your yes be yes, and your no, no.*
- *Let him pray who is suffering.*
- *Let him who is cheerful sing praises.*

- *Let the sick call for the elders.*
- *Let the elders pray over the sick, anointing him with oil.*
- *Confess your sins to one another.*
- *Let him know that he who turns back a sinner will save his soul from death.*

Justification by Faith/Justification by Works

Much controversy has surrounded James 2:14–26 and the issue of *justification by works.* Because of Paul's clear teaching about *justification by faith* (Gal. 3—4; Rom. 3—5), many throughout church history have felt there is a contradiction between Paul and the apostle James. In fact, Martin Luther came close to rejecting the epistle outright as a contradictory work that could not hold up to the writings of Paul. Luther said in his 1522 introduction to his first edition to the German New Testament that James was "a right strawy epistle in comparison with [Paul's writings], for it has no gospel character to it." John MacArthur adds:

> The great Reformer was by no means denying the inspiration of James (as his phrase "in comparison with them" indicates). Nevertheless, his disparaging remarks about the epistle have been echoed by many throughout the history of the church. In fact, due to its brevity, the fact that it was addressed specifically to Jewish Christians, its lack of doctrinal content, and because it was not written by one of the twelve apostles or Paul, James was one of the last books added to the New Testament canon. But such downplaying of the value of James is shortsighted. Luther had little use for James because it contains little teaching about the great doctrines of the Christian faith that he so passionately defended.[4]

James 2:14–26 must be studied carefully to understand the point James is making. But there are clear indicators that show that the apostle is not arguing for works salvation. When he writes about the needy brother or sister, he points out that just saying "Go in peace, be warmed and filled," does not help when the body has certain needs (2:16). Believers must respond to their brothers and sisters in charity. Empty words are meaningless. So, "faith if it has no works, is dead, being by itself" (v. 17). The point James is making is that belief and faith on the *experience* level must perform in order to be seen as genuine.

James further says, "I will show you my faith by my works" (v. 18), and even the demons have an "intellectual" belief about God (v. 19). Thus, for living the Christian life, "faith without works is useless" (v. 20). The example that James then uses is about how faith is seen before human witnesses.

Abraham in Genesis 22 was *justified by works* in the offering of his son Isaac because his trust in God was seen openly by that son and by the servants who saw the drama acted out before their very eyes (James 2:21). James then adds, "Faith was working with his works, and as a result of the works, faith was perfected [matured, made complete]" (v. 22).

In summary, James says that a man is justified by works *before others*, but before God (as with Abraham), one is justified by faith and belief, and made righteous in a *positional* and heavenly sense (v. 23). R. C. H. Lenski writes:

> Trust in works of law is the direct opposite of faith in Christ alone. James deals with gospel works, which ever evidence the presence of gospel faith, which, like this faith, glorify Christ alone, without which all claim of having true faith is spurious, a self-delusion. Both James and Paul attribute salvation to a living faith (Mark 16:16; John 3:16). . . . Paul roots out what destroys and excludes faith; James stimulates sluggish faith. The two are in perfect agreement; in the ethical parts of all his epistles Paul, too, calls for the fruits of faith.[5]

Section I

Working Faith Tested

James 1:1–18

CHAPTER 2

Faith Tested by Trials
James 1:1–12

Preview:

James focuses on practical issues in the Christian life, such as testing, endurance, double-mindedness, and instability. He urges the rich to practice humility because life is short and wealth does not satisfy. A crown of life is given to those who persevere under trials.

The letter of James opens by its author identifying himself modestly, though he was the half brother of Jesus and the leader of the venerable Jerusalem church—an otherwise prestigious claim—as simply "a bond-servant of God and of the Lord Jesus Christ." He does not refer to himself as an apostle, although this office is implied by the apostle Paul in Galatians 1:19 in the words, "But other of the apostles saw I none, save James the Lord's brother" (KJV). Since James was not among the twelve apostles chosen during Jesus' lifetime, and since Paul refers to "the twelve" as that distinct group (1 Cor. 15:5) even when Judas was absent, we are probably safe in inferring that Jesus chose additional apostles during his resurrection appearances or sometime after his ascension to heaven, as in the case of Paul.

The addressees are referred to as "the twelve tribes who are dispersed abroad." "Dispersed abroad" is the translation of the Greek word *diaspora*, from which we also get the English word *dispersion*. This dispersion was likely due to persecution connected ultimately with the one initiated by Saul of Tarsus (Acts, later to be known more widely as the apostle Paul. The opening discussion (1:2–12) dealing with trials reinforces this conclusion. This makes James one of the principal authors to deal with the believer's trials along with

Peter in his first epistle (1 Pet. 1:6–7). The stage is set, therefore, in these opening words for the passage that follows.

James opens his exhortation with the words, "Consider it all joy, my
brethren, when you encounter various trials." When James, like Paul, uses
the address form "brethren," he means both male and female believers,
although the Greek *adelphoi* ordinarily means "brothers." The readers are to
"consider it" a joyful thing. This language implies that although it is not a
joyful thing, they are personally to regard it as something joyful. How is this
possible? "Joy" in New Testament usage is distinct from "happiness." As E.
Beyreuther puts it, "This joy has its source beyond mere earthly, human joy.
It is joy *en kuriō*, in the Lord, and therefore outside ourselves."[1] In other
words, joy is a deep, inner confidence in God to work all things together for
good (Rom. 8:28), while happiness depends on circumstances. In the words
"all joy," the word "all" is used intensively to mean "pure" or "sheer" joy.
Seeing God work in trials is the purest form of joy, as anyone who has suffered can testify.

James's readers are to count it as joy when they "encounter various trials."
The word picture is of someone falling into a pit unexpectedly and not by
one's own fault. It refers to a problem or suffering that comes simply because
of the evil world in which we live. The term *various* implies that there are a
large variety of trials. The Greek word *pierasmois* can refer to what we in
English would call "trials" as well as what we would call "temptations" in the
sense of solicitation to evil, the way it is used in James 1:13. The context determines which is the case. What the two have in common is that in both trials
and temptations there is a temptation not to trust God. In *trials* we are tempted not to trust God for the outcome, while in *temptations* we are tempted not
to wait for God to meet the need the temptation may represent.

The reason we can "consider it all joy" follows in 1:3. It is because we can
know that the trying of our faith "produces endurance" (NIV, "perseverance";
KJV, "patience"). The literal meaning of this word in the original is "to abide
under." One, therefore, who has patience is able to remain under a potential
threat without panicking. When faith is tested, we are faced with trying some
solution of our own or simply trusting God. If we trust God, the experience
leads to greater ability to repeat the experience when other tests come.
Endurance, in turn, leads to our becoming "perfect and complete." The word
perfect in contexts like this is better translated "mature," and this is maturity
in the sense of a state of progress toward a goal. "Complete" here means "fully
equipped," prepared better to endure further trials consistently by trusting
God implicitly.

> ## New Testament Testing (dokimazō)
>
> Prove *what the will of God is* (Rom. 2:18).
>
> *Happy is he who does not condemn himself in what he* approves (Rom. 14:22).
>
> *Fire will* test *the quality of each man's work* (1 Cor. 3:13b).
>
> *Let a man* examine *himself* (1 Cor. 11:28).
>
> *Let each one* examine *his own work* (Gal. 6:4).
>
> *That you may* approve *the things that are excellent* (Phil. 1:10)
>
> *God* examines *our hearts* (1 Thess. 2:4).
>
> Examine *everything carefully* (1 Thess. 5:21).
>
> *The proof of your faith may be* tested *by [persecution] fire* (1 Pet. 1:7).
>
> Test *the spirits* (1 John 4:1).

James 1:5 seems to shift to another thought, but it is actually closely related to enduring trials. "But if any of you lacks wisdom," James adds, "let him ask of God, who gives to all men generously and without reproach, and it will be given to him." What does wisdom have to do with enduring trials? It may refer to some solution or answer to the trial, or it may pertain to the wisdom to trust God. I lean toward the latter, because in the case of the classic trial of Job, no solutions or explanations were given to Job regarding his trial. Instead, God taught him why it was wise to trust Him without knowing why his suffering was taking place. God will help the individual know what course of action is the most "trusting," if indeed some decision to act is required. However, trusting God often means doing nothing at all—simply waiting on God. That God does not reproach us means that God will not find fault with us. God delights in encouraging us to trust Him, for one of the major goals of the Christian life is dependence on God.

However, James warns us that the request for wisdom must itself be made in faith, for the whole process is a test of faith, and tests of faith require the *exercise* of faith. What follows is an interesting illustration of a person who doubts. James describes the "surf of the sea driven and tossed by the wind" (1:6). This points to a frustrating instability, the picture of a person vacillating between faith and doubt. This person will receive nothing from the Lord, except, of course, whatever divine discipline is necessary to get the believer to wake up and repent. Faith is the absolute requirement for God's doing anything for a person. The second illustration James uses is "double-mindedness." Literally, James says, a "two-souled man," a concept probably drawn from the Old Testament ideal of the "undivided heart" (Deut. 6:5)[2] with its opposite, the hypocritical or double heart (Ps. 12:1–2; 1 Chr. 12:33). Double-mindedness comes from neglect of spiritual disciplines, such as prayer, Bible study, meditation, and fellowship, which results in a gradual drift from God. When a crisis comes, a double-minded person wants to believe but is tortured by doubts.

Once again, it appears that James is changing the subject in 1:9–11; however, the "but"[3] that opens the paragraph points us back to what he has been saying. Furthermore, James returns clearly to the subject of trials in verse 12. Here in verses 9–11 he is about to add another reason for considering it all joy when we enter various trials. This reason involves the way we look at our material possessions. Indeed, our view of material possessions is a barometer of our spiritual vitality. This may appear a bit subtle, but the point seems to be that if the brother of humble means realizes his spiritual wealth and the brother of material wealth appreciates the humility that brought him to repentance and faith—and thus the same spiritual wealth—both have genuine reason to rejoice in trials. There is common ground now between both classes due to the gospel and a freedom from worldly concern that might stifle the exercise of faith.

Wealth is relatively temporary, James reminds us (1:10b–11). The figure James employs is familiar to those who live in the semi-desert climate of Palestine. Persons of means are like the desert flowers that bloom readily but remain but a short span of time and become withered by the scorching desert sun. This provides readers with further incentive to disregard the pursuit of wealth in and of itself and provide themselves the freedom from materialism so essential to faith by putting material things in their proper place as mere means to an end.

James 1:12 is the conclusion of this whole section in the form of the final outcome. "Blessed is a man who perseveres under trial, for once he has been approved, he will receive the crown of life, which the Lord has promised to those who love Him." The word *perseveres* is the verb form of the earlier word "endurance" (1:4), which James says the trial of faith will produce. In other words, the exercise of faith produces endurance that in turn enables the person to endure further trial. At the end of this process, he or she becomes "approved," a word that was used of anything that successfully passed a test. A modern equivalent would be the inspection and approval of an automobile that completed the assembly line, ready to be shipped to the dealer. The word is Paul's favorite for divine approval; thus the picture is probably of the judgment seat of Christ (see 1 Cor. 3:10–15; 2 Cor. 5:10). Rewards are granted at that time, symbolized here by the "crown of life." Attempts to distinguish between the various crowns referred to in Scripture (2 Tim. 4:8; Rev. 4:4; 6:2; 12:1) tend to take what is probably symbolic as literal. I prefer the symbolic view, since crowns themselves are symbolic of something in general usage. For example, the crown a monarch wears on festive occasions is a symbol of his authority. The crown of life in this passage simply refers to the goal of the Christian life having been reached successfully. We probably cannot image the precise nature of our rewards, for they will be related to things beyond our present experience.

Study Questions

1. Why does James say that testing is actually good for the believer?

2. What should God's children do when they realize they lack godly wisdom?

3. What is promised to Christians when they persevere under trials?

4. What does it mean to "be approved" after a believer has been tested?

5. Compare the "crown of life" (v. 12) with what Paul writes about running the race in 1 Corinthians 9:24–25.

6. In verse 12, what does loving the Lord have to do with receiving the reward of the crown of life?

CHAPTER 3

Faith Tested by Temptation
James 1:13–18

Preview:

James reminds his readers to understand that trials come from God in order to strengthen the believer. Temptation takes place when the child of God is carried away and enticed by his or her own lust; however, the Christian should not be deceived when under temptation. Every good thing and every perfect gift comes from God, who does not change or shift in His ways.

Although James continues in 1:13–18 with the same Greek word he began with in 1:2, translated there by both NASB and NIV as "trials," it is appropriate in verse 13 to render it as "tempted." Recall from chapter 1 that the semantic range of the Greek word covers both trials that come upon us as well as temptations to disobey one of God's laws. Beginning with James 1:13, the meaning is clarified by the words "tempted by evil." The issue now is not those apparently random occasions on which we suffer because we live in an evil world, but a straightforward solicitation to evil.

Verse 13 immediately arrests our attention: "Let no one say when he is tempted, 'I am tempted by God.'" God is involved in the trials of 1:2–12 at least to the extent of using circumstances for which he is not the immediate cause in order to produce the fruit of tested faith. This, however, is not a trial but a temptation, and temptation is an inward thing, while trials come from the outside. Why would anyone say such a thing? The answer: to blame God who is sovereign and therefore must have brought about the circumstances of the temptation. This is a twist on the excuse "The devil made me do it," except here it means "God got me into this situation, and since I am weak, he is to blame if I fail to resist." This is not an uncommon attitude when the person tempted really wants an excuse for enjoying some sin. The same individual probably hopes that because of God's graciousness, God will not be too hard on him or her in judgment.

New Testament Words to Describe the Problem of Sin

To test as with evil intention to make one fall (pirazō)

Christ was tempted of the devil (Matt. 4:1).

The devil is called "the tempter" (Matt. 4:3).

The Spirit of God can be "tempted" (Acts 5:9).

God can be tempted (Acts 15:10).

Satan can tempt the believer to fall (1 Cor. 7:5).

God will not allow His own to be tempted beyond what one can endure (1 Cor. 10:13).

To sin as missing the moral mark God has set (hamartanō)

Sin can be against heaven (Luke 15:18).

Sin can be against Christ (1 Cor. 8:12).

Sin can be against the fellow Christian (1 Cor. 8:12).

Christ urged sinners to sin no more (John 8:11).

Sinning can be against the Law, or without the Law (Rom. 2:12).

All human beings have sinned (Rom. 3:23).

All have sinned because of the human relationship in Adam (Rom. 5:12).

The believer should serve righteousness and not sin (1 Cor. 15:34).

The believer can sin willfully (Heb. 10:26).

A believer cannot say that he does not sin (1 John 1:10).

To sin as in committing gross transgression (paraptōma)

Adam transgressed against God's command (Rom. 5:15).

The Law magnifies transgressions (Rom. 5:20).

Those who transgress should be restored (Gal. 6:1).

The unsaved are dead in trespasses and sin (Eph. 2:1).

God forgives all our trespasses (Col. 2:13).

To sin as with rebellious wicked intent (kakos, kakia)

Recompense to no one evil for evil (Rom. 12:17).

The government may bring harm upon the believer who does evil (Rom. 13:4).

Christians should not lust after evil things (1 Cor. 10:6).

God cannot be tempted with evil (James 1:13).

Christians should not follow after what is evil (3 John 1:11).

The latter part of verse 13 sternly denies any such foolish idea. Not only does God not tempt with evil, but—and at this point a very profound theological truth is stated—He "cannot be tempted by evil." The Greek phrase literally means "God is untemptable." God is true to His attribute of absolutely holiness, and He is in the business of moving us in the same direction. In our case, it means that things that once drew us into sin cease to do so as our desires become more and more conformed to God's. Incidentally, this statement about God is very important when it comes to our understanding of the fact that Christ never sinned. If He is God—as He indeed is—He is, as the orthodox theology puts it, "unable to sin," not merely "able not to sin." The orthodox theological term is *impeccable.* Jesus' humanity did not make Jesus morally susceptible to sin; instead, His deity welded His humanity into one untemptable person. Jesus was tempted only in the sense that He felt legitimate human needs (Heb. 4:15).

The real source of sin is next exposed. Sin comes from *within* us, not from God (1:14). Sin is lust when we are "carried away," that is, out of control. It is not sin to be tempted, for temptation in the initial phase, at least, is simply the appeal to legitimate human, God-given need. The word translated "lust" is literally "strong desire." Lust in English has the overtones of sinfulness, but the Greek word itself is morally neutral. It is at the point of being "carried away" that sin first enters the picture. This happens when the individual allows his or her mind to dwell on the temptation to the extent of *contemplating* sin. This, incidentally, Jesus never did. He faced the temptation, felt the tug of His human need, but decisively turned away from the contemplation of disobeying His Father. Since Jesus also had no inward sin, His desire could never reach the point of being carried away. His tactic was to quote the Word of God (see Luke 4:3–13), and that is the best antidote against sin for us too.

What follows could be described as the "history of sin" (1:14–15). James uses a fascinating analogy of procreation, all the way from conception to birth, and then extends it for a lifetime to physical death. Conception of sin occurs as a person is "carried away and enticed by his own lust." Two Greek present participles are used to give the following literal meaning: "being drawn out and being enticed." The drawing out or being carried away implies a departure from a position of moral strength to moral weakness. At this point, he becomes vulnerable and is enticed or fascinated by the spell of the temptation. Lust or desire has conceived, and gestation and "birth" are all that remain. We are not to suppose that "gestation" requires much time. "Birth" follows rather quickly if opportunity is available. Sin is "born," and when sin is "accomplished," death occurs. The NASB's "accomplished" is the translation of the Greek aorist participle "having been fully formed," and this points to the full growth of the sin. This is not "spiritual" death or separation from God, for all humans are born into that condition.

This is the sin God warned Adam about that would bring death, not immediately, but in the course of time. Of course, spiritual death occurred immediately, and only faith in the divine provision—perhaps implied by the animal skins given as coverings to Adam and Eve—would remedy that condition. It is possible that James simply has this original sin in mind exclusively. The Christian's sin need not always lead to physical death—although that is an extreme possibility (1 Cor. 11:30)—for ordinarily the Holy Spirit works to bring about repentance and restoration. James wants to remind his readers of the normal course of sin as illustrated by the Garden of Eden account. He uses this to serve as a warning of the extreme possibility and to encourage their repentance.

Does all sin lead to physical death? Not in the immediate sense necessarily. Some sins have more of an immediate effect on the body; others can be practiced for a lifetime. Spiritual, eternal death awaits all those who have not applied the divine remedy of faith in Christ's sacrifice for sin. James may ultimately have this in mind.

James issues a warning in 1:16: "Do not be deceived,[1] my beloved brethren." This serves as a transition to the final paragraph (1:17–18). They are not to be deceived by a fundamental fact that involves faith; namely, that temptation is powerful only when faith is weak. What kind of faith? Verses 17 and 18 will tell us that it is faith in God's ability to provide that which a believer (note the used of "beloved brethren") truly needs in relation to the object of his or her temptation.

God provides "every good thing bestowed and every perfect gift" (1:17). If something is worth having, God gives it. The things that tempt us are related to basic human needs but may be in a form that is not good or perfect. For example, a basic human need is sex,[2] but it is only good and perfect if it takes place within marriage. The temptation may be to satisfy the legitimate need in an illegitimate way—sex outside of marriage, or "fornication."

What James is telling us is that waiting patiently in faith for God to meet our needs "from above" is the bulwark against temptation. Temptation says, "Why wait? Have it now." Furthermore, James says that we can count on God to do it. God's faithfulness is expressed in the words, "Father of lights, with whom there is no variation, or shifting shadow" (1:17). This has become one of the primary texts concerning the attribute of God called "immutability" or unchangeableness of God. The expression "Father of lights" is a reference to creation of the light sources by the One who is characterized by light. Light from God preceded the creation of the light sources such as the sun and the stars (see Gen. 1:3–5, 14–19); and in the New Jerusalem, God himself will be the source of light (Rev. 21:23). James says all this to make the point that God is the provider of good things, not the one who tempts us. He is unchangeably good. Not even a "shifting shadow" of evil exists in him.[3]

The creation motif continues in verse 18, only it becomes *re-creation.* James tells us that we are destined, "in the exercise of His will," for better things than to fall into temptation. To do this God has "brought us forth by the word of truth." James is speaking of regeneration through the Word of God. The purpose of this new birth is to become "the first fruits among His creatures." This phrase changes the motif of creation somewhat into fruit bearing. The point seems to be that sin and the fall have marred the creation from what God intended it to be. Believers are "first fruits," an expression that means the early harvest as the harbinger of the future and final harvest. In other words, believers are intended to be radically different from all the rest of God's creatures. They are to withstand temptation and trust in God to supply their needs. They are to obey, not disobey God. They are intended to show the world what things will be like when sin and evil are abolished someday. This is evangelism at its very best!

Study Questions

1. What does James mean when he writes sin "brings forth death" (v. 15)?
2. Can a believer ever say that he or she is tempted by God?
3. What is the actual source of the Christian's temptation?
4. What did the Lord bring forth in the exercise of His will?
5. What is the difference between a trial and a temptation?

6. What "profession" is James alluding to in the language he uses in verse 14?

7. What illustration about life is James using in verse 15?

8. What does James mean when he writes that we are "the first fruits among [God's] creatures (v. 18)?

Section II

Working Faith Authenticated

James 1:19—2:26

CHAPTER 4

Faith Authenticated by Obedience
James 1:19-27

Preview:

James urges the brethren to be quick to hear, slow to speak, and slow to anger, to be a doer of the Word and not simply a hearer. And finally, he wants the children of God to bridle their tongues and to practice pure "religion," which is to visit and help the orphans and widows who may be in distress.

From the testing of faith, James turns to the authentication of faith. The NASB seems to connect this new section with the previous section about testing in verse 19 with the words, "*This* you know, my beloved brethren." However, as "*This*" in italics indicates in the NASB, the word "this" is supplied by the translators and is not found in the original Greek text. This sort of thing is done by both the KJV and NASB and is a good policy, for it lets the reader know that the translators have tried to clarify the meaning for the English reader. Such a clarification, however, is the judgment of the translators, and others may disagree.[1] My opinion, therefore, is that the NASB should read simply, "You know, my beloved brethren," without the "this." Similarly, NIV translates, "My dear brothers, take note of this."

The upshot of all this is that verse 19 probably introduces a new subject concerning faith, a conclusion I have indicated by calling this section "Section 2," and describing it as the "authentication of faith" following the "test of faith" in Section 1. By "authenticated" I mean demonstrated to be genuine. As we shall see, faith is authenticated by *obedience* (this chapter), *brotherly love* (chapter 5), and *works* (chapter 6).

The obedience that authenticates faith is obedience to the Word of God. This is clear from verse 21 ("the word implanted") and later from verses 22 ("doers of the word"), 23 ("hearer of the word"), and 25 ("the perfect law, the *law* of liberty"). That kind of obedience is described in reference to several kinds of behavior. The first is in relation to listening, speaking, and controlling one's temper (1:19). All three of these are part of a process connected with the tongue, a theme James will revisit in 1:26 and 3:1–12. Here this behavior seems to be in conversation or at least in listening and responding to something like a speech. People who obey the word in this regard are obedient to Proverbs 1:5, "a wise man will hear and increase in learning," and Proverbs 12:15, "The way of a fool is right in his own eyes, but a wise man is he who listens to counsel." These words from the wisdom literature of the Old Testament imply James's advice to be "quick to hear."

The second stage of this process is expressed by the words, "slow to speak." This implies careful consideration of what has been heard. Listening is a lost art. Typical conversations are those experiences in which we really don't listen very intently because we are anxious to express our own ideas. This often leads to listening only partially and even reading in things that are foreign to what a person is actually saying. Listening carefully is one of the purest forms of respect we can show to someone and is essential to good evangelism, for by listening we discover where a person is spiritually.[2]

The third stage in this listening process is being "slow to anger." This suggests a kind of anger that is under control. Such anger is not a sin. Anger is a sin when it is out of control or jumps to unwarranted conclusions. A person is slow to anger when, in spite of what he thinks he has just heard that strikes him as wrong, he patiently asks for clarification. Anger under control never becomes violent but looks for ways to resolve the disagreement once it has been proven that such disagreement actually exists.

As a result, the "righteousness of God" (1:20) is more likely to be achieved. This would involve righteousness in the case of the listener's response to disagreement as well as righteousness in the life of the speaker who needs to be corrected. Such righteousness is the goal of the Word of God that James wants us to obey.

Yet another area of obedience besides speech lies in the moral life (1:21). James's reference to "all filthiness and all that remains of wickedness" will lead him into the book that is the source of all morality, the Word of God, and that is where James will concentrate his remarks through 1:25.

"All filthiness" in its more literal sense involves a word that can be used of dirty garments or even of earwax that prevents good hearing. It becomes in such a use as this a metaphor for moral filth, anything that deviates from

God's moral standards in the Word of God. "All that remains of wickedness" is literally "overflowing amount of wickedness." The NIV translates this as "the evil that is so prevalent." The point is that we all have within us a prevailing amount of wickedness due to our depravity. This depravity expresses itself in varying degrees depending on the restraints—or lack of them—that a person brings to the Christian life. Therefore, whatever sin is not being restrained in us, James commands, must be dealt with, not tolerated.

This brief reference to the lingering sin in the believer is next reinforced by James's exhortation to be doers, not only hearers, of the word. James seems to refrain from a long list of sins and refer us to the basic standard itself. What follows is one of the most famous passages dealing with the implementation of the Scriptures.

To hear the word and not do it is self-delusion (1:22–24). About what are those who fail to do the Word deluded or deceived? They are deceived by their empty profession of faith, by going through the motions of religion (later, in 1:27, James tells what true religion is all about) like church attendance, baptism, and superficial good deeds. They do religious activities but fail to experience a transformation of the inner person leading to a revolution in moral behavior.

To illustrate this duplicity, James uses the illustration of a person looking at himself in the mirror (1:23), which he identifies in verse 25 as the "perfect law, the law of liberty." Once such a person has viewed himself in this mirror, he goes away and forgets "what kind of person he was" (1:24). Knowing human nature, we may speculate that this person took a casual look in the mirror more for vanity's sake than for making any change in his appearance. That one look was enough to confirm what he wanted to know, and so he was able to dismiss the image from his mind. He went through the motions to satisfy his pride but never intended to make any changes in his appearance.

Now change the analogy a bit. Suppose this was a man who stood before the mirror in the bathroom to shave his beard or a woman who sat before a dresser to apply her makeup. In these scenarios, each has every intention of doing something about his or her appearance. The point is, then, we should read the Word of God with the intention of seeing what needs to be changed in our lives. Perhaps we have been reading the Bible to fulfill a legalistic desire to appear devout, as though the mere reading of the words carries with it some sacramental value or merit. Instead, the mind must be engaged fully with a desire on our part to be more fully conformed to the image of Christ.

In verse 25, James writes, "But one who looks intently at the perfect law, the *law* of liberty, and abides by it, not having become a forgetful hearer but an effectual doer, this man shall be blessed in what he does." "Intently" means carefully and with purpose, the purpose of inviting change in character. "Law of liberty" is a strikingly descriptive term for the Word of God. The Old Testament, especially in such places as Psalm 119, frequently uses the word "law" as one of several terms for the Scriptures. Many of us are conditioned to view references to law as likely to be legalistic, and indeed in some places, such as the letter to the Galatians, this is often the case. Legalism is a misuse of the law, even when it is clear that the legal portions of the Pentateuch are in view. Legalism is the use of the law of God—or any law for that matter—to gain merit or achieve some sort of spirituality in one's own strength. To obey the law by the power of the Spirit, in this case the law that governs the believer in the New Testament and that often incorporates the moral law of the Old Testament, is the proper use of the law.

This explanation helps us understand "law of liberty" as a descriptive term for the Bible. This term is James's equivalent of the principle Jesus enunciates in his words, "You shall know the truth and the truth shall make you free" (John 8:32). Whether it is the legal commands or the spiritual principles of the Bible, we are set free by obedience to them. That from which we are made free is sin. Biblical freedom is not the right to do as we selfishly please; it is the freedom God gives us from sin. It begins first in justification as we are *declared* righteous through our faith in Christ and then in sanctification as we are *made* righteous in our behavior and our thinking, equally a matter of faith.

James may appear to change the subject again in verse 26, but he actually continues the theme of the correct use of the Word of God, merely switching to a different word for the misuse of the mirror of God's Word. That word is "religious." "If anyone thinks himself to be religious," James says, "and yet does not bridle his tongue but deceives his own heart, this man's religion is worthless." This use of the word *religious* is equivalent to looking in the mirror of God's Word, or law of liberty, and then leaving and forgetting what he saw. Once again it is mere ritual and legalism. James selects one of the more significant aspects of the law of liberty as his example, the use of the tongue, a subject that occupies a considerable amount of attention in chapter 3.

With failure to control the tongue given as an example of legalistic religion or the misuse of the word of God, James provides an example of *true* religion in verse 27. He calls it "pure and undefiled religion." The word *religion*[3] is relatively rare in the New Testament, but usage in extrabiblical literature, such as Wisdom 14:18, Sirach 22:5, and 4 Maccabees 5:6, as well as biblical usage such as Colossians 2:18, point to religious practices more than religious beliefs. In the Jewish mind such practices would include prayer, fasting, and community worship, things referred to today as "spiritual disciplines." But the problem is, the practices may be mere rituals. One way to determining if this is the case is by our desire to let others know that we are doing them.

So what is "pure and undefiled religion"? It is religion that is pure because it is without any ulterior motives for personal gain. James refers to two ministries that are not likely to be self-serving or ego-boosting and, in fact, may cost more than one is prepared to pay. The first is "to visit orphans and widows in their distress." The Greek word translated "visit" means to "look after" someone out of genuine concern, something more than a social visit. Orphans and widows are two categories of society that are likely to be destitute and lonely, thus in "distress." There will be no reciprocity on their part, no political or social advantage to gain. Serving them may require the sacrifice of time and money.

Such people were in distress, especially in the biblical world, because they received no means of support from the government, no social welfare or job training. The early church engaged in caring for widows who were "widows indeed" (1 Tim. 5:16), those who had no support and were at least sixty years of age. Younger widows were urged to remarry and care for the household, but until that occurred, they needed temporary assistance. The same would have been true for orphans, and James may be implying the possibility of adoption by Christian families.

The other mark of "pure and undefiled religion" was "to keep oneself unstained by the world." The word *unstained* represents a Greek word that means to keep free from the evil influences in the surrounding culture that would alter a believer's values and pursuits. John puts it this way: "Do not love the world, nor the things in the world. . . . For all that is in the world, the lust of the flesh and the lust of the eyes and the boastful pride of life, is not from the Father, but is from the world" (1 John 2:15–16).

Study Questions

1. What does James mean when he writes that sin "brings forth death" (1:15)?

2. What do you think James means when he writes about "the law of liberty"?

3. What is the height of self-deception to James?

4. How can the child of God "stain" himself or herself with the world?

5. How does the word implanted "save the soul"?

6. Why does James focus on visiting the orphans and widows as proof that one has pure "religion." Explain.

CHAPTER 5

Faith Authenticated by Brotherly Love
James 2:1-13

Preview:

James greatly dislikes personal favoritism and prejudice, and he cannot stand the mistreatment of the poor. Christians who are blessed by the royal law and the law of freedom or liberty must not defile their freedom in Christ and must never "show partiality." God will judge those who are merciless; mercy will triumph over judgment!

This section is about showing partiality to people who enter our congregational meetings. Although it may appear that the subject of faith has given way to a different topic, the connection of faith with the problem of partiality is strongly suggested by James's early reference to faith in the very first verse: "My brethren, do not hold your faith in our glorious Lord Jesus Christ with *an attitude of* personal favoritism."[1] To "hold" one's faith in Christ simply means to believe and acknowledge the truth of that faith. Ordinarily it should imply salvation, but to "hold" that faith and then act in partiality or favoritism to someone in the church might call into question the reality of that faith by others. The poor man described in the example would be the victim of such partiality, and he would question the reality of such faith.[2] The literal meaning of "personal favoritism" is "to receive to the face."[3] To receive in this way is to appear (face to face) to receive someone but to have ulterior motives. Such faith is not genuine, as we shall see in the example James gives.

James gives a scenario in which two strangers enter the assembly.[4] The first man is wearing a gold ring and is dressed in fine clothes, indicators of his prestige, wealth, and ostentation. The other man is described as poor and in dirty clothes, signifying his poverty. The "dirty clothes," however, may suggest even more. Many, if not most, poor people are able to keep clean. James may be portraying a person who is without social graces and is thus repugnant as well as poor, one who is in need of social as well as economic help. The response of the congregation (2:3) is to "pay special attention to the one who is wearing the fine clothes" by seating him in a place of honor and to treat with disrespect the poor, socially unacceptable person. He is given a choice of two options, either to stand or sit down on a footstool (NIV takes it as on the floor next to someone's footstool), neither of which is respectful. In an early Christian gathering, the location ordinarily would have been a private home where the token of hospitality would have been to offer him a seat. "By my footstool," where he is told to sit, would contrast with the seat of honor as a place of dishonor. In the Eastern culture this would be an insult.

The Command to Love One's Neighbor	
Jesus commands the believer to love his neighbor	*Matthew 5:43; 19:19; 22:39; Mark 12:31, 33; Luke 10:27*
The believer is commanded to not do his neighbor wrong	*Acts 7:27*
Paul commands the believer to love his neighbor as himself	*Romans 13:9*
Love will not work harm to one's neighbor	*Romans 13:10*
The child of God is to please his neighbor for his good	*Romans 15:2*
The child of God is not to lie to his neighbor	*Ephesians 4:25*
The child of God is to speak truth to his neighbor	*Ephesians 4:25*
In the kingdom, believers will not have to teach their neighbors to know the Lord; they will all know Him	*Hebrews 8:11*

What motives lie behind these actions? James tells us in the words, "Have you not made distinctions among yourselves, and become judges with evil motives?" To "make distinctions" or "discriminate" (NIV) literally means, "to divide between two," or to treat someone differently. Here is where the contradiction with holding faith in Christ occurs. The same kind of faith has brought all believers into equality regardless of their social or economic status. The "evil motives" would include the intention to receive something from the wealthy man. Such motives are selfish, not spiritual.

James goes on to explain this inconsistency in verses 5–7. He addresses his readers as "my beloved brethren," using the approach of gentle rebuke, a technique we all would do well to practice. It implies that there is a better way and encourages change. The rebuke is in the form of a reminder: "Did not God choose the poor of this world to be rich in faith and heirs of the kingdom which He promised to those who love Him?" This choosing of the poor should not be construed as exclusive. God has chosen the rich as well, although there may be far fewer of the rich, because riches tend to obscure a person's need for salvation or provide the temptation for idolatry. James also indicates something of this obstacle to the rich when he describes them as oppressors and blasphemers (2:3–4) and warns them of the perils of luxury as well as their tendency toward injustice (5:1–6). The poor, however, can become spiritually rich in spite of their poverty, and this possibility constitutes one of the missions of the church.

Biblical students have observed from the Gospels that Jesus generally concentrated his ministry among the poor, a fact easily overlooked by many churches today in their quest for larger buildings and the means required to erect them. This is not ground for neglecting ministry and outreach to the rich; it is merely realism. The obstacles that wealth creates require the grace of God to be put into perspective (see 1 Tim 6:17–19).[5]

James further calls attention to the fact that they "drag" believers into court. The word *drag* speaks of violent, disrespectful treatment, not unlike the kind of treatment Jews experienced during the Holocaust at the hands of the Nazis. Furthermore, they "blaspheme" (2:7) the name of Christ, committing verbal abuse in which Christ is ridiculed or His claims denied.

All this treatment by the rich is used by James to point out the naïve act of showing favoritism to them. They could be offended easily by someone in the church, insist on having their way in the church, and consequently turn against the church if denied. In other words, such favoritism would not produce the desired results anyway. God does not need the rich to finance His mission. As the saying goes, "Little is much when God is in it."

The alternative to favoritism, the kind of behavior James's readers should be showing, is to fulfill the "royal law according to the Scripture," namely, to love one's neighbor as oneself. This is called a "royal" law probably because Jesus, when asked what the greatest commandment was, cited both Deuteronomy 6:5, the command to love God completely, and Leviticus 19:18 as those on which all the Law depended. It would be "royal" in the sense of supreme. When Jesus told the parable of the Good Samaritan (Luke 10:25–37),

He illustrated this law of Leviticus 19:18 to show that anyone whose path we crossed and who needed help was our neighbor. His final point was that *everyone*, not just one's friends, was a "neighbor." The application here, then, is that *both* the poor and the rich should be treated the same.

Having brought up the matter of the Law,[6] James next provides an important theological point about the nature and function of the Law (2:9–13). He says that showing partiality is a violation of the Law, thus making his offending readers transgressors. They might imagine that such a violation is a minor offense in their effort to feel better about themselves. The Law "hangs together," or is a unit, because it reflects the nature or character of God. One can keep the "whole law," break one part of it, and "become guilty of all" (2:10–11). In reality, of course, such a person is really not keeping the "whole law," but sinful humanity loves to rate itself on a scale of sorts so that keeping most of the Law is viewed as acceptable. What this leads to is the typical religious idea that at the judgment a tip of the scales toward good determines salvation. Christianity is different in the sense that a person is a lost sinner for having broken but one law. In the case of most "moral" people, this law is the first commandment, to love God unreservedly, one that everyone breaks apart from the grace of God in salvation.

James concludes his exposition of the nature of the Law by exhorting his readers to "act as those who are to be judged by the law of liberty" (2:12). What he means is, keep the judgment in mind whatever you do. James uses another striking designation for the Law: "law of liberty." This, undoubtedly, is another reference to the "royal law" of love. One either views the Law as a means of gaining merit that leads to bondage due to inevitable failure or sees it in terms of its supreme commandment that in turn enables one to obey it: love for God and love for one's neighbor. To love God brings the divine provision of the Holy Spirit for enablement. To love God as well as one's neighbor protects one's motives. This "frees" or "liberates" the believer to obey.

The final word in this section (2:13) adds the capstone to the nature of Law. Everyone fails to keep God's law perfectly. With this in mind, everyone should show mercy the same way God will show mercy to those who believe the gospel. It would be easy for James's readers to condemn self-righteously those who in the future show favoritism. To counter this tendency, he advocates mercy. To be shown what is right does not make a person righteousness, only informed. Correction should humble us. When we do it right the next time, we should maintain that humility and show mercy as we remember that we, too, are sinners. Mercy "triumphs over judgment"; mercy brings salvation that makes judgment unnecessary. This depends, of course, on repentance and faith.

Study Questions

1. From this chapter, list all of the things James says about the poor.

2. In what ways can the rich oppress the poor?

3. In what ways is partiality actually sin?

4. In what ways can a Christian break the whole law of God (2:10)?

5. In the dispensation of grace, if a believer in Christ is a transgressor of the Law, does this mean he is a "Law-keeper" or somehow "under the Law"?

6. Why is the Law called "the law of liberty" (1:25; 2:12)?

7. What would cause God to be "merciless," as is mentioned in verse 13?

CHAPTER 6

Faith Authenticated by Works
James 2:14–26

Preview:

True faith, James says, has to be shown by work; otherwise the world does not know of the genuine godly trust of the child of God. The Christian is justified by faith before God but is justified before humans through the works they can see!

In modern evangelicalism we are less likely to authenticate a person's claim to faith by his or her love for the brethren than we are by the works or deeds that are supposed to result from that faith. Perhaps that is why James referred to love for all kinds of people, poor and rich, before coming to the question of works. Nevertheless, faith should produce works, and those works testify to the genuineness of faith.

The following passage demands careful exegesis, for it is easy, as evidenced by Martin Luther, to misunderstand James's references to the relationship of works to faith in light of the apostle Paul in his letters to the Romans and Galatians. Though a superficial reading of this passage might lead to the conclusion that James and Paul are in disagreement, the apparent difference between them is in perspective, not substance.

James begins with a reference to the uselessness of faith with no works (2:14). What is "useless" faith? The answer is implied in the question, "Can that faith save him?" Useless faith, then, is a faith that cannot bring salvation. This understanding appears to be confirmed by the later reference to faith that is "dead" in 2:26 as well as the discussion about justification in 2:24–25. *Save* can mean salvation from physical death in some contexts, but this context appears to revolve around eternal salvation.

Part of the confusion in the past was due to failure to translate the Greek article that appears before the word "faith" in the phrase, "Can *that* faith save?" in 2:14. The KJV translates it simply, "Can faith save?" Such a translation would appear to contradict Paul's doctrine of justification by faith alone. The first "faith" in 2:14 does not have a definite article in the Greek, whereas the second "faith" found in the question does have the definite article. In other words, James makes a contrast between the first reference to faith that is genuine, the kind to which someone is making claim, and another (with the article), a kind of faith without works. This is why the NASB translates the article with the word "that" and the NIV with the word "such." One final observation on 2:14: The nature of the question, "Can that faith save?" implies a negative answer. An expanded, literal translation would be, "That kind of faith cannot save, can it?"

James never defines faith for his readers; he merely assumes his readers know what he means. Since true faith "saves," James—in light of the rest of the New Testament—must refer to faith in Jesus Christ and his finished work on the cross. That work saves from the power and consequences of sin and brings the believer into an eternal relationship with God that begins with justification, continues with sanctification, and concludes with glorification.

The Christian's Service and Work	
If any man's work remains, he shall receive a reward	1 Corinthians 3:14
If any man's work is burned up, he shall suffer loss	1 Corinthians 3:15
Believers are to be "always abounding in the work of the Lord"	1 Corinthians 15:58
God makes His grace abound to us so that we may have abundance for every good deed	2 Corinthians 9:8
Let each one examine his own work	Galatians 6:4
We are created in Christ Jesus for good works	Ephesians 2:10
He who began a good work in you will perfect it	Philippians 1:6
God saved us not according to our works	2 Timothy 1:9
God saved us not on the basis of works which we have done in righteousness	Titus 3:5
Those who believe in God should engage in good works	Titus 3:8
Let our people learn to engage in good works	Titus 3:14

What follows is an illustration of faith without works (2:15–16). A "brother or sister" is in need of clothing and food, and someone—apparently with this faith without works—merely wishes them well and tells them to go and be warmed and filled without providing what they need. Notice how the illustration clarifies what James has in mind when he uses the word *works*. To meet the need of the brother or sister would require compassion or love, something accomplished in the life of the believer by the Holy Spirit. This work is not in the category of a legalistic work of the Law, but a fruit of the Spirit (Gal. 5:22–23). Thus, faith is authenticated by God's work in the believer's life, not by religious deeds or alms.

James concludes the illustration by pointing out that such faith is "dead, being by itself" (2:17). What does James mean by "dead"? The phrase "being by itself," provides the first clue. We would presume that "living" faith would not be by itself. Later, in 2:26, James offers a similar analogy of the body without the spirit being dead as an illustration of faith without works. This raises the question of how far to carry the analogy of a body whose spirit has departed in death. In other words, is James implying that "dead" faith was once alive with works and therefore was "living" faith at one time? This, then, would imply that James's concern is with believers whose faith has lapsed into a temporary deadness due to lack of works.

However, I prefer the interpretation of "dead" faith as a kind of faith that is not saving faith. Someone has *professed* faith that saves, but it does not. This interpretation is supported by the impression through the passage that someone without works is claiming to have saving faith, especially the challenge in 2:18, "You have faith, and I have works; show me your faith without the works, and I will show you my faith by my works." The one who has faith without works, by implication, cannot show saving faith, because it is some other kind of faith. The illustration indicates that he may believe in God (note 2:19, where the demons "also believe"), perhaps in some intellectual fashion, but his belief does not affect him in any significant way that leads him to compassion.

Such "intellectual" faith is religious faith; its object may even be Jesus and the resurrection. It "makes sense" to someone, and he perhaps has joined the Christian community. There are multitudes like this, but their lives have never been changed. What is missing in this kind of "intellectual" faith? Two things, I believe. What I am about to say goes beyond James's discussion, but I believe James assumes it. The two missing ingredients in "intellectual" faith are repentance and personal trust.

Repentance and faith that saves are closely linked in the New Testament. Note what Paul says in Acts 20:20–21, as reported by the author Luke: "I did not shrink from declaring to you anything that was profitable, and teaching you publicly and from house to house, solemnly testifying to both Jews and Greeks of repentance toward God and faith in our Lord Jesus Christ."

It is true that the words *repentance* and *faith* are sometimes used interchangeably by Luke in Acts (see Acts 16:31, where "believe" appears without "faith" and Acts 2:38 where "repent" is used without "believe"), but Acts 20:20–21, where they both appear in the same text, clarifies their relationship. One repents "toward God" because sin is ultimately against God, one side of the conversion experience, and he or she exercises faith in the Lord Jesus Christ as the concomitant act of will that provides the salvation remedy, the other side of the conversion experience. That makes repentance inseparable from saving faith, an acknowledgment of one's sinfulness coupled with a vital trust in the Savior, the second ingredient of saving faith absent in what James describes as faith without works.

What is this "vital trust," as I have called it? It is common these days to clarify what we mean by saving faith with the word *trust*. Mere intellectual faith accepts something as true because it makes sense, is supported by some recognized authority, or is affirmed often enough in a culture that it takes on the aura of fact. "Vital trust" is faith that depends and acts on something believed. To believe it becomes very important to one's hope or welfare, and complete dependence is placed on it. Furthermore, when required, one acts on it. Another element is the concept of "transfer" of trust. Everyone trusts many things. In the question of eternal salvation, the so-called unbeliever actually believes *something*. Even an atheist "trusts" that there is no God, defying the consequences of discovering that God exists after it is too late, such as after death. When persons are contemplating placing trust in Jesus as Savior, they should be told that they must renounce all other forms of trust or confidence before they place their trust in Him. That is the gospel requirement. For unless they trust in Christ alone, they are merely going through the motions. In other words, they are committing idolatry.

The kind of faith James says cannot save can be labeled "intellectual" faith. One of its deficiencies is lack of repentance. Persons with such intellectual faith have not understood that part of the gospel that announces humanity's lost condition and have merely grasped for the better life that the gospel promises. Another important fact is that repentance in the biblical sense is not self-reformation but a recognition of one's sinfulness produced by the Holy Spirit. Only God can produce reformation through the process of sanctification. Sinners are helpless to change themselves.

Further evidence of the kind of faith that cannot save is found in James's explanation in 2:19: "You believe that God is one. You do well; the demons also believe, and shudder." Demons "believe" that God is one because they cannot deny it in their kind of existence where God is not "hidden." The one whom James addresses in 2:19 does "well," because the evidence points that way. To ignore such evidence, the kind that is related to the so-called theistic arguments for the existence of God and characterized by the law of cause and effect, is to be a "fool" according to such Scriptures as Psalm 14:1. Since such faith on the demons' part means that they simply cannot deny God's existence; it does not meet the requirements of saving faith that we have indicated above. Their belief entails no personal trust. Trust is not even in the picture, for salvation is not an option to them.

There is one further matter of interpretation in 2:19. The belief that "God is one" is probably an allusion to Deuteronomy 6:4 and the Shema.[1] In the ancient world, atheists were rare; almost everyone believed in some god or gods. The issue was more a question of which was the true God. In such a theological culture, "God is one" was therefore an affirmation of the existence of God.

In 2:20 James continues with his remarks to the person who claims to have faith but cannot show it by works. James calls him "you foolish fellow." He was not a fool who denied the existence of God, but a foolish person who ignored the nature of genuine faith. Even the most cynical pagan seems to have the sense to recognize that faith ought to have some sort of evidence, hence the pagan world's contempt for many professing Christians. To reinforce this argument, James continues with an illustration from the faith of Abraham in 2:21–24, probably the most misunderstood part of the book of James.

The most difficult sentence is 2:21: "Was not Abraham our father justified by works when he offered up Isaac his son on the altar?" The word *justify* has two possible meanings in this context:[2] (1) vindication of the reality of something; and (2) to acquit or justify legally. We have reason to believe that James's use of the word *justify* here is in a different category than Paul's use. Paul uses it as a legal pronouncement of righteousness based on faith, the second usage above. When Paul uses Abraham as his example of this kind of justification, he cites as his example Genesis 15, where Abraham believes God and his faith is counted as righteousness. James's example of Abraham is here based on Genesis 22, the occasion when Abraham was commanded to offer up Isaac as a sacrifice, and this corresponds with the first usage referred to above. This was later, following the legal pronouncement based on faith, while Paul cites the original occasion on which Abraham exercised faith and was legally justified. The later occasion with Isaac, therefore, was a *vindication* or proof of Abraham's faith. Thus, James and Paul merely come at the issue of faith and works from different standpoints; they do not contradict each other.

The lesson here is that genuine forensic justification (as in Gen. 15) will be followed by justification as vindication (as in Gen. 22).

James's use of "justify" in the sense of "vindicate" is further confirmed in 2:22–26. James says, "You see that faith was working with his works, and as a result of the works, faith was perfected" (2:22). Abraham's faith originated either when God first appeared to him to call him out of his homeland (Gen. 12:1–4) or when Genesis 15 tells us that his faith was counted as righteousness. It was "perfected" when he showed his willingness to offer Isaac. The word *perfected* means "having reached its goal."[3] The goal of faith is to demonstrate faith in some work enabled by the Holy Spirit. Thus, it is proven to be genuine or is vindicated.

James 2:23 continues with a further explanation of the same thing. "And the Scripture was fulfilled which says, 'And Abraham believed God, and it was reckoned to him as righteousness,' and he was called the friend of God."

To "fulfill" the original exercise of Abraham as the quotation of Genesis 15:6 indicates is to prove that the original identification of Abraham's faith was accurate. Furthermore, a more expansive reason is given at the end of the sentence: "He was called the friend of God." This speaks of an ongoing relation between Abraham and God. All who share the faith of Abraham in this way are not only children of Abraham by faith (Gal. 3:7) but friends of God.

James begins a conclusion of his discussion of genuine, saving faith with the statement, "You see that a man is justified by works, and not by faith alone" (2:24). "Justified," as we have learned, is *vindication*, and "faith alone" is faith in the sense of intellectual acceptance of some belief or fact. This is not "faith alone" in the sense of one of the great affirmations of the Reformation, *sola fide* referring to forensic justification, but faith that is alone or devoid of works.

The final part of the conclusion involves a reference to one of the great believers of the Old Testament, Rahab (2:25). She occupies a place in the "faith hall of fame" of Hebrews 11, and James includes her along with Abraham as an example. This is a fascinating study in contrasts. Abraham is the man to whom God first personally appeared, and he is characterized by tremendous faith at the crucial points of his life, but he was no stranger to lapses of faith. He is the great "friend of God" and apparently bore that reputation throughout the land of Canaan. Rahab, on the other hand, was a prostitute[4] in a pagan society, and she never had the benefit of a personal appearance of God. Rather, she came to faith by hearing of Israel's great exploits by God's power, facts kept alive by fear in her neighbors' thinking but kept alive by faith in her case. Rahab's faith was thus "justified" by her courageous decision to take her place with the people of God. Her decision flowed out of her justifying faith.

James's final word is given in a kind of maxim: "For just as the body without the spirit is dead, so also faith without works is dead" (2:26). The body without the spirit (and I would include the soul as a correlating aspect) is a corpse. Whatever modern medical science may deem as the point of death, we learn here that the departure of the spirit/soul is the time when God regards someone as dead. By analogy, faith and works bear a similar relationship. They are inseparable in James's saving faith, and works will bear out the reality of one's faith. Faith without works has no "action." It is a kind of religion that is private and for the sole benefit of the one who professes it; it makes no difference to anyone else.

Study Questions

1. In what way do the demons "believe"? Explain.

2. By what concrete means is the faith of the Christian seen?

3. Explain the difference between justification by faith and justification by works. Is this a contradiction?

4. Does justification by works imply salvation by works?

5. What does James mean when he writes, "Faith without works is dead" (2:26)?

Section III

Working Faith Demonstrated

James 3:1 — 5:20

CHAPTER 7

Faith Demonstrated by Controlling the Tongue
James 3:1–12

Preview:

The tongue is one of the most powerful instruments in the world because it can destroy people, and at the same time, it can bless our Lord and heavenly Father! Without the Lord's intervention, the tongue cannot be tamed.

James 3:8 says that no one can tame the tongue. However, 3:2 says that the one who does not stumble in what he says is a "perfect man, able to bridle the whole body as well." What these two apparently contradictory statements imply is that taming the tongue cannot be done in ordinary human strength. Who, though, is "perfect"? No one is—in the absolute sense, at least. But faith can make the otherwise impossible attainable to some degree, for it appeals to God for His divine ability. Thus, this section has a tie to faith, even though James makes no explicit reference to faith. If one tames the tongue, he or she does so by faith, relying on the divine ability, and success therefore becomes a demonstration of faith.

The connection with faith, though not mentioned by James explicitly, lies in the previous context (2:22–26). In 2:22 James stated that faith works through works and is thus perfected, and in 2:24 he tells us that a man is justified (his faith is vindicated) by works. Taming the tongue is certainly a "work" as James earlier defined a work (2:15–16). I identified it further as a work energized by the Holy Spirit, not an effort of our own ability. James thus sets the stage for his discussion of the work of taming the tongue, which he clearly states is beyond any human being's ability (3:8). In summary, taming the tongue is a work of the Holy Spirit as we in faith allow it to happen.

James begins his discussion on the tongue with perhaps the most unlikely or unexpected person, the teacher. Surely one would expect the teacher, the person of experience and maturity, to have a handle on the tongue. We might expect that if one were to warn the teacher, it would be in connection with the teacher *practicing* what he or she teaches. But James thinks of the teacher's tongue as being a most fertile area for offense. "Let not many of you become teachers, my brethren, knowing that as such we shall incur a stricter judgment" (3:1) rarely has been interpreted in light of its following context. It tends to be quoted most often in connection with the awesome responsibility of practicing what one preaches, not so much in connection with offending by what one says.

The teacher had considerable status in ancient Judaism. Jesus warned against those who presumptuously assumed this office. Speaking particularly of the Pharisees, Jesus said, "They love the place of honor at banquets and the chief seats in the synagogues, and respectful greetings in the market places, and being called by men, Rabbi. But do not be called Rabbi, for One is your Teacher, and you are all brothers" (Matt. 23:6–8). Indeed, Jesus is thinking of the sin of love of position, but the point is that such position puts a person in a place of influence that gives him the power to manipulate Scripture as well as people. Jesus is foreseeing the days of the church, and not to be called "Rabbi" would be an effort to disassociate from the abuse of the Pharisees. The teacher in the church should not be one who, like the Pharisees, loves the position and abuses the Scripture in an effort to advance his own personal prestige. Likewise, James does not preclude the role of teacher but rather the abuse of the role. For James to say, "Let not many of you become teachers," means that only certain individuals are called by God to that position and are gifted to expound the Word of God.

But the warning is applicable as well to those who are called to the office of teacher, and this includes the pastoral ministry if it is truly biblical, for today's pastors and teachers face the temptation to misinterpret Scripture as well. Think of the modern situation—not essentially that different in terms of abuse than that in the early church. Pastors and teachers today must regularly preach or teach *new* material, to cover a "curriculum," whether in the specific teaching role or the pulpit. But they may be so burdened by pastoral duties that they fail to spend adequate time preparing to teach. This in turn may result in careless interpretation and superficial content. Part of the answer to the pressures of modern ministry is to get rid of unbiblical duties, and focus on biblical duties, or, as the apostle Peter put it, to "devote ourselves to prayer, and to the ministry of the word" (Acts 6:4).

The "stricter judgment" that James warns about in 3:1 pertains to the fact that those in places of responsibility are held more accountable; there are fewer extenuating circumstances that can relieve them partially of responsibility. In 3:2 James says that we "all stumble in many ways." But his focus is on stumbling in what we *say*, as the following context makes clear.

What James says next is significant in regard to sin. "If anyone does not stumble in what he says, he is a perfect man, able to bridle the whole body as well" (3:2b). The ability to control the tongue implies the ability to control the whole body. Since sin usually involves the body (see Rom. 6), the ability to control the whole body involves the ability to control all forms of sin. This would seem to place control of the tongue at the pinnacle of Christian achievement. This means that control of the tongue is control of inward sin that drives the tongue to utter sinful things, and as James proceeds to discuss control in detail, we must realize that the physical organ and some sort of mechanical capability to make it say what we want is surely not James's point here.

James's reference to bridling the tongue leads him to illustrate his point with analogies to bridling horses and steering ships. Here again the determinative nature of the ability to control our speech comes into view. The ability to control the tongue becomes the key to dealing with all other sins. The bridle in the horse's mouth controls the whole horse in spite the horse's great strength (3:3). The rudder of the ship controls the whole ship in spite of the force of the wind. The point is that control of the tongue is a fundamental achievement toward dealing with sin of all kinds.

Perhaps the comparative size of the bridle to the horse and the rudder to the ship next suggests to James the comparative size of the tongue to the body (3:5). We need to realize, however, that what lies behind these physical comparisons is the spiritual or ethical reality behind them. Behind the organ we call the tongue is indwelling sin. Behind the comparatively greater size of the body to the tongue is the extensiveness of sin. Control of indwelling sin through the avenue of speech is what James has in mind.

The tongue "boasts of great things" (3:5), yet it is relatively small. James has in mind the sin of pride, an immense aspect of human sin that finds its expression in the tiny tongue. Swiftly James uses another analogy of a tiny spark setting a great forest into flame. The sins of the tongue, more than any other part of the body, far exceed all other sins in which the body is involved. Remember Paul's references to the fact that sin uses the body for its great variety of expressions (Rom. 6).

The Problem of the Tongue

The lost deceive with their tongues *(Rom. 3:13)*.

Those who are religious should bridle their tongues *(James 1:26)*.

Refrain the tongue from evil *(1 Pet. 3:10)*.

Love not with tongue but in deed and truth *(1 John 3:18)*.

James further expands on this idea in 3:6. Not only is the tongue something of a key to the battle against sin because of the kinds of sins that occur through it, but also the damage it can do is frightening. Earlier the metaphor for the tongue was "a small fire" (3:5b). James extends that metaphor to a full-fledged fire out of control that sparks new fires, a danger any firefighter is well aware of as flames often jump by way of their sparks over acres of land to ignite trees far removed from the main fire (3:6). James refers to the tongue as "the very world of iniquity." If the tongue does not itself perpetate every sin in the world, it can *express* every sin. In this way it "defiles the entire body," and this reminds us of Jesus' words, "Do you not understand that everything that goes into the mouth passes into the stomach, and is eliminated? But the things that proceed out of the mouth come from the heart, and those defile the man" (Matt. 15:17–18). The chain of sinful events concludes with the fact that the tongue "sets on fire the course of our life." In other words, the tongue can alter a person's whole life if not ruin it.

The most frightening statement is that the tongue "is set on fire by hell [Greek, *Gehenna*]" (3:6b), the place of future eternal suffering as opposed to the present Hades. Here it stands for Satan, like White House stands for the president of the United States. However Satan incites sin, whether by himself or by one of his demons, he gets the tongue to wagging out its sinful poison. This raises the practical question of "how?" Does he plant ideas in our minds, or does he utilize circumstances? Since ideas can occur apart from any cause outside us, I am inclined to view planting of ideas as a possibility. The same can happen from the Holy Spirit, although the Spirit predominantly works through the Scriptures. I am suspicious of any claims to divine inspiration, because the Bible is complete, and the placing of ideas in the mind by the Holy Spirit comes close to that, unless, of course, those ideas are in the form of already revealed Scripture. On the other hand, most of what we say comes from within, and so the reference to hell may refer to Satan as the ultimate cause traced back to Eden.

Finally, to stress the comparative difficulty of taming the tongue, James refers to the "taming" of various animals. "Tame" here is not domestication as in the case of horses, dogs, or cats, but *subduing* as in God's mandate to humans to subdue all creatures (Gen. 1:28), for reptiles and "every species" of animals have not been so "domesticated." The larger creatures such as whales and dinosaurs[1] have been subdued in spite of the relatively small size of human beings, and James gives the comparison to get his point across about the mighty power of the tongue though it is such a relatively small organ.

Next comes the depressing statement, "But no one can tame the tongue; it is a restless evil and full of deadly poison" (3:8). "No one" undoubtedly refers to no human being. James is, through the tongue, referring to what Paul calls the "flesh," that propensity toward sin that remains powerful even in Christians. The tongue is one of the flesh's primary avenues of expression. Since in verse 10 James says the tongue's evils "ought not to be this way," we must infer that *someone* is able to tame the tongue. Surely this is to be done in faith in the ability of the Holy Spirit to do so. The answer is found in Galatians 5:16, "Walk by the Spirit, and you will not carry out the desire of the flesh." Walking by the Spirit is a decision of faith in the Spirit's power, always available to us if we will simply ask in faith for it.

James adds two descriptions of the tongue: "restless evil" and "full of deadly poison." The word *restless* appeared in 1:8 in connection with the double-minded, unstable person. Here it seems to suggest the tongue's unpredictable and continuous activity, two factors that make it difficult to control. The flesh that can control the tongue on occasion never sleeps. Only constant vigilance—something hard to maintain—can contain it. In a weak moment it suddenly emerges and we wish we could recapture that moment of thoughtless outburst and say something worthwhile in its place. Being "full of deadly poison," it does its damage like snake's venom (for this comparison see Ps. 140:3), eventually penetrating to every part of the body and destroying us. The deadly words we utter spread rapidly, usually through the speech of those who report what we say, often in the form of gossip. It threatens the work of God in the church and in evangelism. It destroys friendships and reputations. The only antidote is apology, and that often is ineffective due to bitterness and resentment.

A paradox follows as James concludes his words about the tongue. The paradox is that from the same source, the tongue, both praise for God and cursing for our fellow human beings come. James reminds us that in cursing human beings we are assaulting God also, for we humans were created in the "likeness" of God. This term is one of two ways to describe our similarity to God. In Genesis 1:26 God makes man in His image, according to His likeness. The term *image* is something that represents something. It can be an idol or it can be something unseen, as in this case. To clarify that the "image" is an unseen reality so far as humanity is concerned, God adds the words "according to Our likeness." The likeness of God is not found in anything material, for God is a spirit. Rather, it is found in personality, moral consciousness, and dignity.

This paradox of cursing and praise from the same source is contrasted with the fact that all other "sources," like fountains that pour forth water and fig trees that bear fruit, do not issue forth with contradictory ingredients. Either fresh water or bitter water flows from a fountain, not both. Only figs come from fig trees, and salt water cannot produce fresh water.

The Old Testament on Cursing and Blessing

God will bless those who bless Abraham and His children (Gen. 12:3).

He will curse those who curse Abraham and His children (Gen. 12:3).

When Israel entered the land of Canaan they would be blessed or cursed depending if they kept the Law of Moses or not (Deut. 11:26-28).

To the new generation of Jews entering the land, Joshua reminds them of the blessing or the curse of the Law (Josh. 8:34).

When David was cursed by those who hated him, He still asked God to bless them (Ps. 109:38).

There are certain people who curse their fathers and refuse to bless their mothers (Prov. 30:11).

God will send a curse upon those who do not listen to Him, also He will curse their "blessings" (Mal. 2:2).

Under the theocracy of Israel, the Jews were blessed who brought their tithes to the storehouse (Malachi 3:10).

Under the theocracy of Israel, the Jews were cursed who failed to bring their tithes to the storehouse (Malachi 3:9).

The hearts of the Jews who accept Elijah the prophet will be blessed (Malachi 4:6).

If the Jews do not accept the coming of Elijah the prophet, their land will be cursed (Malachi 4:6).

The human tongue is unique because of our duality, our capability for both good and evil. James is pointing not merely to the paradox of human duality among the singleness of nature, but to the tragedy of the human condition. This tragedy needs a remedy, as I discussed above, and that remedy is God Himself.

Study Questions

1. What does James mean when he writes that teachers are held to a stricter judgment?

2. How are teachers held to this "stricter judgment"?

3. Since Christians are able to both bless and curse, what does this say theologically about the issues of sin in the life of the believer?

4. What ignites the tongue? Explain.

5. Why is it impossible to tame the tongue?

6. From James 3:8–12, list the different descriptions James uses to show the folly and sinfulness of the tongue.

7. Why is James so specific in his detailed indictment against the sins of the tongue?

CHAPTER 8

Faith Demonstrated by Seeking Heavenly Wisdom
James 3:13–18

Preview:
The gentleness of wisdom is shown by good behavior. Jealousy and selfish ambition are forms of lying against the truth and are actually "wisdom" that does not come from God. The wisdom that comes from above produces moral and spiritual fruit that can be seen by all.

Once again, the connection of this section with the overall theme is subtle. James begins (3:13) with the question, "Who among you is wise and understanding?" This wisdom is to be shown by the person's "good behavior," a statement reminiscent of the discussion of chapter 2, in which faith is to be demonstrated by good works. This idea ties this section with the theme of the book. Wisdom, like faith, is seen in action. Wisdom will always be a component of faith if it is wisdom "from above" (3:15), which is divine wisdom. The apostle Paul contrasts earthly wisdom with God's wisdom in 1 Corinthians 1:18–31. In that discussion, the end result of the wisdom of this world is that through its wisdom the world "did not come to know God" (1 Cor. 1:21). James tells us that the wisdom of this world is "earthly, natural, demonic" (3:15). Both Paul and James, argee that true wisdom comes through faith.

The second part of verse 13 in the NASB is an attempt to be more literal but yields a somewhat tortured sentence: "Let him show by his good behavior his deeds in the gentleness of wisdom." The actual Greek is difficult for the English translator because of such a difference in syntax, but the meaning seems to be:

"Let him show out of good conduct his works in meekness of wisdom." Or, to put it another way, "Let him show his wisdom in meekness through good conduct." Verse 14 continues with a reference to the opposite of gentle or humble wisdom, "bitter jealousy and selfish ambition." If that lies behind an attempt to be wise and understanding, then the person is advised by James not to be arrogant so as to "lie against the truth." James seems to be warning against an attempt to be wise for the wrong reasons. To answer according to earthly wisdom is always a matter of pride and arrogance. This is intriguing and shocking. Two kinds of wisdom and understanding are immediately available to us, one from the earth, the other from above. At the very moment wisdom is needed, one of two possibilities will take place depending on the motivation that lies behind it. We will express ourselves either in God's wisdom from above or earthly wisdom from below ("demonic" according to verse 15).

The very ease with which we can express the wisdom from below is alarming, because to answer with that kind of "wisdom" is to "lie against the truth" (3:14). We are people of two radically different realms, the heavenly and the earthly/demonic. This world is more influenced by the demonic, and this kind of "wisdom" can easily seep into everything we do, even ministry. Thus, we find the church being run, evangelism being done, counsel being offered by wisdom from the world. The church gets run by worldly management techniques, evangelism gets watered down by a half gospel that avoids the harsh reality of human depravity in order to avoid offending someone, and counseling gets corrupted by secular psychology.

James pulls no punches as he continues in 3:16: "For where jealousy and selfish ambition exist"—and this reflects the wrong motivation he warned against in verse 14—"there is disorder and every evil thing." This last phrase describes the chaotic situation that exists in our nation and our world today. People have turned their backs on God's wisdom as found in Scripture, and we have gradually seen "disorder and every evil thing." Tragically, this is too often the state of affairs in our churches also, places that ought to resemble the conditions of heaven, not earth.

Contrasting with the disorder and evil of the earth is the "wisdom from above" (3:17). There is an implied progression of qualities about this wisdom. James says that it is "first pure," the "first" suggesting a progression to follow. To be "pure" means that any form of evil from this fallen world does not corrupt it. We often corrupt God's wisdom by mixing worldly wisdom with it; that is, we compromise and mix worldly principles with biblical principles. Much of worldly wisdom is a blend of true wisdom with earthly wisdom, something the evil one uses to enhance the world's approach to things—something that gives earthly wisdom some measure of credibility.

Next, wisdom from above is "peaceable." This means that it does not spawn friction like personal opinions often do. To reasonable people this wisdom is obvious. What follow are reasons why this wisdom is peaceable. First, it is "gentle." This means it is sensitive to peoples' needs and patient with them. Next, it is "reasonable." The Greek word means "well persuaded" in the sense of recognizing, when there is no moral issue involved, the good sense of an argument without being detracted by some personal bias. It is also "full of mercy and good fruits," a quality already defined in 2:8–13, where someone in need has that need met by one with working faith. Then wisdom from above is "unwavering." This NASB translation is one possible meaning, but it can also mean "impartial" (NIV). The context here favors this latter meaning, because reasons for why wisdom from above is "peaceable" are the overall thrust of verse 17. Last, this wisdom is "without hypocrisy" (NIV, "sincere"). Hypocrisy would exist in a society where intelligence and cleverness are virtues, things often mistaken as wisdom. Those who have looked to God for their wisdom have no reason to pretend or impress anyone with a show of worldly wisdom.

Verse 18 concludes, "And the seed whose fruit is righteousness is sown in peace by those who make peace." Without an explicit reference to wisdom, the sentence does not appear at first to fit here. Earlier, in verse 17, James said that wisdom from above was "peaceable." Perhaps he now focuses on that quality because quarrels were plaguing the church (3:16 and 4:1–2). The statement may have originally been a proverb that James is now quoting, and the point is that wisdom from above ultimately produces righteousness instead of strife.

James has thus provided for us a prescription for harmony in the body of Christ. That harmony is threatened by worldly wisdom. Worldly wisdom, in turn, lurks within all our minds, and our pride in trying to accomplish God's work in our own ability leads to the doing of God's work in man's way. Since everyone has an opinion on how something should be done, friction results. The prescription James offers is to seek the wisdom from above. This, I believe, comes through Scripture. If we look earnestly and in faith, we can find God's way for doing ministry in Scripture, often the last place we go.

Study Questions

1. In what way is good behavior seen and measured?

2. Where does bitter jealously and selfish ambition come from?

3. What is the source of earthly "wisdom"?

4. Might we say from verse 17 that the qualities of heavenly wisdom are actually the fruit of the Holy Spirit?

5. Compare 3:17 with Paul's fruit of the Spirit in Galatians 5:22–23.

6. How are the two lists different? How are the two lists similar or the same?

7. When James writes of "seed" in verse 18, is he writing about the qualities he has just listed in verse 17, or is he referring to the "seed" as one, as a complete spiritual entity, or as a cluster reflecting the characteristics he has just mentioned?

CHAPTER 9

Faith Demonstrated by Avoiding Worldliness
James 4:1-12

Preview:

The believer in Christ is capable of the greatest sin. Jealousy and pride bring on sins that are destructive to the Christian walk. James again urges the child of God to be humble and to draw near to God with clean hands. He further commands believers to refrain from speaking against the brethren since God is the One and only Lawgiver and Judge.

James asks the opening question of this section in order to diagnose a problem among his readers. His question calls attention to one of their symptoms and offers a reason for it. "What is the source of quarrels and conflicts among you? Is not the source your pleasures that wage war in your members?" (4:1) He goes on to list other symptoms like their lust, envy, and self-serving prayer (4:2-3) and finally identifies the problem as "friendship with the world" (4:4). Their faith has taken a backseat. This is further substantiated by the indirect references James makes to prayer. The latter part of verse 2 says, "You do not have because you do not ask," words that imply that they were not praying because they did not have faith. Then verse 3 continues with the remark that even when they do ask, they do so with wrong motives, which again suggests lack of faith. Furthermore, worldliness seems to increase as faith grows weak.

James begins (4:1) by asking the source of quarrels and conflicts among the believing community. The word for "quarrels" in the NASB is a softened translation of the Greek word *polemoi*, which actually means "wars." Likewise, the NASB translates the next word, *machai*, as "conflicts," and it means "fights." This is rather serious terminology in reference to a Christian fellowship, terms that are used more often in armed conflict between nations or individuals. However, these words can be used metaphorically for violent verbal disputes, and James wants to shock his readers into realizing that the same kinds of motives, emotions, and disagreements that engender strife among believers are the same feelings that lead to physical conflicts. What happens to believers when this happens? In light of the discussion to follow concerning loving the world, I would say they have a love for self-gratification and a desire to have their own way, and this is pure worldliness.

From whence do these kinds of conflicts arise? James points to "your pleasures that wage war in your members" (4:1). This has been James's subject indirectly in his discussion of the tongue. Behind the sins of the tongue lies indwelling sin, that which Paul calls the "flesh." War is waged in precisely the way Paul describes in Galatians 5:17: "For the flesh sets its desire against the Spirit, and the Spirit against the flesh; for these are in opposition to one another, so that you may not do the things that you please." The conflict, according to Paul, takes place between indwelling sin (the flesh) and the Holy Spirit. The conflict is resolved only by "walking by means of the Spirit"—a metaphor for depending on the Spirit to enable us to say "no" to sin in such moral situations.

James uses even more explicit and strong language in 4:2: "You lust and do not have; so you commit murder. And you are envious and cannot obtain; so you fight and quarrel. You do not have because you do not ask." If "wars" sounded out of place among Christians, "murder" sounds even more unbelievable among believers. Once again James is dealing in hyperbole as he did with "wars" and "fights." Jesus, remember, said that to hate one's brother is to commit murder in one's heart (Matt. 5:22). Although physical murder is rare among believers, such hatred unfortunately is not. Frustrated desire is James's subject here. Depravity within the believer is fully capable of everything James says here and, in extreme cases, even murder.

Hard on the heels of James's statement that his readers fail to ask and therefore don't receive (4:2), he adds that even when prayer is offered under these conditions of inner worldliness, the motives are not pure or in faith. Such prayer does not yield answers from God, because the motives are purely selfish. Some people imagine that God is a "celestial Santa Claus," existing solely for their desires.

What happens to believers who work their way into such godlessness? James tells in 4:4: "You adulteresses, do you not know that friendship with the world is hostility toward God? Therefore whoever wishes to be a friend of the world makes himself an enemy of God." For believers this means reverting to the lifestyle that enslaved them before they believed. James's language has become even more severe. He bluntly calls worldly Christians "adulteresses." The feminine form of the word arises out of the Old Testament imagery of God's unfaithful people, Israel. Jeremiah 3:20 provides an example of such imagery:

"Surely, as a woman treacherously departs from her lover,
So you have dealt treacherously with Me,
O house of Israel," declares the Lord.

James thus implies that the New Testament people of God, the church, are capable of the same thing.

The Christian and the World

The world cannot give peace (John 14:27).

The world hates believers (John 15:19).

Satan is the prince of the world (John 16:11).

Christians do not belong to this world (John 17:16).

The wisdom of the world is foolish (1 Cor. 1:20).

The world by its wisdom knew not God (1 Cor. 1:21).

The things of the world are foolish (1 Cor. 1:27).

The world sees believers as scum (1 Cor. 4:13).

The form of this world is passing away (1 Cor. 7:31).

The sorrow of the world produces death (2 Cor. 7:10).

Believers are to shine as lights in the world (Phil. 2:15).

Believers are to keep themselves unstained by the world (James 1:27).

The world is corrupt (2 Pet. 1:4).

Believers are not to love the world nor the things in it (1 John 2:15).

The world is full of the lust of the flesh, the lust of the eyes, and the pride of life (1 John 2:16).

The world is passing away (1 John 2:17).

The believer's faith overcomes the world (1 John 5:4).

The world lies in the power of the evil one (1 John 5:19).

James's only explicit reference to the Holy Spirit (in 4:5–6) appears as a warning of the consequences or disciplinary work of the Spirit in believers who have come to love the world. Admittedly this meaning is not clear in the NASB: "Or do you think that the Scripture[1] speaks to no purpose: 'He jealously desires the Spirit which He has made to dwell in us'"? The NIV is even less clear, not even capitalizing the word for "spirit."[2] The literal translation is: "Toward jealously yearns the Spirit which dwelt in you." The wording has puzzled translators, and they have debated whether the Greek word, *pneuma*, "spirit," is the Holy Spirit given in baptism or the human spirit given by God at creation or birth.

The only translation that makes sense in connection with spiritual adultery is that believers who become momentarily lovers of the world are headed for the work of the Holy Spirit that will restore them to spirituality. Thus my translation would be quite legitimate: "The Spirit that dwelt in you jealously yearns." "Jealously yearns" in what way? Once again, Paul's words in Galatians 5:17 come to mind: "The Spirit [sets His desire] against the flesh," and he will not rest until we have been brought to the place where we once again "walk by of the Spirit" (Gal. 5:16).

A quotation from Proverbs 3:34 concludes James's thought (4:6) and supports my translation: "But He gives a greater grace. Therefore it says, 'God is opposed to the proud, but gives grace to the humble.'" The opposition of God to pride is God's fundamental reaction to all sin. It will lead Him to judge those who persist in their pride (the basic nature of sin, incidentally) and require Him to discipline His people who have fallen into it. The "greater grace" is the work of the Spirit, and such grace is granted to those who humbly submit to the Spirit's efforts to rid them of their worldliness.

In light of the quotation from Proverbs above, James clearly states the remedy for loving the world.

> Submit therefore to God. Resist the devil and he will flee from you. Draw near to God and He will draw near to you. Cleanse your hands, you sinners; and purify your hearts, you double-minded. Be miserable and mourn and weep; let your laughter be turned into mourning, and your joy to gloom. Humble yourselves in the presence of the Lord, and He will exalt you (4:7–10).

This is obviously the language of what we often call "revival," although I prefer the term *reformation*, because the remedy is so comprehensive and revolutionary.

The first remedy—and most essential—is to submit to God. To submit to God is to acknowledge His absolute sovereignty, but it requires a renewal of memory about all the attributes of God including His holiness. Submission to

God is the opposite of hostility toward God (4:4) and is totally contrary to indwelling sin. If God through the Holy Spirit energizes our obedience, all that remains for us is to submit, but we tend to resist this vigorously. This conflict begins at conversion and continues for the rest of our lives, making faith absolutely necessary throughout. As Paul puts it in Romans 1:17, "the righteousness of God is revealed from faith to faith," or to capture the idiom a bit more accurately, "faith from beginning to end."

The second part of the remedy is to "resist the devil." In light of the devil's great power and cleverness, it may seem presumptuous to add, "he will flee from you." What we need to remember is that the devil has already been defeated at the cross, his power over believers broken. Thus the words of Colossians 2:15: "He had disarmed the rulers and authorities, He made a public display of them, having triumphed over them through Him."

The power of the devil originally lay in man's fall in the garden where man was in bondage to sin. Having paid for sin, Jesus broke this power. Thus, in the principal passage on spiritual warfare against "principalities and powers," Ephesians 6:10–20, we merely "put on the full armor of God," a metaphor for appropriating the salvation victory already achieved. We do this by affirming the truths symbolized by the various pieces of armor.

Third, we "draw near to God" (4:8), and as a consequence He draws near to us. This involves the spiritual disciplines of prayer, meditation, study of Scripture, fellowship with other believers, worship, fasting, and suffering in a godly manner.

Next we cleanse our hands and purify our hearts (4:8). These metaphors refer to confession of sin as well as to steps to overcome and avoid sin. The reference to hands has in mind the ritual washings of Judaism that symbolized spiritual cleansing, whereas the heart is seen as the essential self, the most comprehensive biblical term for the person's inner self. James's readers are addressed in this connection as "sinners" and "double-minded." "Sinners" reminds us of our proneness toward sin. James used "double-minded" in 1:8 of unstable people. It serves here as a reminder of one of the reasons worldliness had taken over.

Repentance is expressed also in Old Testament words. "Be miserable and mourn and weep" (4:9) are throughout Scripture acts of genuine sorrow for sin. The laughter of sin (this is implied by the context) must be "turned into mourning" and "joy to gloom." God was sorrow for sin instead of laughter when repentance is needed. True repentance will lead us to the appropriate laughter and joy.

Finally, we are to "humble" ourselves "in the presence of the Lord" (4:10). This is not mere repetition of the early prescription but a full-circle result of all the previous remedies. The final result is to be exalted by the Lord. This exaltation is not for personal satisfaction or glory but for God's glory. God lifts up people who have thus been revived before the world so that God can attract people to Himself through us.

James 4:11–12 is not obviously connected to the previous context: "Do not speak against one another, brethren. He who speaks against a brother, or judges his brother, speaks against the law, and judges the law; but if you judge the law, you are not a doer of the law but a judge of it. There is only one Lawgiver and Judge, the One who is able to save and to destroy; but who are you who judge your neighbor?"

Although the connection is somewhat subtle, the most logical possibility is that these verses continue the exhortations to the worldly begun in 4:7. James 4:7–10 looks toward God, while these involve one's fellow human beings. The revival proposed as the remedy should work its way into relations with others.

Apparently the dissensions that plagued the church were resulting in personal attacks. To "speak against" someone can include a number of kinds of attacks and includes the questioning of authority, as when the Israelites "spoke against God and Moses" (Num. 21:5), slandering someone in secret (Ps. 101:5), and falsely accusing someone (1 Pet. 2:12).

What is intriguing about James's exhortation is that he explains that whoever speaks against his brother "speaks against the law, and judges the law" (4:11). The word *law* is without the article in both cases (even though most modern translations supply the article for smooth English) and thus refers to the law governing the Christian life in general, not the specific Law of Moses. James has already referred to it as the "perfect law, the law of liberty," (1:25) and the "royal law" or law of Christian love (2:8). In what sense, then, does the one speaking against another believer speak against and judge this law? It is clear that he is violating that law, and James appropriately describes the situation as a person's "speaking against" the Law as he has spoken against a fellow believer. To speak against or judge someone is, in effect, to slander, misrepresent, and accuse the law that forbids what he is doing.

In the words "There is only one Lawgiver and Judge" (4:12), James indicates that the one speaking against another is setting himself up as a judge, and this too is presumptuously becoming a law to oneself. James seems to be saying, "Let God's law judge; don't you." Only God is qualified. Only God "is able to save and to destroy." In fact, such a person is setting himself up as God, a fact implied in the words "Who are you who judge your neighbor?"

Bear in mind, of course, that discernment of the behavior of others is something else. For example, we are not violating James's prohibition when we evaluate a person as a candidate for elder or when we examine a person's qualifications for ministry. The judging forbidden here is that which arises out of animosity and worldliness.

Study Questions

1. Is James speaking about Christians murdering people physically, or does he speak of murder in an emotional or spiritual sense?

2. In this section, what does James want the child of God to ask for?

3. Why do believers often ask but fail to receive what they petitioned the Lord for?

4. In James 4:11–12, is James putting believers in this age of the Church back under the Old Testament Law?

5. How can a Christian "judge" the Law?

CHAPTER 10

Faith Demonstrated by Submission to God's Will
James 4:13-17

Preview:

James warns against presumption and forgetting the sovereign will of the Lord in the matters of daily living. James illustrates the quickness and shortness of life for children of God by describing us simply as a wind, or vapor. By not considering God in the affairs of daily living, believers show their arrogance, which James says is evil.

Submission to God's will is yet another act that requires faith. To say confidently, "If the Lord wills, we will live and also do this or that" (4:15), is to have implicit, unwavering faith in God's way as the best. One of the primary factors of sin is independence from God, the opposite of submission and faith. This was the essence of Eve's temptation, when she acted not only contrary to but also independently of God's will and took the fruit.

The opening words, "Come now," are a strong rebuke. This time James uses an exclamation filled with disdain and unbelief instead of an accusing question (2:14; 4:1). James understood that life was hazardous and uncertain. Only God knows the future, and for each day's new awakening, there is no guarantee. We humans merely have an illusion of continuity and control. The words "Today or tomorrow" imply a sense of personal sovereignty, a confidence that the speaker is able to direct his life on a whim. James refers to something typical a wealthy merchant might say to his associates: "We shall go to such and such a city, and spend a year there and engage in business and make a profit" (4:13). People of wealth entertain the illusion—after some successes in doing as they please and succeeding in a competitive world—that they are in complete command. Such people are often the least prepared to be thwarted in their purposes and often, when they fail, have extreme difficulty coping with unexpected bad fortune.

The fundamental error in such confident planning is that no one knows nor can really plan for the future with any assurance (4:14): "You do not know what your life will be like tomorrow." No matter how long anyone lives, a human being is "just a vapor that appears for a little while and then vanishes away." The word *vapor* is often used to refer to smoke—here one minute, gone the next. The brevity of life strikes us all from time to time, but only the wise among us truly take it seriously.

What is the godly course of action? James says, "Instead, you ought to say, 'If the Lord wills, we shall live and also do this or that'" (4:15). From this passage has come the expression "Lord willing." This expression too often merely serves to make the one using it appear pious, while in reality it is uttered as a habit with little conviction. The person using the expression honestly will have a respect for divine sovereignty and be willing to have something interrupt his or her plans and cheerfully make the most of it. It expresses an attitude of willingness to conform to the divine will, whatever it may be. Such a person indeed makes plans, but he or she does not worship those plans. Everything is contingent on God's will.

What lies behind the presumptuous making of plans? James says, "You boast in your arrogance" (4:16). This translation does not quite capture the meaning. The more literal translation is, "You boast in your arrogances [plural]." The meaning involves what the boasting is *all about*, not the way the boasting occurs. This individual, in other words, boasts in his ability to make plans as though nothing could stop him: his *arrogances*. This is the epitome of pride, the heart and core of human depravity. No wonder James says, "All such boasting is evil." One could boast in God and His wonders—that would be no sin. But when you boast in your illusion of sovereignty, you are usurping an attribute of God. This is called self-deification, the desire of the Devil from the beginning (Isa. 14:14)[1] and the future act of the Antichrist himself (see 2 Thess. 2:4; Rev. 13:11–15).

James concludes this discussion with a proverbial-sounding statement: "Therefore, to one who knows the right thing to do, and does not do it, to him it is sin" (4:17). The connection (as implied by the "therefore") is straightforward. James seems to be saying, "You have been sinning by your arrogant belief that you, like God, can plan your future with utmost confidence. I have told you that that is sin. Now you know what is *right*. Therefore do not ignore what I have said and thus sin by omission. Do the right thing."

Study Questions

1. From James 4:13, in what way is the child of God cutting the Lord out of the way he or she lives?

2. In verse 14, What is James reminding us of?

3. In what way can a believer "boast in arrogance"?

4. What are the consequences of knowing how to do right but failing to do so?

5. What should believers be saying about their own "plans" in life?

6. Does God's will override all of our life or just part of our existence?

7. How does verse 17 refer to what James has just written about God's will?

CHAPTER 11

Faith Demonstrated by One's Attitude toward Wealth
James 5:1-6

Preview:

James takes the wealthy Christian to task for failing to handle his riches properly. Again, he is concerned about the poor and the laborer who have nothing and who may be mistreated by the wealthy believer. He also accuses the rich of living frivolously and wantonly and, by this, even condemning "to death" the righteous man, because he is unable to resist the power of wealth.

Earlier, in James 2:6–7, the rich were distinguished from the believers as those who "blaspheme the fair name" by which they were called. In all likelihood, here also James has in mind unsaved people, although at times he has addressed arrogant people—either believers or unbelievers—who plan their lives without God. Nevertheless, what James says here is a warning also to believers who achieve wealth not to be tempted to put their confidence in that wealth. This, indeed, was the essence of Paul's warning to the rich in 1 Timothy 6:17–18.

Faith ties in to this subject in a similar way as James suggested back in chapter 1 in connection with temptation. Faith looks to God for every provision (1:16–18).

James's rebuke is a scathing denunciation of excessive luxury. It was not unusual for Jews of the Second Temple period to regard *all* the rich as favored by God. The New Testament makes it clear, however, that wealth does not imply divine favor.

James begins with the same exclamation as he did in 4:13 toward the presumptuous planners of the future, "Come now." Earlier we saw these words as contemptuous of those who ought to know better. James tells them to "weep and howl" for the miseries to come upon them. We must remember that the wrong attitude toward riches is the object of God's future judgment, whether on earth or in the final judgment.

Using the "prophetic perfect" approach, one in which the prophet of the Old Testament would speak in the past tense as though the certainty of his predictions was emphasized by their being viewed as already accomplished, James says that their wealth had rotted, their garments had become moth-eaten (5:2), and their gold and silver had rusted (5:3). Given time, the material things in which they had placed their hopes and confidence would deteriorate. They were putting hope in things that were not enduring. This condition (specifically the rust) would be a witness against them and "consume your flesh like fire." This is the imagery of judgment, something used even of believers, some of whose works will be consumed by fire at the Judgment Seat of Christ (1 Cor. 3:13). Fire is an appropriate symbol, because it penetrates and consumes everything of little endurance. Thus shall be God's judgment of both believers (for rewards) and unbelievers (for degrees of punishment). This judgment is reserved for the "last days," and these people are seen as storing up "treasure" for that day, a time described in Revelation 20:11–15 after the end of the millennial kingdom at the Great White Throne. The judgment of believers, of course, is distinct in place and time from this occasion. Their judgment will occur in heaven following the removal of the Church before the Tribulation. The reference to "treasure" here is ironic, since it is not really treasure, something lasting, on which they had placed their hope, but something worthless in light of eternity.

James next turns to the social sins that these wealthy people had perpetrated (5:4–6). First of all, they had withheld wages from their workers (5:4). A typical Hebraic form appears in the accusation that the unpaid wages of the workers in the fields "cries out" against them. This is a favorite way of stating an injustice, as though the crime itself were testifying against the guilty in court. One of the firm biblical economic principles is that a laborer is worthy of his or her wages (Luke 10:7), but the wealthy, in their comfortable places of power, frequently underpay their workers. New Testament Palestine had reached a place where most land was in the hands of a few. Thus, James's scenario is quite typical. Not much has changed in modern times—wealth and the abuses that accompany it are in the hands of a very few. The "outcry of those who did the harvesting has reached the ears of the Lord of Sabaoth," which means that judgment is certain. The word transliterated "Sabaoth" in the NASB means "hosts" or "army" and is a name suggesting God's power. It usually refers to angels, but the armies of Israel were also referred to as the "host" of the Lord (1 Sam. 17:45).

The Bible's Teaching about Wealth
Solomon was granted wisdom because he did not ask for wealth from God (2 Chr. 1:11).
The wicked are not granted enduring wealth (Job 15:29).
The evil trust their wealth and boast in their riches (Ps. 49:6).
The fools and those who are senseless leave their wealth to others (Ps. 49:10).
The righteous should honor the Lord with their wealth (Prov. 3:9).
Some pretend to be wealthy but have nothing (Prov. 13:7).
Some pretend to be poor but have great wealth (Prov. 13:7).
Wealth obtained by fraud dwindles away (Prov. 13:11).
Wealth obtained by labor increases (Prov. 13:11).
Do not grow weary trying to be wealthy (Prov. 23:4).
Wealth can have wings and fly away! (Prov. 23:5).
Those who are evil run after wealth (Prov. 28:22).
To some God gives riches and honor, but often others are blessed and not the one who became wealthy (Eccl. 6:2).
For some who are wealthy, their riches make it hard to enter the kingdom of God (Luke 18:24).
The Laodicean Christians boasted of their wealth but did no realize they were spiritually wretched, miserable, poor, blind, and naked (Rev. 3:17).

The next charge against the wealthy is that they "have lived luxuriously on the earth and led a life of wanton pleasure" (5:5). This accusation must be put in tandem with the previous one. Kings, for example, were expected to live luxuriously. Luxury itself was not necessarily a sin. The sin lay in the wealthy living luxuriously while those for whom they were responsible went without. Paul teaches that failure to be generous and share, not the wealth itself, was the sin of the rich (1 Tim. 6:17–19). The "wanton pleasure" they enjoyed points up another aspect of their sin. Pleasure had become an occupation, not merely a diversion. Since sin causes people to go to extremes, self-discipline must be exercised to keep it in check. We actually enjoy pleasure more when ✳

we experience it in moderation. A final metaphor sums up the fate of James's wealthy readers: "You have fattened your hearts in a day of slaughter." This is another of James's picturesque figures of speech for judgment. As a farmer fattens his cow for the slaughter and a sumptuous meal, so they had "fattened" their own hearts for judgment.

The final indictment against the rich is found in James 5:6: "You have condemned and put to death the righteous man; he does not resist you." In 2:6 James already said in similar words that the rich oppressed the people of God: "Is it not the rich who oppress you and personally drag you into court?" Both remarks reflect a court situation, and I am inclined to think, after two such references in the same book, that the court system was a favorite locale for the persecution of Christians. Saul's persecution took a similar approach, according to Acts 8:3, where the reference to prison implies this. The fact that the righteous did not resist probably reflects obedience to Jesus' command not to resist evil in Matthew 5:38–42.

Study Questions

1. Why does James appeal to the Old Testament description of God as "the Lord of Sabaoth" in this chapter?

2. In what way has the rich cheated the average laborer in his fields?

3. How has the wealthy condemned the righteous man who is unable to resist him?

4. Why do you think James keeps coming down so hard on the rich?

5. Is James writing about the lifestyle and sins of wealthy believers, or does the reference and context relate to unbelievers?

6. Why is it difficult for the righteous to resist the influence of the wealthy?

CHAPTER 12

Faith Demonstrated by Patience in Trials
James 5:7–12

Preview:

James seems to be clearly writing about the rapture of the Church when he says, "The Judge is standing right at the door." By this he means the Lord may come at any time, because "He is at hand." As an example of patiently waiting for that day, James reminds the readers of the suffering of the prophets who have gone before. It is a blessing to endure troubles as that which Job suffered.

This section of the letter of James is the only eschatological portion in the letter except for the references to judgment and human mortality in 2:13; 4:12, 14; 5:3, 5. James uses one of the most common forms of the words for the second coming of Christ, *parousia,* which means basically, "presence" or "coming," translated with the latter term throughout the New Testament. In ancient classical and *koine* (biblical) Greek, the word was used most often in connection with the visit of royalty to a city; thus, it was an appropriate term for the biblical writers to select. From a dispensational standpoint, the word is somewhat vague, except for the fact that the other two words for Christ's second advent, *epiphaneia* ("appearing") and *apocalupsis* ("revelation"), lend themselves by virtue of their intrinsic meaning to the aspect of the return of Christ to earth to establish his millennial kingdom. *Parousia* is used of both the assembling of living and dead believers before the Tribulation period as well as the triumphant return to earth following the Tribulation period.[1]

James has no particular trials in mind. What he says is rather general: "Be patient, therefore, brethren, until the coming of the Lord" (5:7). This patience is needed for the entire Christian life as well as the entirety of Christian history. Since this commentary is written from the classical or traditional dispensational perspective, I will here propose reasons for interpreting this "coming" of the Lord as the pretribulational rapture and resurrection of the Church.

Several words or phrases in the section (5:7-11) imply the concept of "imminence," and imminence, if it is a valid concept, in turn implies a distinction between the coming of Christ *for* His own and the coming of Christ *with* His own. If one were to assemble all the promises to the Christian of the coming of Christ (excluding those references that apply to His coming to establish His kingdom), a concept of imminency would legitimately emerge requiring the following definition of the word: *Biblical imminency means that the coming of Christ to translate living believers and resurrect dead believers could have been and still could be possible at any moment.* This definition is reached on the basis that such words as *wait* are used as though the event might be the next eschatological event on the calendar. Furthermore, it does not mean *will* occur in the near future, for that would mean that it already would have occurred.

The words to which I refer that imply imminency are "be patient" (5:7-8), "the coming of the Lord is at hand" (5:8), and "the Judge is standing right at the door" (5:9). In the case of the word *near*, it must be obvious now after two thousand years of Christian history that the biblical writers did not mean "near" in the sense of "about to happen." The reference to the Judge "right at the door" is the strongest statement of imminency[2] in the passage. The picture is of a judge standing at the door of the courtroom waiting for just the right time to enter. Even the words of Revelation 22:20, "Yes, I am coming quickly," connote this very technical concept of "any moment" rather than "very soon."

I am well aware that my line of argument—and more could be said that cannot be justified in this commentary—is not conclusive but reasonable. There are a number of reasons for believing in the pretribulational rapture and resurrection, and the concept of imminency is merely one of them.

What does James mean by "be patient" besides "wait for an imminent event"? The translation "be patient" represents the Greek word *makrothumeō* in 5:7 twice and in 5:8, 10 four times. It means enduring a trial or experience for a very long time, as long as it takes to do so without panicking. Some have used the illustration of a very long fuse. Another similar word, *hupomenō*, occurs twice in 5:11 and is translated "endured" and "endurance." It connotes remaining under a threat without moving or confidence in God's care. Believers are to allow the hope of Christ's intervening return to condition their attitude toward all of life's unexpected and unpleasant events.

James gives as his illustration of the principle of patience the farmer who waits patiently for his harvest "until it gets the early and late rains" (5:7b). These rains[3] came in Palestine during late autumn and early spring and were vital to the success of the crop (Deut. 11:14). In a semi-desert land, great dependence was placed on such moisture. The illustration implies the patience of faith in the divine provision. The farmer has his work to do in preparing the soil, planting the seed, and harvesting, but the rest he must leave up to these rains.

Thus James continues, "You too be patient; strengthen your hearts, for the coming of the Lord is near" (5:8). The believer is to be patient in the work he or she has been assigned, a factor that will nurture patience. But the waiting times come when no work can be done, and an even greater measure of faith and patience is required. For two thousand years now the Church has been waiting, and its faithfulness has depended much on the understanding it has had regarding the meaning of "near." This imminence is not greatly unlike the possibility of death itself, something that might seem remote at times yet in our hazardous world is always possible "at any moment."

Faith and Patience

The Thessalonian Christians were known by their patience and faith (2 Thess. 1:4).

Believers are to pursue faith and patience (1 Tim. 6:11).

Believers are to follow after and pursue both faith and longsuffering (2 Tim. 3:10).

Older men are to be characterized as sound in faith and patience (Titus 2:2).

Believers are to imitate others who inherit God's promises through faith and longsuffering (Heb. 6:12).

In the Tribulation, those who have come to trust in Christ are to live by patience and faith (Rev. 13:10, see 14:12).

The coming of the Lord is a reason for patience because of the vindication and fulfillment it will provide. Whatever goes without justice and closure at the present time must be assigned to the Lord's coming when justice will be carried out and rewards distributed. Meanwhile, this world is not fair.

Lack of patience and endurance results in complaining against our brothers and sisters in Christ (5:9). Instead, we should be occupied with encouraging one another. The seriousness of this kind of behavior—it tears down rather than builds up the Church—is indicated by a reference to the Judge "right at the door." Since James is probably referring to the translation and resurrection of the Church, this judge would be Jesus Christ, and the occasion would be the Judgment Seat of Christ (1 Cor. 3:13–15; 2 Cor. 5:10).[4]

James offers the prophets as an example of suffering and patience (5:10). The prophets, both of the Old and New Testaments, suffered abuse and persecution. They bore this patiently, hence the meaning of "suffering and patience" when coupled together. The first word, *suffering,* is what they experienced; the second word, *patience,* is how they did it. The reason they suffered is implied in the words, "who spoke in the name of the Lord." There is a price to pay for speaking the truth, but there is no greater privilege. Thus, it is always worth it.

Job is the next example, this time of the other word, *endurance* (5:11). The "outcome of the Lord's dealings" probably refers to the outcome of the Lord's dealings with Job. Job, according to Job 42:10–17, had his fortunes restored beyond what he had suffered (see especially v. 12). Though Job was baffled about why God had allowed his sufferings and accordingly protested to God about them, he never lost faith in and loyalty to God and was consoled by God's revelation to him of His power and greatness (Job 40–41) as well as His compassion and mercy.

James 5:12 has puzzled interpreters from the very beginning as to its connection with the preceding passage. The expression, "But above all," implies a reference back to the preceding material. My feeling is that it forms a conclusion to the broader section and embraces the discussion of worldliness as well as patience and endurance in trials in light of the Lord's return. Whether in reference to worldliness or to trials, the danger of oaths is ever present. Swearing by heaven, earth, or any other thing is tempting when attempting to justify one's friendship with the world. Likewise, it is tempting to swear by something greater than oneself to justify one's lack of patience and endurance in the face of trials.

What kind of swearing is involved here? The flippant use of the name of God in profanity is not what is specifically condemned, either here or in the similar prohibition in Matthew 23:16–22. We have here an appeal to Someone or something greater than ourselves to give credence to what we claim or affirm. The point is that this should not be necessary. We should have established our integrity and credibility to such an extent that this will not be necessary. A simple, straightforward "yes" or "no" should establish what we say as the truth. Therefore, the danger of judgment is for lack of integrity, not for the use of God's name or the name of something else.

Study Questions

1. In what way does James refer to patience in this section? And how many times does he mention patience?

2. How does James use the sufferings of Job to help the reader?

3. How have the readers "seen the outcome of the Lord's dealings" with Job?

4. Why is James so adamant against believers swearing an oath by heaven or earth?

5. Why are believers told to "strengthen their hearts" because the coming of the Lord is at hand?

6. What is it about verse 9 that could make it a "rapture" of the Church passage?

7. In the context of James, how would the believer fall under the condemnation of judgment for not living consistently?

CHAPTER 13

Faith Demonstrated by Powerful Prayer
James 5:13–18

Preview:

James calls for prayer to be offered for the sick and reminds his readers that "the effective prayer of a righteous man can accomplish much." He urges believers to "keep on keeping on" by praying, being cheerful, and singing praises to the Lord. In case sickness is brought on by sin, he calls for confession. He uses the illustration of righteous Elijah to show how much can be accomplished by prayer.

James indicates the connection between prayer and faith in verse 15 when he refers to "the prayer offered in faith." The references to Elijah (5:17) and effective prayer (5:16) tell us that prayer offered in faith is powerful.

Whatever our mood or condition, Christians are to remember their dependence on God. We do this by praying when we suffer and by singing praises in good times (5:13). Actually, singing praises is a form of prayer, so our attitude in either case is one of recognition of our dependence on God. Whatever happens to believers is ordered or permitted by God.

James turns then to an occasion requiring prayer. "Is anyone among you sick?" James asks (5:14). The word translated "sick" (Greek, *astheneō*) by usage throughout the Bible (the Greek Septuagint of the Old Testament and the Greek of the New Testament) means weakness of any kind.[1] In the Gospels it is used most often in the sense of physical illness, and the context here points to physical illness in that "sick" is contrasted with "suffering" (5:13), which would be emotional. This is coupled with the fact that in verse 15 James's subject is referred to as "the one who is sick" a word that has only two possible meanings, weak or ill, and the extremity of this situation suggests much more than mere weakness. Furthermore, the elders go to the one who is sick. A person suffering emotionally or spiritually ordinarily could go to the elders. Because healing appears to be guaranteed if the prayer is offered in faith, some have made efforts to avoid what seems to be contradictory to other biblical passages that teach that God does not heal all sicknesses. Thus, the word "sick," since it can include emotional or spiritual weakness (as in the Pauline epistles), is interpreted as spiritual depression or emotional illness, something God never wants for the believer.

Praying Believers

Believers often do not know what they should pray for (Rom. 8:26).

Pray at all times (Eph. 6:18).

Prayer can be for increased love (Phil. 1:9).

Prayer should be without ceasing (Phil. 1:9).

Paul always prayed for the believers (Col. 1:3).

Paul did not stop praying for believers to be filled with the knowledge of Christ (Col. 3:9).

Paul wanted believers to pray for an open door of witness while he was imprisoned (Col. 4:3).

Paul wanted Christian men to pray, lifting up holy hands (1 Tim. 2:8).

Prayer should be done with dependence on the Holy Spirit (Jude 1:20).

Paul continually asked prayer for his ministry and for those who served with him (Col. 4:8; 1 Thess. 5:25; 2 Thess. 3:1).

However, the problem probably does not exist if we understand James's thinking as a whole. The promise that the "prayer offered in faith will restore the one who is sick" (5:15) is contingent upon James's earlier teaching about the will of God (4:15). The "prayer offered in faith" is faith that God is *able* to heal. Those who take faith healing to the unbiblical extreme, such as the "name it and claim it" faith cult, intimidate people with accusations of lack of faith. They claim that God *will* heal all who make requests "offered in faith." It is quite possible to believe God is able to heal without insisting that He must heal. Prayer exists for God, not humanity. It provides occasions for Him to teach us about Himself—what He can do as well as how He wants us to trust Him when prayer is not answered in a way suitable to us.

The one who is sick calls the elders,[2] which suggests that the person is seriously incapacitated. This may imply the extent of illness that warrants such extraordinary measures. Prayer for the sick ordinarily can be offered without the presence of the elders; thus, calling the elders may signal an exceptional situation.

Anointing with oil (5:14) has occasioned considerable debate among interpreters. The word *anoint* is the Greek *aleiphō*. The problem as to its meaning here lies in the fact that it sometimes means a ceremonial anointing (Luke 7:38, 46) and at other times the application of a household remedy for the ill (Mark 6:13).[3] Since this anointing is to be carried out "in the name of the Lord," it is likely to be ceremonial. The problem with seeing it as a healing remedy is that such a remedy was never for *all* illnesses as implied here, only specific ones in which such a remedy would be appropriate. And why should it be necessary for the elders to apply a healing remedy when their purpose is spiritual, not medical?

The question is, what is the purpose of ceremonial or religious anointing? God is being called upon ("in the name of the Lord") to heal, and anointing is frequently for the purpose of consecration of the individual and a means of divine healing.[4] Therefore, this is a solemn act on an extremely critical occasion. The elders gather to pray that, if God is willing, their prayer of faith that God is able to perform such a miracle will be used by God to bring about physical restoration.

One further issue needs to be resolved. James refers to the possibility of the sick person's having committed any sins, and if so they will be forgiven (5:15). A misreading of the Old Testament led many Jews to believe that all illness was the result of sin. That notion should be laid to rest, for the wording is "if" the person has committed sin, not "since." True, all instances of illness should raise this question, since illness is one of God's means of discipline to bring about repentance and spiritual restoration. But illness can also be a trial God allows to bring about the strengthening of faith and refinement of character, as James has already taught (1:2–4).

The reference to confession of sin leads James to recommend that believers confess their sins to "one another" (5:16). This verse has suffered much abuse in an unwarranted general interpretation and application. The Roman Catholic confessional is based partly on this passage, which ignores the context in which the elders come to the sick person, and instead picture it as one going to a priest to confess. When I refer to "an unwarranted *general* interpretation," I mean an interpretation that we should confess to one another publicly and indiscriminately about matters that are better reserved for a select and mature group of people, as is the case here with the elders of the church. There is merit in the dictum "confess private sins privately and public sins publicly." Otherwise, a public display of personal sins may violate Paul's warning in Ephesians 5:12: "For it is disgraceful even to speak of the things which are done by the disobedient in secret."

To summarize the matter, James's recommendation to confess sin to one another is restricted to the context in which it is found. "One another" admittedly could suggest *mutual* confession, but this need not imply an exchange of confessions, each person taking his or her turn. All this requires is that from one believer to another (in this case one believer to several others) confession take place. The elders—mature and spiritual men—are to be those who do not commit the same sins (Gal. 6:1). They are hearing this confession and God is applying its benefits to the sick person to bring about his healing, perhaps physical healing if God so wills, but at least spiritual healing (forgiveness) when sin has been involved.

When and Where Can Prayers Be Said?

- *Prayers can be said kneeling (Luke 22:41).*
- *Praying should take place while waiting (Acts 1:14).*
- *Leaders should devote themselves to prayer (Acts 6:4).*
- *Leaders should pray in decision making (Acts 6:6).*
- *Prayers can be offered on the housetop (Acts 10:9).*
- *Prayers can be said in the house (Acts 10:30).*
- *Prayers can be said in the city (Acts 11:5).*
- *Prayers can be said in a group (Acts 12:12).*
- *Prayers can be coupled with fasting (Acts 13:3).*
- *Prayers can be accompanied with singing (Acts 16:25).*
- *Elders should pray (Acts 20:36).*
- *Prayers can be said by the seashore (Acts 21:5).*
- *Women should pray (1 Cor. 11:5).*
- *Men should pray (1 Tim. 2:8).*

Verse 16 concludes with a description of what makes prayer powerful: "The effective prayer of a righteous man can accomplish much" (NASB). The KJV translates, "The effectual, fervent prayer of a righteous man availeth much," and the NIV offers, "The prayer of a righteous man is powerful and effective." The order of words in the original Greek is difficult to translate, hence the variations.[5] My own fairly literal translation is: "A prayer of a righteous man is very strong being made effective." The participle, if in the passive voice, means "being made effective" (one word in Greek) and implies that something makes it effective because it is from a righteous man. The participle could be in the middle voice and would then be translated "in its working." Admittedly, there is no reference to anything empowering prayer up to this point, but I would prefer to understand it as passive. Thus, the divine energizer is implied. This prayer is made effective by God because it meets the requirements of intensity and righteousness.

Elijah is James's next example of powerful prayer, in this case prayer that changed the weather (5:17). Mark Twain was wrong when he wrote that everyone talks about the weather but no one ever does anything about it. Elijah was an exception to Twain's generalization. Elijah is described as "a man with a nature like ours," which means he was a man with human limitations (who could not control the weather himself) and a fallen nature. James intends to encourage prayer with this statement. Powerful prayer is possible for any one of us. One requirement, however, was that it should be earnest. This would accord with 5:16, where the prayer is described as very strong.

A problem occurs when we read the account of the drought in 1 Kings 17 and 18. Elijah is described as announcing the drought by the word of the Lord, but there is no explicit reference to his praying, nor is there a specific reference to its length. As the time approached for the drought to end (1 Kgs. 18:42) Elijah climbed to the top of Mount Carmel and putting his face between his knees in what appears to be a posture for prayer. In light of the fact that James selected this as an example of fervent prayer, I am inclined to believe that he was aware of facts that are not preserved in our canonical Scriptures, facts that were known also to Jesus, who referred to the drought as lasting three and one-half years in Luke 4:25. When James wrote, a tradition was probably widely known about Elijah's praying, so that his original readers would have understood his use of that event. Second Esdras, an apocryphal book, may be a witness to this tradition. It records the fact that Elijah prayed in connection with this drought (2 Esdras 7:109).

Study Questions

1. What is the importance of anointing the sick with oil?
2. Does the oil heal the sick, or does prayer?
3. From James 5:15–16, what would make us think that the sickness James describes came about by sin?
4. What is the role of the church elders in this section?
5. Does the prayer of the elders guarantee healing?

CHAPTER 14

Faith Demonstrated by Restoring the Erring
James 5:19–20

Preview:

Finally, James closes this epistle with a great concern that his readers do not stray from the truth. He urges others to help in turning the wayward Christian around. Sparing those who are in error is like covering a multitude of sins and saving the soul from death.

The final two verses of James provide an appropriate conclusion to the entire letter. We have seen a potpourri of valuable advice for the Christian life, much reminiscent of the Sermon on the Mount. James's final word involves our responsibility to this truth so far as our obligation to one another is concerned. We are to "turn back" the one who errs and be ready to accept that same discipline ourselves. This advice coincides with Galatians 6:1, where Paul commands those who are spiritual to restore one overtaken in some sin.

The translation "if any among you strays" involves the aorist subjunctive, passive voice, of the Greek verb "to cause to stray" and literally means "should be led astray," implying inducement by a tempter. This is a straying from the "truth," and the warning may not at this point be a warning not to commit some sin as much as wander from the truth. To wander from the truth is a step *toward* committing some moral sin; thus, the fundamental preventative from moral sin is adherence to truth, primarily theological truth. Such theological truth underlies all of James's teaching in this letter. For example, believing that God is the rich provider prevents us for giving in to temptation; believing that God tests and refines faith prevents us from becoming impatient when we face trials; believing that God shows no favoritism prevents us from showing favoritism toward anyone.

James refers to the one who strays as being "among you." This implies that this person is a believer, a member of their Christian community. In the New Testament, it is common for writers to make a sharp distinction between pagans and themselves. Frequently it is done by the use of the first person plural pronouns "we" and "us." The apostle John addresses his readers as "my little children" (1 John 2:1 et al.). Furthermore, he states that the spirit of antichrist is already in the world, and they are those who "went out from us, but they were not really of us; for if they had been of us, they would have remained with us" (1 John 2:19). In James 5:20 the erring one is called a "sinner," and this may appear to some to point to this person's being an unbeliever. On occasion, however, one finds passages that describe the sin of the believer, and although the believer is more often referred to as a "saint," he is capable of sin and, as this reference shows, may even be called a sinner in exceptional instances.

James encourages his readers to turn back the one who is caused to stray from the truth he has proclaimed in the letter. His reward is twofold: First, he will "save his soul from death," and second, he "will cover a multitude of sins." The first problem in interpreting the first phrase is what kind of death James has in mind.

The Bible speaks of three kinds of death: (1) separation from God, or spiritual death, the condition into which we all are born; (2) separation of the soul/spirit from the body, or physical death (note James 2:26); and (3) final separation of the soul from God, or eternal punishment in the lake of fire. The issue boils down to one of the latter two, since no one can be saved from the condition inherited through his or her parents. The issue ultimately is whether a true believer can ever be lost again, a complex issue involving the hermeneutical principle of interpreting equivocal salvation passages in light of unequivocal salvation passages.[1] This principle leads me to interpret this passage as physical death, the ultimate form of divine discipline.

The second result of turning a straying believer from the error of his way is that the one turning him "will cover a multitude of sins." First Peter 4:8 uses the same expression: "Above all, keep fervent in your love for one another, because love covers a multitude of sins." The expression seems to be an allusion to Proverbs 10:12, where hate stirs up strife, while love "covers all transgressions" in the sense that we overlook offenses against us in the interest of peace among brethren. In the Petrine text also, the likelihood is that the covering of sins is the result of a love that does not hold grudges and maintains peace among brethren. One view is that the expression was common during the first century for the love of God covering sin through Christ's death on the cross. In James, then, the meaning would be that when a sinning Christian is converted from his or her error, the love of God is available to cover that sin. The problem with this interpretation is that the text seems to be saying that the one who restores is accomplishing the covering of a multitude of sins, not God. My own conclusion regarding the best interpretation of James's usage of the phrase is from the standpoint of the *prevention of sin*. When we restore an erring brother or sister to the truth, many sins that would otherwise flow from that error are prevented from occurring.

Study Questions

1. What is the place of truth in the Christian life?

2. How far can a fellow believer go in turning around the erring one who is going astray? When does such help become "meddling"?

3. Is James referring to loss of salvation when he speaks of "saving the soul" of the wayward?

4. When James writes about "covering a multitude of sins," is he arguing for simply "hiding" sins in some kind of secrecy?

THE BOOK OF FIRST PETER

Godly Suffering

CHAPTER 15

Background of First Peter

Martin Luther called this book one of the most outstanding in the New Testament: "This epistle of Peter is one of the grandest of the New Testament, and it is the true, pure gospel. For Peter does also the very same thing as Paul and all the evangelists do in that he includes the true doctrine of faith—how Christ has been given to us, who takes away our sins and saves us."[1]

First Peter was written just as the early church came near the threshold of violent persecution. The book is addressed to "aliens, scattered throughout Pontus, Galatia, Cappadocia, Asia, and Bithynia, who are chosen" (1:1). These were probably descendants of Jewish Christians who had been living in Asia Minor, now the region of modern Turkey, who had made pilgrimage to Jerusalem and were witnesses to the dramatic events of Pentecost (Acts 2:9–11). When they returned, they must have shared with great enthusiasm about the risen Christ.

It is not inconceivable that the audience Peter was writing to was mainly Jewish, though the doctrine of the church was by now fully developed, bringing together both Gentiles and Jews into the spiritual body of Christ. But it still seems fair to say that this apostle was focusing his ministry with the scattered Jewish communities of believers throughout the Mediterranean basin. Kistermaker writes:

> Considering the population mixture in the provinces of Asia Minor, we think that both Jews and Gentiles received the gospel of Christ and responded in faith to the call of the apostles. Moreover, some of the people Peter addresses were slaves. We infer that many of these slaves were Gentiles (2:18–20).
>
> Jewish people through their local synagogues in Asia Minor, Macedonia, and Greece evangelized the Gentile population, so that many Gentiles

were known as "God-fearers" (Acts 10:2; 13:26, 50; 17:4, 17). God-fearing Gentiles readily accepted the gospel of Christ and became members in the church together with Jewish Christians.2

No matter what the audience ratio for Peter's readership, the basic principles that governed the New Testament church were in place and were applicable to whatever ethnic group read these words of the apostle.

External and Internal Evidence of Authorship

The book of 1 Peter was never seriously disputed among the early church fathers. This epistle went unchallenged, and there was never any doubt that it was written by the apostle Peter. Traces of quotes can be found in the Corinthian letter of Clement of Rome. Up to twenty allusions are found in early church writings. By the time of Polycarp's Epistle to the Philippians, additional quotes and references are abundant. While 1 Peter is not listed in the Muratorian Fragment, it is thoroughly attested to by Irenaeus, Clement of Alexander, and Tertullian.

The internal evidence has all the marks of being from the apostle Peter. Second Peter 3:1 mentions "the second epistle," which many believe would certainly be this first letter. The book was obviously written by one who held great authority in the church. It claims Petrine authorship (1:1); points strongly to the resurrection of Christ from the dead, which Peter personally attested to (v. 3); and speaks of Christ as the Holy One (v. 15), as Peter quoted from Psalm 16:8 in Acts 2:27. Peter also uses the word *foreknown* (v. 20) as he did in a similar manner in Acts 2:23. Peter's emphasis on shepherding in 1 Peter 2:25 and 5:1-3 may signify that he was recalling Christ's words in John 21:15-16, where the Lord told him to "Shepherd My sheep" (v. 16). Finally, Peter says outright that he was a "witness of the sufferings of Christ, and a partaker also of the glory that is to be revealed" (1 Peter 5:1). The first statement would refer to the fact that he was a witness to Jesus' crucifixion, and the second statement is probably distinct reference to the transfiguration of the Lord as recorded in Matthew 17:1-6.

Date and Purpose

The persecution of Nero would fall hard on the church in A.D. 64. The pressure seems to be building about the time this letter was written; therefore, most scholars place the date of the writing of 1 Peter around A.D. 63. Some have thought that since Peter mentions Babylon (5:13) this may have been where he was staying at the time of writing. He mentions a woman there who sends her greetings to the readers. Many have surmised that this was his wife, but more than likely, if this was the case, he would have mentioned her in a specific manner. A traditional view is that his reference to Babylon was a code name for Rome used to keep his location secret in such dangerous times.

Some have further speculated that the "she" in 5:13 is a collective of the church in Babylon, but the way the verse ends makes this doubtful. "She" is "chosen together with you, sends you greetings, and so does my son, Mark." In normal language, and by the way this is written, the most likely answer is that this is a prominent and well-known woman whom the readers recognized.

While this epistle truly reflects the mind of the apostle Peter, his secretary and scribe was Silas, or Silvanus (5:12), who was with Paul on his second missionary journey. To have a close associate take down dictation was quite common in biblical days. This fact in no way affects the doctrine of the inspiration of Scripture, nor does it take away from the fact that this is indeed a letter from Peter, reflecting his ideas and thoughts.

> Tradition holds that Peter spent time in the imperial city and in its vicinity met martyrdom. The assumption that Peter wrote this epistle from Rome seems credible, for the evidence from tradition points to Rome as the place of composition. Papias, bishop of Hierapolis D. 125), reports that Mark was Peter's interpreter. And Irenaeus comments that both Peter and Paul had preached in Rome, and that afterward "Mark, the disciple and interpreter of Peter, did also hand down to us in writing what had been preached by Peter."[3]

Some have asked, "Why did Peter write this letter?" At first glance there seems to be no obvious theme or clear intended purpose. But the more the epistle is examined, especially in the final chapters, patterns begin to emerge. In 5:12 Peter writes, "I have written to you briefly, exhorting and testifying that this is the true grace of God. Stand firm in it." The increased persecution of the church is the backdrop for this summary statement. God's grace will sustain all those about to face the fiery trials ahead. Many passages prove this point.

Further, Peter writes, "The end of all things is at hand" (4:7), "Do not be surprised at the fiery ordeal among you, which comes upon you for your testing," (v. 12a), "but to the degree that you share the sufferings of Christ, keep on rejoicing" (v. 13). Peter reminds his readers that they are not to suffer as criminals (v. 15), but they should take persecution as Christians (v. 16), whose suffering is really part of the larger purpose of God: "Therefore, let those also who suffer according to the will of God entrust their souls to a faithful Creator in doing what is right" (v. 19). The apostle further writes that such troubles were coming upon other brothers (5:9), but a glorious end was in sight: "And after you have suffered for a little while, the God of all grace who called you to His eternal glory in Christ, will Himself perfect, confirm, strengthen and establish you" (v. 10).

The Isaiah 53 Connection

The crucifixion of the Lord Jesus made a lasting and permanent impression on the apostle. He refers to Christ's body on the cross (2:24) and His dying for our sins (3:18). He speaks about the suffering of Jesus in His body (4:1) and the fact that he observed Jesus' agony (5:1).

Peter refers to Isaiah 53:9 in teaching that the Lord "committed no sin, nor was deceit found in His mouth" (2:22). The apostle writes that Christ "also suffered for you," a reference to Jesus' chastening and scourging for our well-being (Is. 53:5).

Peter also mentions Christ's sinlessness (2:22) and that He was "a lamb unblemished and spotless" (1:19 cf. Is. 53:7). He writes that the Lord died for the unrighteous (1 Pet. 3:18 cf. Is. 53:12) and sprinkled His blood on sinners (1 Pet. 1:2 cf. Is. 52:15;), who were given healing by His wounds (1 Pet. 2:24 cf. Is. 53:5).

Conclusion

While at first glance 1 Peter may not appear to be *doctrinal*, in reality it is full of teaching nuggets. Besides what has already been mentioned, the apostle refers to Christ's resurrection and ascension. He writes that God "has caused us to be born again to a living hope through the resurrection of Jesus Christ from the dead" (1 Pet. 1:3), that the resurrection of the Lord saves you (3:21), and that He now has "eternal glory" (5:10). And though Peter mentions the ascension only one time, his statement is powerful and dramatic: We are saved by "the resurrection of Jesus Christ, who is at the right hand of God, having gone into heaven, after angels and authorities and powers had been subjected to Him" (3:21b–22). This last statement seems to be an allusion to Daniel 7:13, where it is prophesied that the Messiah will be "presented before Him," that is, the Ancient of Days, and He will then be given "the sovereignty, the dominion, and the greatness of all the kingdoms under the whole heaven" (v. 27).

Section I

The Resources for Suffering

1 Peter 1:1 — 2:3

CHAPTER 16

The Resource of Salvation
1 Peter 1:1-12

Preview:

God is the author of our salvation who has caused us to be born again to a living hope. Our faith is more precious than gold, and the outcome of our trust is the salvation of our souls. The ancient prophets inquired about the sufferings and the glory of the prophesied Christ, and they were told that they were not "serving themselves," but a future generation who would hear the gospel preached to them.

After identifying himself as "Peter, an apostle of Jesus Christ," and describing his readers as those scattered in the part of the ancient Roman Empire known today as Turkey, Peter describes them also as "aliens" (1:1). This single reference to their spiritual position as those who are "in the world but not of the world" sets the tone for the rest of the letter. This part of the empire had been Paul's mission field. Peter, however, felt the same kinship with his readers that we sense when we meet a believer in some remote, unfamiliar place and suddenly no longer feel alone. As an apostle, Peter was concerned for them and wrote to help prepare them for the coming holocaust.

Peter's very next statement introduces the topic of salvation. He describes his readers as "chosen according to the foreknowledge of God the Father, by the sanctifying work of the Spirit" (1:1-2). This choosing or election (the English transliteration) is theologically the fundamental basis for salvation. According to Romans 9:11, election is based not on anything within the chosen person but according to God's "purpose . . . not because of works, but because of Him who calls." Furthermore, this choosing is according to God's "foreknowledge." One view is that this is foreknowledge of who would someday believe, but this view may create a problem with the sense of Romans 9:11, where election is according to God's purpose, not according to His knowledge of who would someday believe. How would the purpose of God relate to His foreknowledge? Does God's foreknowledge precede His purpose? Or does His purpose precede his foreknowledge? The evangelical world, of course, is divided over how to answer this question. Arminian believers say foreknowledge comes first, then purpose. Calvinist believers say purpose always precedes foreknowledge. Note that the text says that believers are chosen according to foreknowledge, but this has to be reconciled with Romans 9:11.

Calvinists prefer to reconcile these two views by thinking of foreknowledge as the consequence of God's eternal plan or decree. They define "foreknowledge" as God's perfect knowledge of all future actualities and possibilities. In this case, the election and salvation of people are an actuality and can only be an actuality because God decreed that it would be so. Election is God's act of will, while foreknowledge is the prescience of that certainty. When put this way, election is a sovereign choice made by God for reasons undisclosed to us.

Arminians, on the other hand, prefer to reconcile the two views by saying that God, who knows the future perfectly because of His perfect knowledge of all things past, present, and future, knows who will believe and purposes at that point to elect them, thus guaranteeing that they will someday actually be saved. God does not decree all things but allows for human will to operate without causing it, unless, of course, you prefer to say that He decrees to give humans freedom of choice without determining that choice Himself.

Some Calvinists put another spin on foreknowledge by saying that it actually is, in this text, not mere knowledge of the future, but is related to the Old Testament concept of "intimate, personal, covenantal love." This is an idea based on the Old Testament word translated "to know" (Hebrew, *yadah*) in the King James Version, which can mean sexual intercourse, as in Genesis 4:1, or as in the case of Amos 3:2, to be chosen as the nation Israel. The New Testament equivalent is found in Romans 11:2, where the nation of Israel was "foreknown" by God. In this latter case, mere knowledge of something in advance makes no sense, because Paul is saying that God has not forsaken Israel whom He foreknew. Only the concept of a prior covenant relationship makes sense in that passage, because Paul is arguing the faithfulness of God toward Israel. This lends strength to this theory that foreknow—when used in salvation passages like 1 Peter 1:2—means something like "fore-love."

I prefer the meaning that can be paraphrased "elect according to the previously made covenant [fore-love] of God." This emphasizes the sovereignty of God and His grace in salvation.[2]

What is more intriguing is Peter's reference to sanctification in connection with this eternal, unconditional election. Sanctification means "to make holy" and is twofold. It begins with an initial setting apart of the elect at the time of justification (1 Cor. 6:11), which is an act, not a process, and continues as a process throughout the Christian life (1 Thess. 4:3). When Peter says that their choosing or election is "by the sanctifying work of the Spirit, that you may obey Jesus Christ" (1:2), he makes it clear that salvation involves a work of God within the believer, not merely getting a person into heaven.

This sanctification by the Spirit has as its purpose "that you may obey Jesus Christ and be sprinkled with His blood." One cannot separate sanctification from obedience, a fact often overlooked by the monastic tradition. People who separate themselves from the world in an effort to be holier ignore the command to make disciples of all the nations (Matt. 28:19). Holiness is therefore an inner work of the Holy Spirit that is possible in spite of the believer's surroundings. It may be necessary to separate ourselves from certain practices, but we cannot obey Christ and separate ourselves from people.

If there is no evidence of this progressive holiness, there is reason to warn such a person concerning the reality of his or her faith. We cannot pass final judgment on a person's faith, for there may be much we do not know that God knows.

The expression, "sprinkled with His blood" (1:2), is Old Testament language that speaks of sacrifice for sin. In this context it refers symbolically to the ongoing cleansing from sin that is a part of sanctification. It is accomplished, according to 1 John 1:9, by confession of sin: "If we confess our sins, He is faithful and righteous to forgive us our sins and to cleanse us from all unrighteousness."

Peter concludes his rather long salutation at the end of verse 2 by wishing his readers "grace and peace" to "the fullest measure." Neither of these is a worldly benefit. Since believers are recipients already of the grace of salvation, grace here in all likelihood is divine enablement. The broadest definition I know of the word *grace* is that it is what God does for us that we cannot do for ourselves. We cannot save ourselves, so God by grace saves us by faith. We cannot live godly lives in the midst of suffering, so God by grace grants us the ability. The peace he wishes for his readers is peace in the midst of suffering in light of the overall theme, since believers already have been reconciled to God and thus have peace with Him.

Peter launches his discussion of the salvation resources for suffering by pronouncing a blessing on God (1:3). Since God does not need to be blessed, this kind of blessing constitutes an expression of praise. God is referred to as the "Father of our Lord Jesus Christ." This is another fundamental basis for salvation and is probably therefore a reference to the Incarnation, the first earthly step toward salvation, the act by which God became man.[3]

It is by God's "great mercy" that He "has caused us to be born again to a living hope through the resurrection of Jesus Christ from the dead." There is a close relationship between mercy and grace in the New Testament, so much so that the two words are almost interchangeable. When they appear together, as in Hebrews 4:16, "Let us therefore draw near with confidence to the throne of grace, that we may receive mercy and may find grace to help in time of need," their difference must be noted. That difference may be stated in the following convenient statement: Mercy is what God *does not do* to us even though we deserve it (condemn us), while grace is what God *does* for us even though we *do not* deserve it. Mercy, therefore, is the remedy for sin committed, while grace is the preventative for sin not yet committed, at least so far as the Hebrews text is concerned.[3]

Peter's Use of Faith and Belief

God grants protection by the power of God through faith for a salvation ready to be revealed in the last days (1 Pet. 1:5).

For the Christians trials exhibit the proof of faith (1 Pet. 1:7).

Though believers do not now see the Lord, they still believe in Him (1 Pet. 1:8).

The outcome is the salvation of the soul (1 Pet. 1:9).

Because of Christ, Christians become believers in God (1 Pet. 1:21).

Isaiah prophesied (Isa. 28:16) that those who believed in Christ, the "precious stone," would not be disappointed (1 Pet. 2:6).

Jesus is of "precious value" to those who believe in Him (1 Pet. 2:7).

God is called our Faithful Creator (1 Pet. 4:19).

Believers are urged to be steadfast of soul (1 Pet. 5:9).

All believers receive a faith "of the same kind," by the righteousness of our God (2 Pet. 1:1).

To saving faith can be added moral excellence, knowledge, self-control, perseverance, godliness, brotherly kindness, and love (2 Pet. 1:5–7).

God's mercy, Peter adds, has caused us to be born again. "Born again" (Greek, *anagennao*) here is the translation of a different but essentially same expression in the famous discourse with Nicodemus in John 3:3. Jesus uses a word that literally is translated "born from above" (Greek, *gennao anothen*). This concept is theologically referred to as regeneration, the act by which God restores spiritual life to all of us who were once spiritually dead in sin. It makes us "partakers of the divine nature" (2 Pet. 1:4) so that we now are no longer rebels against God but are desirous of obeying God.

The "living hope" to which we are born again is the hope of the future that comes "through the resurrection of Jesus Christ." If death has been overcome and someday will be abolished (Rev. 21:4), we indeed have hope, for death casts a shadow over earthly hopes by bringing them to an end. Without Jesus' resurrection, there would be no basis for our hope in something beyond the grave; we would merely have a wish. This hope is *living*. It animates our life now and serves as a powerful force in taking us through suffering.

Peter continues the thought by identifying this living hope as the eventual obtaining of "an inheritance which is imperishable and undefiled and will not fade away, reserved in heaven for you" (1:4). The Christian's hope is centered on an inheritance. He is an heir of God and joint heir with Christ (Rom. 8:17). This inheritance is the logical consequence of being a child of God through the new birth that Peter has been describing. This inheritance is absolutely secure as compared to an earthly inheritance that can perish, be defiled, and fade away. In contrast, the heavenly inheritance is "imperishable" (it will not rot or decay), "undefiled" (it is morally pure), and "will not fade away" (unlike a flower, it maintains its beauty and is timeless). Its security is emphasized by the words, "reserved in heaven," language that suggests the security of a bank that cannot be broken into because it is inaccessible.

Verse 5 continues the sentence that ends with verse 4, "reserved in heaven for you," turning the thought to the plural "you," referring to believers. Peter goes on: "who are protected by the power of God through faith for a salvation ready to be revealed in the last time." Not only is the inheritance secure, but so is the believer. This balances the beauty of a secure, eternal inheritance with the ultimate perseverance of the believer.[5] This protection is by the power of God, a power that stands ever ready to thwart the evil intentions of the devil and enable the believer to obey God. It is a power that maintains the believer's faith, which is itself a gift from God.

This salvation is "to be revealed in the last time." Even though salvation is an accomplished fact, it nevertheless has three "tenses," past (justification), present (sanctification), and future (glorification). Primarily "salvation" here pertains to glorification and the actual reception of the inheritance. We are "substantially" saved now; we await only the eradication of sin and the resurrection of the body. The "last time" would have to refer to the coming of Christ, the gathering of both living and dead believers in the air (1 Thess. 4:13–18). Further events follow the Rapture, such as the judgment of believers, the seventieth week of Daniel, the judgment of the Gentiles, the thousand-year reign of Christ on earth, and the Great White Throne Judgment. Broadly speaking, all these events are included in "the last time," while here, narrowly speaking, James refers to the rapture and resurrection of the Church.

Peter says that believers "greatly rejoice" at this prospect (1:6). This rejoicing more than compensates, he adds, for their being "distressed by various trials." With this, he goes on to show how the hope of salvation comes to bear upon the believer's endurance during trials (1:6–9), the primary theme of this letter. First, rejoicing in trials—note the resemblance here with James 1:2–4—will serve as "the proof of [their] faith" (1:7). God needs no such "proof," because He knows all things. He is the one who could justify Abraham without any spoken testimony and count his faith as righteousness (Gen. 15:6). The "proof" of one's faith is probably more for the benefit of the one with faith as an evidence and encouragement through trials. It works this way: We face a trial and a measure of fear and uncertainty strikes us. We may falter momentarily, but our faith overcomes this temporary uncertainty. As we continue to face trials, the remembrance of past victories over doubt gives us greater confidence and consistency in exercising faith. This becomes "more precious than gold which is perishable," because we are able to face all the unexpected dangers of life and live victoriously.

The metaphor of being "tested by fire" is selected from the refining of metals and is appropriate to describe the test of the believer's faith. Such refining of metals had the purpose also of removing impurities, and this may be implied by Peter's use of the figure. Perhaps the impurities would be the fears, uncertainties, and doubts that are purged from us during a test of faith, so that in the course of time faith comes more readily and becomes stronger. This serves as a kind of deposit that will "result in praise and glory and honor at the revelation of Jesus Christ." I understand this praise, glory, and honor to be for Jesus, not us. It is He, after all, who works in us to give us this victory, not we ourselves.

The term revelation (Greek, apocalupsis) is one of the three major New Testament words for the second coming of Christ. The other two words are "coming" (Greek, parousia) and "appearance" (Greek, epiphaneia). All three of these words are appropriate to describe the pretribulational rapture and resurrection of the church or the glorious return of Christ to earth to establish the millennial kingdom. This is obviously so for the latter event, but it is not a strain on their meaning to use them of the former event. After all, Jesus will indeed be "revealed" to dead and living believers. He will "appear" in the air to believers, and he will "come" from heaven to meet believers in the air. I am inclined to identify the "last time" as specifically the pretribulational Rapture (1 Thess. 4:13–18), and thus, to be consistent, I am inclined to refer this "revelation" of Christ to the same event.

This hope that exists even though we "have not seen Him" nevertheless is strong because we "love Him" (1:8). A relationship exists between believers and their Lord without the Lord's visible presence, because love can come into existence even under such conditions. Recently a friend of mine developed a great deal of affection for someone by email. The qualities that really count and make for an enduring relationship are those that cannot be seen. We will not love Jesus more by merely seeing his physical appearance, though we certainly will not be disappointed.

Peter describes this present relationship with Christ as one that causes the believer to "greatly rejoice with joy inexpressible and full of glory." Joy is not dependent on circumstances as is the case with happiness. This joy is the undergirding force that will protect the believer's faith through all kinds of trials. The believer is "full of glory" because of this expectation. This is not the same glory he or she will experience at the revelation of Christ, but a glory in anticipation of faith provided by the description of that glory in Scripture.

I consider verse 9 to be the end of a paragraph, although the NASB makes no note of this. Peter is finishing one idea and going on to another. He concludes with the words "obtaining as the outcome of your faith the salvation of your souls." This "outcome of your faith" probably refers to the future aspect of their salvation. I say this because the word used (Greek, *telos*) means "goal" of their faith. This seems to point more toward the future, final salvation (glorification or entire sanctification) than the past justification by faith. The person facing trials can know the ultimate outcome. His or her salvation is never in jeopardy.

What follows in the new paragraph (1:10–12) is somewhat parenthetical, a digression by Peter to enhance the salvation resource he has been describing. This is indicated by the words "As to this salvation" (1:10). What follows connects this salvation with the Old Testament and indicates that it was somewhat of a mystery[6] about which those in the Old Testament could only speculate as they reviewed and pondered certain statements given by the Holy Spirit to those who prophesied.

The "prophets who prophesied of the grace that would come . . . made careful search and inquiry." In light of what Peter is about to say, these prophecies were largely concerning the coming Messiah, summed up with the word *grace*. It would be by God's grace that the Messiah would be sent into the world. The words *search* and *inquiry* imply a lack of knowledge about *how* the prophecies would be fulfilled, not about what they meant. They were "seeking to know what person or time the Spirit of Christ within them was indicating as He predicted the sufferings of Christ and the glories to follow" (1:11). The NASB translation, "what person or time," should be, according to most authorities, "what time or manner of time."[7] They had difficulty reconciling the suffering prophecies with the glory prophecies of the Messiah. As Peter says, the glories would *follow*. He means they would follow at another advent, not within the Messiah's first advent, something now clear to all.

Peter concludes, "It was revealed to them that they were not serving themselves, but you" (1:12). The prophets understood, eventually at least, that these predictions would not be fulfilled within their lifetimes but were concerning the future. They served a future age that would experience the First Advent as well as an even more distant age that would see the Second Advent. The First Advent had been "announced" now through "those who preached the gospel . . . by the Holy Spirit sent from heaven," a reference to the apostles like Peter.

Peter adds one more fact that makes this salvation so significant and such an incomparable resource for suffering. This salvation is something "into which angels long to look." God's salvation of human beings is an object lesson concerning the grace of God, a grace not available to the angels who disobeyed and fell with Satan. Apparently the choice of some of the angels to follow Satan in his rebellion was such a clear and radical repudiation of God that their destiny was fixed at that moment. The grace of God in human salvation therefore becomes an example of a quality of God they never would know about apart from the object lesson of human history.

Study Questions

1. What does "sprinkled with His blood" mean?

2. List the blessings that are a part of the imperishable inheritance.

3   What does the faith of the believer produce?

4. How many times is the Spirit of God mentioned in these verses, and what does Peter say the Spirit is doing in each of the references he makes?

5. What were the prophets seeking to know?

6. Is the "Spirit of Christ" the Holy Spirit? How do we know?

7. In 1 Peter 1:10–12, what was the ultimate message the prophets received?

CHAPTER 17

The Resource of Godly Behavior
1 Peter 1:13–2:3

Preview:

As obedient children, we Christians are to gird our minds for action, keeping our spirits sober and avoiding worldly lusts to which we conformed in ignorance in former days. As believers in Christ, we saints should conduct ourselves in fear, knowing that God will someday judge our actions. Jesus bought us with His precious blood, and God raised Him from the dead, giving Him glory for His work on the cross. Having been born again, we obeyed the truth and purified our souls.

Peter begins this section with a call to prepare for action. He uses the language of military preparation: "Therefore, gird your minds for action" (1:13). Literally, this is "gird up the loins of your mind," a figure the apostle Paul uses partly in Ephesians 6:14. There he calls upon believers to "gird their loins with truth," a figure drawn there as here with Peter for the first step the Roman soldier was required to do before battle: tighten his belt and thus restrict the flow of his outer garment. This figure in turn suggests personal discipline of mind by way of getting ready emotionally and planning strategy.

Further clarification comes next: "Keep sober *in spirit*, fix your hope completely on the grace to be brought to you at the revelation of Jesus Christ." The words "in spirit" are not in the Greek text but are placed there for the sake of clarification by the translators, hence the italics in the NASB. It probably refers to soberness in the sense of having all of one's faculties, not merely the spirit, under control. To fix one's hope completely on the grace to be brought with the return of Christ is simply to have that eventual consummation and victory as an ongoing focus. The trials ahead will be daunting at times, and a reminder of the ultimate victory will give the believer courage.

Peter further issues a call to leave the old way of life behind. "As obedient children, do not be conformed to the former lusts *which were yours* in your ignorance" (1:14). The call to obedience is a call to conform to a new standard of morality. The old way was one of ignorance, although, according to Paul, it originally came about through suppression of the truth that originally was possessed by everyone through creation (Rom. 1:18–32). The human conscience tells us what is right and wrong, but when we disregard that truth, it eventually passes beyond our consciousness. Thus, this ignorance is blameworthy, and humanity is without excuse (Rom. 1:20).

Instead of conforming to the old ways, believers are to be "like the Holy One who called [them]" (1:15). This "Holy One" is, of course, the Lord Jesus Christ. To be like the Holy One is to be holy. To this every believer is called. This holiness sets us apart, and God is able to use it to attract others whom He is drawing to Himself. For confirmation of this, Peter calls upon Leviticus 11:44, a text that sets forth the basic theme of the entire book of Leviticus: "You shall be holy, for I am holy." This, of course, has to be a relative statement, for no one is capable of absolutely perfect holiness, as some have mistakenly assumed. Only God is absolutely holy, but He means business when He desires a substantial measure of holiness for those He uses.

The motivation for this follows in 1:17–21. The first motivation is that if we "address as Father the One who impartially judges according to each man's work" (1:17), we had better conduct ourselves "in fear during the time of [our] stay upon earth." In other words, if we want a relationship with the Father, it comes at the price of holiness.

The next motivation is the priceless redemption we enjoy (1:18). "Redemption" is a word taken from the commerce of the market, in this case the slave market. The word means "to purchase a slave in the market by the payment of a price." The upshot of this is that we belong to another. We are not our own (1 Cor. 6:19). We have become slaves to Jesus Christ, a most desirable bondage. It is "desirable" because the life from which we were delivered was a "futile way of life inherited from [our] forefathers." It had no future except eternal condemnation. Redeemed life has the joy of service and obedience to Christ now and an inheritance in the eternal future.

Finally, there is motivation for holiness in the fact of our worth to God (1:19–21). This worth is measure in terms of the "precious blood, as of a lamb unblemished and spotless, *the blood* of Christ" (1:19). We have been purchased out of the slave market of sin by the ultimate price, and that price, the blood of Christ, indicates our corresponding worth to God. Human beings created in the image of God are of inestimable worth, and thus the redemption price is equal to it. This is why Paul in 1 Corinthians 6:19–20 says, "Or do you not know that your body is a temple of the Holy Spirit who is in you, whom you have from God, and that you are not your own? For you have been bought with a price: therefore glorify God in your body." To glorify God is to obey God, and to obey God is to strive for holiness.

With this redemptive work in mind, Peter continues by expounding on his favorite theme, God's provision of salvation through Christ. He begins by tracing it into eternity past in the words, "For He was foreknown before the foundation of the world, but has appeared in these last times for the sake of you who through Him are believers in God, who raised Him from the dead and gave Him glory, so that your faith and hope are in God" (1:20–21). Peter's use of the word *foreknow* here is the same as it was earlier in 1:2. No other meaning really makes any sense. If Christ is the eternal Second Person of the Trinity, it would not be theologically accurate to say that God foreknew Him in the sense of knowledge of Him before He came into actual existence before the foundation of the world. He was already in existence. For Christ to be "foreknown" must therefore refer to an eternal covenant arrangement to provide salvation for the elect.

The next step in the divine plan was that Christ should appear for our sakes to provide salvation. "Through Him" we have entered into belief in God (1:21). This is an interesting statement in light of the fact that so many non-Christians believe in God. Peter must be assuming a qualitative difference between belief in the existence of God and belief *in* God. The latter belief is saving trust mediated by Jesus Christ. A famous theologian responded to the question, "Do you believe in the devil?" with a flat "No." But he hastened to add the following clarification: "I believe in the *existence* of the devil, but I believe *in* God only."

This belief in God includes the fact that He raised Jesus from the dead; the two must go together, for believing *in* God is belief that He provided salvation in Christ. This also involved giving Christ glory, a glory that attracted us so that our faith and hope are in Him.

The subject of godly behavior takes a minor turn starting with 1:22 and moves toward godly behavior that largely concerns our relationships with fellow believers (1:22—2:3). Christians have "in obedience to the truth purified [their] souls for a sincere love of the brethren" (1:22). This is Peter's way of saying that in obeying the gospel message by repenting and believing, they have through that obedience brought about the purification of their souls, which in turn has as its goal this sincere love for one another. Peter's exhortation is, "Fervently love one another from the heart." The capacity has been granted, and that resource needs to be tapped wholeheartedly. Remember, love is more an *act* in the New Testament than a feeling. The act of loving brings about the feeling of love.

This kind of love is possible, he goes on to explain, because "you have been born again not of seed which is perishable but imperishable, *that is*, through the living and abiding word of God" (1:23). The new birth provides resources for Christian living. We are born again by the Holy Spirit, and this Spirit comes to indwell, thus providing all the resources we need. Peter's reference to "seed which is perishable" is to biological birth that provides resources for physical life. In contrast, the "imperishable" seed arises out of the Word of God. Peter's picture is an analogy of human intercourse. The Holy Spirit impregnates the believer with the seed of the Word of God. This is a conception that results in eternal life, not merely temporary physical life.

To impress this eternal nature of the new birth upon his readers, Peter quotes in 1:24–25 from Isaiah 40:6–8. Isaiah declares that human life is transitory, but spiritual life is eternal and comes from the "word [literally, in Peter's version of the quotation, "utterance"] of the Lord." Peter concludes with the affirmation, "and this is the word which was preached to you," to stress the identity of the gospel message with Isaiah's reference to the word of God.

The chapter break in our English versions is misplaced.[1] First Peter 1 should continue on through 2:3, because the subject obviously continues through to that point as indicated by the "therefore" that connects it with the material that began with 1:22. What we find in this final part of the paragraph is further appeal and instruction on tapping the resource of the new birth. Peter exhorts his readers, "Therefore, putting aside all malice and all guile and hypocrisy and envy and all slander, like newborn babes, long for the pure milk of the word, that by it you may grow in respect to salvation" (2:1–2). The putting aside of these sins is to be done by imbibing with an insatiable hunger the Word of God that brings about spiritual growth. Believers cannot change themselves. The Holy Spirit uses, among other things like trial and suffering, the implanted seed of the word of God.

The vices of malice, guile, hypocrisy, envy, and slander are those kinds of sins that disrupt the fellowship of the church and prevent the church from accomplishing its corporate part in the believer's growth. Malice is an evil or belligerent attitude toward another believer, usually for selfish reasons. Guile is the desire to trick someone. Hypocrisy is pretending to be something one is not, and envy is wishing to be like someone or have something someone has. Slander is a misrepresentation of another to his or her harm.

To desire the "pure milk of the word" like a newborn babe does not necessarily imply that Peter's readers were all new believers, because this is a simile ("like" or "as") that makes a comparison with something. What Peter means is that one's hunger for the Word of God should be as intense and persistent as milk is to a baby. This kind of spiritual desire is one of the surest signs of a genuine conversion. If it is lacking, there is reason for concern about a lack of genuine faith or a falling back into spiritual indifference on the part of an older believer.

Peter's final remark (2:3), "if you have tasted the kindness of the Lord," is an "if" that in Greek is called a first-class condition, which means that it is a fact. They *had* tasted this kindness, and that should spur them on to spiritual growth since that kindness was so sweet.

Study Questions

1. From verse 13, when will this grace be brought to the believers?

2. Who empowers believers to live in godly behavior?

3. What specifically will the Father judge when we face Him?

4. Why does Peter quote Isaiah 40:6–8 in verses 24–25? How does he apply the verse to what he has just written?

5. List what believers are to put aside and to put on.

6. On what basis and for what reason are Christians to be holy?

7. What should drive the believer's life here on earth? Explain.

Section II

The Relationships for Suffering

1 Peter 2:4—3:12

CHAPTER 18

Relationships toward Those Who Reject the Believer
1 Peter 2:4–12

Preview:
The Lord Jesus is described as a living stone, precious in God's sight. Believers also are seen as living stones who are to be built up as a spiritual house to carry out a holy priesthood. Christ fulfills several Old Testament prophecies as God's choice stone and as a rock of offense to the world. Believers are to live godly lives, glorifying God until the "day of visitation."

Christians find themselves in relationships with a variety of people. In this "chapter"[1] Peter starts with people in general who reject the believer because of his or her faith. He notes that the believer has come to Christ, who was also rejected. The believer has come to Him "as to a living stone, rejected by men, but choice and precious in the sight of God" (2:4). The metaphor of the stone is common throughout Scripture, but Peter's allusion here is probably to the rejected stone of Psalm 118:22–23:

> The stone which the builders rejected
> Has become the chief corner stone.
> This is the LORD's doing;
> It is marvelous in our eyes.

Rejection is much easier to cope with if the greatest Person who ever lived was also rejected.

But Christ's rejection led to the building of something new and "marvelous." It appears that the building and stone metaphor refers to the Church. Jesus is the "living stone," not dead, and we have come to him also as living stones to be "built up as a spiritual house for a holy priesthood, to offer up spiritual sacrifices acceptable to God through Jesus Christ" (2:5). The place of Jesus as the living stone is not stated here, but the quotation from Psalm 118, where Messiah is the corner stone, and similar language in 1 Corinthians 3:11, where Jesus is the foundation, give us two possibilities, both of which are valid, depending on how we want to view the building.

In this building, the Church, we are to offer "spiritual sacrifices" as a "holy priesthood." The Church *has* no formal priesthood but *is* a priesthood. Our sacrifices are the various ministries we perform as we exercise our spiritual gifts. Our priestly duties involve mediating between God and the world in our mission to the world. This idea, Peter continues, is "contained in Scripture" (2:6–8). What follows is a series of quotations, the first from Isaiah 28:16, which refers to Messiah as the corner stone who is believed upon without disappointment (2:6); the next from Psalm 118:22–23, which refers to the stone rejected by the builders that became the corner stone (2:7); and the final one, Isaiah 8:14, which warns that those who reject the stone will stumble over it and be offended by it (2:8a).

Peter concludes his stone metaphor with a sobering explanation (2:8b). Those who stumble over this messianic stone did so because they were "disobedient to the word." It was not the appearance of the stone that offended them; it was the message of repentance and faith he preached that they rejected, the least welcome message to depraved humanity. The most ominous statement Peter makes is, "To this *doom* they were also appointed" (2:8). This is one of several texts that those who believe in the doctrine of reprobation call upon for evidence.[2] Two primary words are used in the New Testament to express the idea of predestination, *protithemi* and *prohorizō*. The first literally means "to place beforehand," while the second means "to appoint beforehand." Both words are translated as "predestine" or "foreordain," the latter word found in the KJV. The word in our text here is related to the first of these words, the aorist passive tense of *tithemi*, "to place." It lacks the prefix *pro*, "beforehand," and thus may not mean eternal appointment. Instead, it may simply mean destined to this doom by choices they themselves made. Whether you prefer eternally predestined or appointed or temporally (by one's own choices) appointed, the concept of appointment suggests a destiny, and destiny points to a fixed order of things according to the justice of God.

With verse 9 Peter gives a strong contrast to the fate of those who are disobedient to the gospel. "But," he declares, "you are a chosen race, a royal priesthood, a holy nation, a people for *God's* own possession." Such language is strongly reminiscent of the kinds of things that pertained to the earthly nation of Israel. The fact that keeps us from identifying the Church with Israel is the way the Bible maintains the distinction between those born as Jews as opposed to those who are not. A Jew is always a Jew, and a Gentile is always a Gentile, although both may happen to be Christians.

Another factor that precludes what is today called "replacement theology"[3] (the Church *replaces* Israel) is a passage like Romans 11:11–27, where a distinction is maintained between Israel and the Church even though both are related to the figure of the olive tree that probably represents the Abrahamic covenant. That passage concludes with a clear promise of the restoration of national Israel:

> A partial hardening has happened to Israel until the fulness of the Gentiles has come in; and thus all Israel will be saved; just as it is written,
>
> 'The Deliverer will come from Zion,
>
> He will remove ungodliness from Jacob."
>
> "And this is My covenant with them,
>
> When I take away their sins." (Rom. 11:25b–27)

In what sense do the ideas of "a chosen race, a royal priesthood, a holy nation, a people for God's own possession" apply to the Church today? If the Church is distinct from Israel, why does Peter use language that points to identity as replacement theologians claim? Part of the answer is that there are similarities between the Church and Israel. But there are more dissimilarities than similarities, and that forms part of the basis for the dispensational viewpoint.

But to return to these figures and their interpretation regarding the Church, the Church can be said to be "a chosen race" in the sense of a new, special people (Greek, *genos,* which in some contexts as this can be translated "people"). All believers are priests, not just the members of a particular tribe, as in the case of Israel. As priests, all believers are representatives of God and proclaimers of Scripture. The Church is a "holy nation" in contrast to other nations of the earth that are something less than holy, and it is drawn from all the nations of the earth. In contrast to Israel, however, the Church is not a political entity. Finally, the Church is a people for God's own possession in a manner very similar to Israel. This latter designation implies a people through whom God intends to accomplish a very special purpose. That purpose is described next in the latter part of 2:9. The Church is to "proclaim the excellencies of Him who has called [them] out of darkness into His marvelous light." This is done by declaring through word and lifestyle that God knows how people need to live in a sinful world.

Peter continues this section on relationships to people in general by reminding his readers what they once were. "For you once were not a people, but now you are the people of God; you had not received mercy, but now you have received mercy" (2:10). They may suffer for being a people of God, but their suffering will be more than worth it. The references to "not a people" and "people of God" are from Hosea 1:10 and 2:23 and are an interesting use of the passage. They actually are prophetic of Israel's judgment, dispersion, and eventual restoration. As the prophet Hosea was commanded to divorce his unfaithful wife, Gomer, so God "divorced" his people. But as Hosea received Gomer back, so God would receive his people back eventually. In the case of the people to whom Peter was writing, they *never* had been a people. But when they heard the message of redemption, they *became* a people.

Peter concludes this section by urging his readers to live in light of what they now are. "Beloved, I urge you as aliens and strangers to abstain from fleshly lusts which wage war against the soul. Keep your behavior excellent among the Gentiles, so that in the thing in which they slander you as evildoers, they may on account of your good deeds, as they observe *them*, glorify God in the day of visitation" (2:11–12). This is the sum of the matter about relationships with people who reject believers.

First, God's new people must realize that they are "aliens and strangers" in this world. Christians are not to expect good treatment from a hostile world. Second, they must turn away from the bondage of the evil desires that will conquer them if they do not. In other words, believers are to regard themselves as aliens and strangers to sinful impulses. Third, and on a positive note, their behavior must be "excellent among the Gentiles." The word translated "excellent" means "noble" or "good." This means not only moral living but respectful, kind, and friendly behavior. Non-Christians observe this lifestyle, and it may eventually be the basis for their glorifying God. This probably expresses the hope for their salvation, based on the use of the expression "day of visitation." It could mean the return of Christ, but it more likely means God's visitation of salvation, especially in light of the fact that they have observed the Christians' good way of life and turned to God to achieve the same quality of life.

One matter remains, and that is Peter's use of the word *Gentiles* to refer to those outside the Church. Those who compose the Church are both Jews and Gentiles, but the early Church soon began to adopt the "we/they" mentality that characterized the nation of Israel and was encouraged by the Old Testament. The word more literally means "nations" and is best translated that way in some contexts. In this context, however, I prefer the translation "pagans," because it expresses in our day that which was intended in the early Church and is less ethnic in tone.

Study Questions

1. What are all the things said about Christ in 1 Peter 2:4–8?

2. List the ways Jesus is described as a stone and as a rock.

3. List the ways believers in Christ are described by Peter in 2:5–10.

4. What is the reason for keeping our behavior excellent? Who is watching what we do?

5. On what basis should children of God abstain from fleshly lusts? What kind of struggle will they encounter in this life?

6. What does 2:12 say is the result of a godly walk?

CHAPTER 19

Relationships toward Worldly Authorities
1 Peter 2:13–17

Preview:
Believers are to submit to human authority, for this is the will of God, and by doing right, they may silence "the ignorance of foolish men." They are also not to use freedom as a covering for evil, but are to act as bondslaves of God. They are to honor men, love the brothers, fear God, and honor the king.

Peter may well have anticipated the fact that the Roman government would turn against Christianity in the course of time. It would be easy for believers to regard government with contempt when that time came, but such contempt would not be good for their testimony. If suffering was going to be used for the glory of God, believers had to recognize the divine origin of all authority. The apostle Paul made this clear in another passage that has great similarity with this one (Rom. 13:1–7). In particular, this divinely delegated authority is affirmed in Romans 13:1: "For there is no authority except from God, and those which exist are established by God."

The basic principle governing the believer's relationship with civil authorities is that authority must be respected even when that authority is abused. The abuse of authority, however, is not even mentioned in either of these two passages. One must go to several other biblical texts to find out what to do when worldly authorities abuse their power by overstepping their authority. One of the most significant passages is Acts 4, where the governing authority—in this case the Jewish Sanhedrin—forbade the early Christians to preach the gospel. Peter makes it clear that they must obey God when there is a conflict between God's law and government's law (Acts 4:18–20). This is the subject of civil disobedience, and there are ways in which the believer must do this properly, based on a number of biblical texts.

Peter's purpose is to maintain among believers a general stance toward worldly authorities that will be conducive to their testimony before the world. This is clear from his opening statement: "Submit yourselves for the Lord's sake to every human institution, whether to a king as the one in authority, or to governors as sent by him for the punishment of evildoers and the praise of those who do right" (2:13–14).

Submission is "for the Lord's sake," for the sake of His honor based on the behavior of His people. *Submit* is a military term that means to "rank yourselves under" someone or something. This submission is here stated in terms of the common ruling authorities of biblical times but applies to the whole hierarchy of governmental authorities, as we would know them today, whether the supreme leader or those delegated to carry out the law under him.

The word translated by the NASB as "institution" is the Greek *ktisis*, which generally means "creature" and may mean more broadly "every human being." This would reflect the fact that believers are commanded to submit to all people in the interest of their welfare, especially their salvation. While this is true in a general way, I believe "institution" or "authority" is intended here in this particular context because of the references to governmental authorities that follow.

Peter states the fundamental purpose of human government as being for the punishment of evildoers and the praise of those who do right. The same thing is said by Paul in Romans 13:3–5, where he calls the civil authority a "minister of God to you for good" and "an avenger who brings wrath upon the one who practices evil." This is the administration of justice. In our modern world, government has taken on the aspect of enforcer of general social welfare, and as it moves in that direction, the public loses more of its liberty. The various degrees of socialism as well as totalitarianism sometimes make life more comfortable for those who prefer to be provided for and told what to do, but such governments tend to be oppressive, and change is always in the direction of greater and greater oppression and less and less liberty. It seems that the biblical ideal is to limit government to the realm of protection and justice. In light of the trend of the age toward a world government headed up by the Antichrist, any change toward less government will only be temporary. But whatever shape government takes, the general rule is to submit. Thus, Peter concludes, "For such is the will of God that by doing right you may silence the ignorance of foolish men" (2:15).

Early Christians indeed were misunderstood as anarchists of sorts because they claimed a heavenly citizenship. Peter wants, for the sake of the gospel, to set these false claims to rest.

Relationship to Government and Authority

Render to Caesar the things that are Caesar's (Matt. 22:21).

Paul reminded the Jews that Moses said (Ex. 22:28) it was evil to speak against rulers (Acts 23:5).

Government rulers are not to be considered a terror to those who do good (Rom. 13:3).

Those who are evil despise authority (2 Pet. 2:10).

Those who are evil reject authority (Jude 1:8).

First Peter 2:16 actually is a continuation of 2:15. The whole sentence is linked with the command "you may silence the ignorance of foolish men." Such silencing is accomplished by doing right and, according to 2:16, doing this as "free men" and not using such freedom as a "covering for evil" but as "bondslaves of God." The reference to a "covering for evil" means they would do it as a pretense to cause people to think they are good. The reference to "free men" means they do right as people who make their own decisions to do so, not out of compulsion or pretense.

It is at this point (2:17) that Peter expands the idea of submission to include "all men," except the more appropriate term here is *honor* or *respect*. Then he becomes more specific by commanding them to "love the brotherhood,"[1] meaning the Christian brotherhood. Admittedly, he implies a qualitative greater love for fellow Christians with his use of "love." "Fear God," he adds, supplying the upward dimension. Then finally he concludes with another reference to the king to round out his exhortation.

Study Questions

1. What should be the believer's relation to human authority?

2. What does God want the believer to do, and why?

3. What a Christian does right, what effect does that have on those who are foolish?

CHAPTER 20

Relationships toward Worldly Masters
1 Peter 2:18–25

Preview:
Servants are to submit to their masters, even to those who are unjust, for by doing so they find favor with God. Christians are to follow the example of the Lord and walk in His steps. When reviled, the Lord did not repay in kind those who brought suffering upon Him. In fact, Christ went so far as to die on the cross to heal us. He is now the Shepherd and Guardian of our souls.

Of all the classes of people in the Roman Empire, the slave was the lowest and was therefore subject to the most abuse. Peter found it fitting to address the situation that existed for such believers. One of the questions this passage raises—and others like it in the New Testament, such as Ephesians 6:5–9 and Philemon 1:1–25—is why the writers, Peter and Paul, do not directly address the social evil that is involved.

First of all, slavery in the first-century Mediterranean world cannot be compared to slavery in America prior to the Civil War. In the latter case, most slave owners regarded black people who had been captured and imported from Africa and sold to wealthy landowners as somehow inferior and destined for subjugation. Abuses were much more prevalent because blacks were treated as subhuman. Slavery in the Greco-Roman world was generally more in line with management and labor today. Of course, Roman masters could be very cruel, and in the final analysis, slaves were also regarded as property.

Some people actually sold themselves into slavery for periods of time in order to improve their standard of living.

The Old Testament legislation concerning slaves was, in light of the culture of the time, redemptive by comparison. Every fiftieth year was set aside as a Year of Jubilee during which slaves were to be set free (Lev. 25:1–7, 47–55). In the New Testament, slaves were free to attend Christian assemblies, something implied by the fact that they are addressed in these letters. Paul offers the following significant advice to slaves in 1 Corinthians 7:20–23: "Let each man remain in that condition in which he was called. Were you called while a slave? Do not worry about it; but if you are able also to become free, rather do that. For he who was called in the Lord while a slave, is the Lord's freedman; likewise he who was called while free, is Christ's slave. You were bought with a price; do not become slaves of men."

We reach, at this point in history, what I regard as the final state of the biblical ethic concerning slavery. A slave is regarded with dignity as "the Lord's freedman." If he is able, he should seek freedom, but if not, he is to remain in slavery. Paul does not criticize the cultural institution but provides for change through the effects of the gospel. He states precisely what that final condition should be—freedom from slavery[1]—although that final condition might not be achieved immediately.

The term translated "slaves" is different from the word ordinarily used in the New Testament. The usual word, *douloi*, is not used; instead, the term *oiketai* is utilized, which means "domestic servants." This may be due to the fact that Peter has just referred to all believers as *douloi*, "bondslaves" (2:16), and wants to specify this social group more definitively. In any case, there is no observable difference between the two words so far as their usage is concerned, because the same kind of household servant is referred to elsewhere as a *doulos*.

Slaves are to submit "in all respect." Peter will require this whether the master is good or "unreasonable," which shows that the respect might not be personal esteem but respect for authority. This is what this section on relationships with government and masters is all about: respect for authority in order to maintain a good testimony. The next verse clarifies this: "For this *finds* favor, if for the sake of conscience toward God a man bears up under sorrows when suffering unjustly" (2:19). "Conscience toward God" means a sense of obligation toward God in bringing about glory for his sake. Once again, the value of suffering is seen in suffering patiently when that suffering is inflicted unjustly (2:20). Ordinarily, unjust treatment would arouse seething anger in the slave, who would rebel in retaliation when an opportunity presented itself. Many cruel masters would expect this and look forward to killing or at least punishing the slave. A lack of retaliation might capture the slave master's attention and arouse curiosity, so that he asked the believing slave to give the reason for his or her hope (see 3:15).

What benefit, Peter asks, is it if a slave bears up under just punishment (2:20)? That is to be expected, because if the slave is learning a lesson, he does not retaliate. The master may not appreciate the slave's suffering bravely for injustice, but the slave would "find favor with God" anyway, and that should be enough so far as the believer is concerned.

The Christian and Labor

Those who work hard should be compensated quickly (Matt. 20:8).

Paul worked with his hands so that no one could accuse him of living off the charity of the churches (1 Cor. 4:12).

In order to be able to share with those who have little, Christians are to work with their hands (Eph. 4:28).

If one does not work, he should not be fed (2 Thess. 10).

The laborer is worthy of his hire (1 Tim. 5:18).

The hard-working farmer should be the first to receive the bounty of his crops (2 Tim. 2:6).

To withhold the pay of the hard worker brings on God's judgment (James 5:4).

Before going on to other domestic relationships, Peter finds it appropriate to appeal to the example of Christ, the One who suffered unjustly in behalf of the world (2:21–25). Peter links suffering with the believer's purpose as a Christian. "For you have been called for this purpose, since Christ also suffered for you, leaving you an example for you to follow in His steps" (2:21). It is easy for us to think of a call to salvation and a call to ministry, but a call to suffering is not a widely understood concept. Christ's suffering sets an example, not so much of *why* we suffer, but of *how* we suffer. Christ suffered unjustly, yes, but He suffered for sin as a payment for sin. The suffering to which Peter refers is specifically the suffering of the trial and crucifixion.

According to 2:22, Jesus suffered without sinning. He "committed no sin, nor was any deceit found in His mouth." This is a quotation from Isaiah 53:9, eight hundred years before the cross. Throughout His life, Jesus uttered no deception to gain a following. At His trial he told no lies to escape from suffering. In fact, He made no defense at all.

Jesus suffered without retaliating (2:23a). He was "reviled" or insulted but took this abuse without repaying in kind. As God He could have warned His abusers of God's just punishment to come or exchanged insults that would in their case have been accurate. The problem humans have with retaliation is that those who strike back usually strike back harder than the blow they receive. This becomes more hateful vengeance than just retribution, which is what justice is all about.

Jesus endured suffering by entrusting Himself to His Father (2:23b). To do this requires that a person have absolute trust in God's sovereignty and in His working some good in the suffering. If we suffer, God has allowed but not caused it. His sovereignty is uniquely seen in His taking the evil that He has not caused but is due to the sinful choices of creatures He has created in His image and turning it into something good (Rom. 8:28).

Finally, the example of Christ is seen in His suffering for the salvation of those who would someday believe (2:24–25). This example is limited, of course, to the *effects* of godly suffering on those who witness our suffering. Jesus' suffering the penalty of our sins cannot be emulated, for that is something only the eternal, perfectly righteous Son of God could accomplish. In these two verses, Peter sets forth the essence of the gospel. Usually literal, the NASB translates the Greek word *xulon*, "tree," as "cross." This, of course, is what Peter has in mind, but it is interesting that NIV translates it literally, when it leans more toward a "dynamic equivalent"[2] policy. Peter's selection of this term probably is based on Deuteronomy 21:23, "His corpse shall not hang all night on the tree, but you shall surely bury him on the same day (for he who is hanged is accursed of God), so that you do not defile your land which the LORD your God gives you as an inheritance." Peter desires to allude to the fact that Jesus was cursed by bearing our sin.

The ultimate goal of Jesus' "accursed" death is that "we might die to sin and live to righteousness" (2:24b). By comparison we suffer so that possibly in a godly manner of suffering we might influence some to consider faith in Christ. To put it another way, we strangely reenact the death of Christ before a watching world! Jesus' very wounds, Peter adds, are the means by which we are "healed." This text supplies a clarification of the text in Isaiah 53:5 that in part says, "And by his scourging we are healed," and must therefore refer to spiritual healing, not physical healing as some have interpreted it.

Verse 25 also confirms this interpretation: "For you were continually straying like sheep, but now you have returned to the Shepherd and Guardian of your souls." This rounds out nicely Peter's reference to the gospel. Our straying like sheep refers to our sinfulness in the most fundamental way, as a rebellion against God. And the final reference to the "Shepherd and

Guardian" is to the soul-care carried out by the Savior. The term *Shepherd* suggests guidance, while *Guardian* speaks of protection. The salvation we have received is permanent.

Study Questions

1. Why should a servant be submissive to his or her master regardless of the master's behavior?

2. If you are punished when you have done nothing wrong, how should you react?

3. What was the example given for all suffering servants to follow?

4. What does it mean for believers to "die to sin and live to righteousness"?

5. In this section of verses, how many ways does Peter draw upon Isaiah 53?

6. In what way did Jesus trust God in doing what was right with Him?

CHAPTER 21

Relationship with One's Spouse
1 Peter 3:1-7

Preview:

Wives are to submit to their husbands so that those who are disobedient to the Word of the Lord may observe the chaste and respectful behavior of their wives. The adornment of wives should be the hidden person of the heart, which is precious in the sight of God. Sarah is an example of a submissive wife. Husbands likewise are to live with their wives in an understanding way so that their prayers are not hindered.

Another form of suffering for the faith is inflicted on a woman who has become a Christian while her spouse remains an unbeliever. Yet she can turn her situation into an opportunity for witness to Christ as she responds in a godly fashion. Peter offers advice on this topic that cannot be found anywhere else in the Bible. And he also offers advice to Christian couples, because harmony in married life strengthens believers as they face trials in a godly manner.

Peter begins with a generality that at first appears to be a statement about Christian marriage: "In the same way, you wives, be submissive to your own husbands" (3:1). This leads us to believe that Peter's ethic for the Christian marriage matches Paul's (Eph. 5:22–33). The Greek word translated "submit" is the same as that found in chapter 2. It involves recognition of authority, invested here in the husband. Paul bases his ethic on what he calls the "headship" of the husband, a concept of authority.[1]

This passage is not intended to provide advice to the believing woman who disobediently marries an unbeliever. The Old Testament forbids marriages between Israelites and pagan women (Deut. 7:1–4); the New Testament commands believers to marry only other believers (1 Cor. 7:39).

But this submission based on headship takes a different twist for the Christian woman who has become a Christian after marriage. In addition to submission as any Christian woman would render to her believing husband, she is to attempt to win the unbelieving husband "without a word" and by her behavior. This behavior is to be centered in "chaste and respectful behavior" (3:2). Why does Peter suggest this sort of nonverbal testimony? Why would a verbal witness be inappropriate? The answer to this question lies partly in the historical background and partly in a careful examination of what is said and not said.

As to the historical background, Christianity had raised women's status, and this new measure of freedom among believers sometimes spilled over into the home, making pagan husbands resentful in a society in which the wife was expected to follow the religion of her husband.[2] It is likely that some Christian women went beyond the actual apostolic teaching that called for submission among all believers and domestic submission on the part of wives (Eph. 5:22–33) based on the creation order (1 Tim. 2:11–15). It was probably to this situation that Peter spoke these words. Peter is trying to bring the situation under control and to suggest a more pleasing approach that might win such husbands. His advice is timeless, not necessarily merely cultural, even in our modern society that leans toward egalitarianism, at least among the newer generation.

But we must be careful not to read too much into Peter's advice. First Peter 3:15 applies in this situation. There Peter tells believers to be ready to give an answer *when asked* about the hope that lies within them. In this text he does not forbid speaking. He only recommends the silent message of a beautiful life that might elicit a question from the husband.

Peter describes these husbands as "disobedient" to the word of the gospel. This implies that they have heard the message and turned aside from it, but it does not necessarily mean a permanent rejection. They "may be won." The word translated "win" appears in 1 Corinthians 9:20 in an evangelistic sense of winning converts and thus probably means that in this text also.

To clarify his point further, Peter encourages not only "chaste and respectful behavior" (3:2), but an appropriate "adornment" that goes beyond the "external" grooming of the hair, jewelry, and clothes (3:3) and extends to "the hidden person of the heart, with the imperishable quality of a gentle and quiet spirit, which is precious in the sight of God" (3:4). The NASB attempts to clarify the spirit of Peter's remarks about external adornment—which in the KJV sounds more like a prohibition against such adornment—with a word in italics: "Let not your adornment be *merely* external" (3:3). Peter wants beauty to arise from internal qualities, not external, but he is not necessarily forbidding the external. It is safe to assume that Peter, as the apostle Paul, would simply encourage modesty in the way that women dress (1 Tim. 2:9).

As to these internal qualities, Peter asks for a "gentle and quiet spirit" and adds that this is precious in the sight of God. This is not Peter's way of imposing a strict code of silence among women, for "quiet" does not mean "silent." These are qualities produced by the Holy Spirit and apply to both men and women. Such qualities are attractive to most people, and Peter is interested in winning the pagan husband.

To strengthen his instruction, Peter appeals to the conduct of the great women of the Old Testament, who with these same qualities "used to adorn themselves, being submissive to their own husbands" (3:5). Sarah is used as an example of one who "obeyed Abraham, calling him lord" (3:6). This is a reference to Genesis 18:12, where Sarah says to herself after receiving the news of her forthcoming conception in her old age, "After I have become old, shall I have pleasure, my lord being old also?" We have no biblical reference to Sarah's speaking directly to Abraham and addressing him as "lord," which means "master" and is a title of respect, not a reference to slavery. Peter is not proposing that all Christian women address their husbands as "lord" or "master." His point is that there was a genuine feeling of respect on Sarah's part, because Sarah referred to Abraham this way out of earshot, not as a pretense in his presence. Peter adds that Christian women become Sarah's "children" if they "do what is right without being frightened by any fear." Peter's use of the expression, becoming Sarah's children, is similar to all believers becoming Abraham's children if they emulate Abraham's faith (Gal. 3:7). A spiritual kinship is suggested, and this should be an honor to Christian women to be able to claim such a kinship.

What is the fear that women should disregard when showing respect to their husbands? In spite of showing submission and thus "doing what is right," they must also "do what is right" in terms of their obligations to God to grow spiritually. A woman's husband may continue to resent her new allegiance to the Christian God and may threaten her. In face of this, she must not give way to fear but continue to do right. I would include as "right" the obligation to continue reasonable spiritual disciplines including assembling together with other believers. These obligations need not interfere with her proper wifely duties anymore than they do with the duties of women with believing husbands.

Before Peter leaves the subject of the relation of believers to their spouses, he rounds out the discussion with a reference to husbands (3:7). When Peter says, "You husbands likewise," he is not stating a strict adherence to the code for wives. Wives submit, but husbands must likewise do what is right. In the husbands' case, that which is right is to "live with *your wives* in an understanding way." Peter puts his finger on the essence of a good marriage from the standpoint of the husband's obligation and the wife's point of view. Men and women are different, and the tendency is for women to understand their husbands better than their husbands understand them. This statement provides a complementary addition to the general command of Paul in Ephesians 5:25, "Husbands, love your wives, just as Christ also loved the church and gave Himself up for her."

The Christian and Marriage

Husbands and wives are to be faithful to each other (1 Cor. 7:1-2).

The husband and wife have conjugal responsibilities to each other (1 Cor. 7:3-5).

If the marriage is made intolerable by the unbelieving spouse, he or she is allowed to leave the relationship (1 Cor. 7:10-17).

The husband must be attentive as to how to please his wife (1 Cor. 7:33).

The husband is the head of the wife, as Christ is the church (Eph. 5:23).

Wives are to be subject to their husbands (Eph. 5:24; Col. 3:18).

Husbands are to love their wives as Christ loves the church (Eph. 5:5).

Husbands are to love their wives as their own bodies (Eph. 5:28a).

A husbands is to love his wife as he loves himself (Eph. 5:28b).

In marriage, the husband is to leave his father and mother, and cling to his wife (Eph. 5:31a).

The husband and wife are to become one flesh (Eph. 5:31b).

The husband is to love his own wife (Eph. 5:33a).

The wife is to respect her husband (Eph. 5:33b).

Husbands are not to be embittered toward their wives (Col. 3:19).

A husband is to have one wife (Titus 1:6).

Older women are to teach younger women how to love their husbands, be good homemakers, and to care for their children (Titus 2:3-5).

Peter's further unique contribution to the relationship between husbands and wives is his first reason for understanding the wife's being the "weaker vessel." This refers to the woman in her physical aspect, since the term "vessel" is sometimes a metaphor for the body, as in 1 Thessalonians 4:4, "that each of you know how to possess his own vessel in sanctification and honor."[3] The woman is ideally the equal of the husband intellectually and spiritually, something strongly implied in Peter's second reason for understanding in verse 7: "And grant her honor as a fellow heir of the grace of life." This probably refers to the creation of Eve, along with Adam, in the image of God and as a "helper equal to him" (Gen. 2:20; NASB translates, "helper suitable for him").

The importance that Peter attaches to good marital relations is sobering. The husband's granting honor to the wife as a fellow heir will enable their prayers to be effective. This strong connection between a good marriage and effective prayer is based on the fact that the marriage is a portrayal of Christ and the church according to the apostle Paul (Eph. 5:22–33). This is why Paul in another place requires overseers to be good husbands and managers of their homes (1 Tim. 3:2, 5). The functional family is a high priority to God. After all, it was God's first institution (Gen. 2:24).

Study Questions

1. What is Peter referring back to in the previous verses when he writes, "In the same way, you wives . . ."?

2. Is Peter saying that being "fashionable" for women is wrong?

3. Could 1 Peter 3:4 characterize many modern women today?

4. In what way is the woman the "weaker vessel"?

CHAPTER 22

Relationships in Summary
1 Peter 3:8-12

Preview:
After giving detailed instructions to men and women about interacting as husbands and wives, Peter summarizes this section by giving real life examples that exhibit qualities that will bring greater glory to God.

Peter brings to a conclusion the section I have called "relationships" with the words "To sum up" (literal Greek, "now the end") with what appear to be the most significant virtues that govern human relationships. These virtues, with the quotation from Psalm 34:12–16, provide a grand finale for how to deal with people of all kinds.

The five virtues (3:8) Peter commands are "harmonious, sympathetic, brotherly, kindhearted, and humble in spirit." "Harmonious" means a desire to cooperate so long as the purpose is in harmony with biblical principles and the mission of the believer. He does not mean to compromise at any cost. "Sympathetic" literally means, "to feel together," and it involves an ability to understand and comfort people. "Brotherly" represents the familiar term *philadelphoi* for "brotherly love." It connotes a sense of family ties and loyalty to one another. The fourth word, "kindhearted," means compassion, a quality of hurting when someone else is hurting. Finally, "humble in spirit" is literally humble-minded. A person who possesses this attribute is willing to listen to others' ideas even when he or she disagrees.

This verse punctuates the idea that believers should have a strong feeling for the welfare of the other Christians. Compassion and sympathy are two hallmarks of the Christian life. Loving the brother is so often enjoined and even enforced in the New Testament, the child of God cannot escape this responsibility. The believer is to consider that he or she now lives in a family, a spiritual family, with Christ as the Head. Friendliness is also to prevail, as well as humility. Christianity requires that both of these virtues be enforced as important injunctions in the walk of faith.

Qualities like these encourage harmony and cooperation. Sometimes they fail when pagans—or even believers—refuse to respond in kind, but often they will turn away wrath, because they involve a "gentle answer" (Prov. 15:1).

Peter reminds us of what he said about Christ's example earlier in 2:21–25 with the words, "not returning evil for evil, or insult for insult, but giving a blessing instead" (3:9). Vengeance is a powerful inclination when we believe we have been unjustly treated. Possibly what Peter is implying by putting this comment in juxtaposition with the five listed virtues is that these virtues lie behind the ability to control the urge to seek revenge physically or verbally.

Giving a blessing instead of returning insult for insult should characterize those who were "called" to inherit a blessing. The logic of this follows in a quotation from Psalm 34:12–16. This part of the psalm is addressed to "the one who desires life, to love and see good days" the one who is called to inherit a blessing. That covenant blessing in the Old Testament, which Psalm 34 has primarily in mind, would have centered on the land, peace, length of life, and prosperity, the kinds of blessing associated with God's earthly people. Peter intends us to convert this by way of application to the people of God under the new covenant, a heavenly people promised primarily spiritual blessings.

A brief examination of the requirements set forth by Psalm 34 will be profitable and serve as a fitting conclusion of these relationships in summary. Bear in mind that Christ did everything in the psalm by way of example but did not experience the blessings that were promised. This was due, of course, to the fact that He came to suffer for sin. And we are called to suffer with Him. Thus, we take the advice more for our testimony's sake than for any earthly benefits.

Barnes adds:

> Knowing that you were called to be Christians in order that you should obtain a blessing infinite and eternal in the heavens. Expecting such a blessing yourselves, you should be ready to scatter blessings on all others. You should be ready to bear all their reproaches, and even to wish them well. The hope of eternal life should make your minds calm; and the prospect that you are to be so exalted in heaven should fill your hearts with ... love.[1]

The first prescription of Psalm 34 is to keep our tongue from evil and our lips from speaking deceit (3:10). We cannot prevent evil speech on the part of others, but we can avoid perpetrating evil speech ourselves. The next prescription is to turn away from evil and do good (3:11). The negative side, turning from evil, is not enough. The positive side, doing good, must accompany it. We may suffer, but let it be for good, not evil, a theme already dealt with by Peter. Instead, we must seek peace. The guarantee is that the "eyes of the Lord are upon the righteous" (3:12), and He will hear our prayers.

Kistemaker makes this point:

God sees the people who do that which is right. When they pray to him, he hears their prayers. This comforting word means that God's favor rests upon all who fear him (Ps. 33:18), that nothing escapes his attention, and that he answers prayer. ... The contrast is clear, for as God sees the works of righteous people so he sees those of people who practice evil. Nothing escapes his view. And no one should think that God does not care. Those who delight in doing evil do not have God as their friend but as their adversary. He is against them. In fact, [Peter] does not finish the quotation from Psalm 34:16, which describes the end of God's adversaries. The desire is to give the evildoer time and opportunity to repent and establish a living relationship with God.[2]

With direct encouragement to the child of God, Leighton writes:

You whose hearts are set towards God, and your feet entered into his ways, I hope will find no reason for a change, but many reasons to commend and endear those ways to you every day more than the last, and, amongst the rest, even this, that in them you escape many even present mischiefs which you see the ways of the world are full of. And, if you will be careful to ply your rule and study your copy better, you shall find it more so. The more you follow that which is good, the more shall you avoid a number of outward evils, which are ordinarily drawn upon men by their own enormities and passions.[3]

Without a doubt a peaceful spirit contributes to extended days in life. Such a spirit, and an equal attitude of mind, adds to health, without such there can be a wearing down of the emotions and even the physical. As well, God is our Lord and our Protector who continually gives us His guardianship and Fatherly care. He hears our prayers and He keeps us from the wrong path.

It is God who is the Author of our lives; He protects the righteous and saves from vices that kill and maim, and shorten the time on earth. He hears our prayers, and saves the righteous from an early grave. No one will know the number of times He has snatched the child of God from the jaws of danger. This is not to say that all believers have guaranteed long life because we understand that often the child of God is cut down in the prime of existence. Sometimes the righteous are caught up in the harm that comes upon earth: war, famine, storm, etc. But the overall general rule is that believers who walk in righteous integrity, are spared and are blessed with longevity. Too, in regard to the sins in this world, He saves us and others from sins that are likewise destructive. The Lord throws a protecting shield over His children who may be in harm's way. When the believer dies it is because it is time for him or her to go home and be in His presence.

Study Questions

1. What is Peter referring back to when he writes, "To sum up. . ." (3:8)?

2. Do the characteristics Peter lists in verses 8–9 also apply to the relationship between husbands and wives?

3. What is Peter trying to get across when he quotes Psalm 34?

4. From these verses, list and sum up all Peter says about how believers are to treat each other.

5. Since Peter has just addressed wives and husbands in the previous verses, could this section apply then to how wives and husbands should treat each other?

6. What does 3:12 mean when it says, "For the eyes of the Lord are upon the righteous?"

Section III

The Attitudes for Suffering

1 Peter 3:13—5:14

CHAPTER 23

The Attitude of Capitalizing on Suffering
1 Peter 3:13–22

Preview:

Strange as it may seem, believers in Christ are blessed when suffering for the sake of righteousness. Christ is to be sanctified in the hearts of believers that they might give an answer to those who ask about the hope within. Christ died to bring people to God. Baptism is a picture and a type of what the Lord did for us in His death and resurrection. Jesus has gone into heaven and is now at the right hand of God the Father.

Peter's opening statement, "Who is there to harm you if you prove zealous for what is good?" is at first glance paradoxical. He has already warned us that we will suffer for doing good (2:20). The next verse (3:14) even seems to contradict the opening statement: "But even if you should suffer for the sake of righteousness, *you are* blessed." Evidently Peter does not equate the word "harm" with the word "suffer." There is no "harm" for the believer whose physical existence and well-being are not most important. He or she is ultimately secure in the truth that "if God is for us, who is against us?" (Rom. 8:31). But the believer will certainly suffer.

In an allusion to Isaiah 8:12–13, Peter encourages his readers not to fear intimidation by those who would try to harm them. Isaiah 8:13 instead advises the godly to face the coming invasion, unlike the unbelievers among them, with the fear of God. Peter's version of this is that they "sanctify Christ as Lord" (3:15). "Do not fear their intimidation" translates the literal original,

"Do not fear their fear," that is, their enemies' "fear" being their efforts to frighten them. It makes no sense to the pagan world, but the fear of God is the best antidote to the fear of man, because for Christians it carries with it a confidence in the supreme power of God to deal with enemies and grant eternal life to those who fear Him.

In this section that closes chapter 3, Peter is setting forth the attitudes that ought to undergird believers during persecution. They are (1) preparedness to state the hope we have (3:15), (2) a good conscience (3:16–17), and (3) an awareness of Christ's purpose in suffering when we are cosufferers with Him (3:18–22).

The first of these is to "sanctify Christ as Lord" (3:15). This is an unusual use of the word *sanctify* for the New Testament. Ordinarily, the word pertains to making people holy, that which occupies believers, so far as God is concerned, for their entire lives. The order of divine undertakings for believers is first *justification* as an event, then *sanctification* as a process, and ultimately *glorification*, also an event. Peter's use here is more in keeping with its Old Testament domain, in fact, its original use. That use had to do with setting apart something like an article of the tabernacle for God's exclusive use. The word in turn gradually became more moral in its use and gradually took on the meaning of making something holy.

In this context, to sanctify Jesus as Lord in our hearts is to make Jesus our master by placing Him in the center of our lives. Peter is not thinking of a single event but of an ongoing attitude, an attitude that prepares us for any crisis that might call for "a defense to everyone who asks you to give an account for the hope that is in you." Such a "defense" (Greek, *apologia*, from which we get the word *apologetic*) is necessary when believers, in the midst of the most unjust and horrendous situations, demonstrate courage for the future that comes from above. In the early Church this took place as Christians stood before rulers, pagan courts, and individuals.

Peter cautions his readers about making this defense in two regards. The first is about the perennial problem connected with such a witness. During persecution a kind of arrogance could creep into a believers' attitudes toward those who might be interrogating them. They are to give their answer "with gentleness and reverence." They are not to preach sermons. This situation is like a court of law where only the facts about one's Christian experience and hope are appropriate. The second caution is in regard to their personal behavior. They are to "keep a good conscience so that in the thing in which [they] are slandered, those who revile [their] good behavior in Christ may be put to shame" (3:16). An attitude of obedience to biblical moral and ethical standards must be their preparation for this moment, so that any slander will be baseless, and objective observers will know the accusations are lies. There were occasions, of course, when Christians were not vindicated at the time. God Himself has since put to shame those who persecuted and even killed them, and history also vindicates the brave people who died for the cause of Christ.

Peter's final exhortation is that it is better to "suffer for doing what is right rather than for doing what is wrong" (3:17). Note the additional words, "if God should will it so." Ordinarily, at least in the Old Testament, one suffers for doing wrong, and when he does right, God blesses him, but the dominant New Testament principle is to expect to suffer for doing what is right. This arrangement is in keeping with the church's mission of witnessing to the truth throughout the world, not merely in the stronghold of a geographical nation. Such a mission thrusts believers into harm's way as they live out the Christian life in a hostile world.

Peter concludes this section about capitalizing on suffering by reminding his readers of the way Christ capitalized on his suffering, in a fashion similar to 2:21–25. Besides reminding his readers that Christ's suffering provided for their salvation, Peter also talks about other aspects of the cross and presents as well a rather difficult section (3:19–21). The essence of Christ's example in suffering is in dying for sin and bringing His people to God (3:18).

The first significant matter of the theology of the cross is that "Christ also died for sins once for all" (3:18). This is quite similar to Hebrews 7:27. Jesus the Great High Priest "does not need daily, like those high priests, to offer up sacrifices, first for His own sins and then for the *sins* of the people, because this He did once for all when He offered up Himself." The value of Christ's sacrifice is infinite as opposed to the relative value of sacrificial animals. His death is sufficient to cover the sins of the whole world.[1] Therefore, that one sacrifice needed to be made only once. This doctrine is one of the essentials in the spectrum of the "doctrines of grace," because it makes all good works for salvation unnecessary.

Another significant theological concept regarding the cross is found in the words "the just for the unjust." This concept is more fully developed in Romans 3:21–30, where Paul describes the doctrine of justification. The heart of the passage (vv. 23–26) goes as follows:

> For all have sinned and fall short of the glory of God, being justified as a gift by His grace through the redemption which is in Christ Jesus; whom God displayed publicly as a propitiation in His blood through faith. This was to demonstrate His righteousness, because in the forbearance of God He passed over the sins previously committed; for the demonstration, I say, of His righteousness at the present time, that He might be just and the justifier of the one who has faith in Jesus.

The point is that since Christ, the just, could die in behalf of the unjust, He retains His justice due to His sacrifice for sin. Those for whom He died thus become *justified* through their faith in Jesus' sacrifice and are then counted righteous by the legal pronouncement of God even though in reality they are unjust in their behavior.

The words, "so that He might bring us to God," pertain to the doctrine of the cross in which believers are reconciled to God. This is accomplished by the removal of the barrier of sin through payment of the price required by the Law. The believer is then at peace with God, no longer alienated.

The Suffering of Christ

It was in God's plan that Christ would go to Jerusalem and suffer at the hands of the Jewish elders, die, and be raised on the third day (Matt. 16:21).

Christ, the Son of Man (Messianic term), would suffer "many things" (Mark 8:31).

God announced through His prophets that Christ must suffer before He would reign (Acts 3:18).

Before Christ would come to reign, He first had to suffer and be rejected by that generation of the nation of Israel (Luke 17:24-25).

Christ Himself predicted He would suffer at the hands of the Jews (Matt. 17:12).

Christ appeared to His disciples alive after His suffering (Acts 1:3)

Christ suffered death only once and does not have to so suffer again (Heb. 9:25-26).

Christ suffered outside the gates of Jerusalem in order to sanctify the people through His blood (Heb. 13:12).

Believers become heirs of the world through their suffering with Christ (Rom. 8:17).

Because of Christ's suffering He could come alongside of believers who are tempted (Heb. 2:18).

Believers are granted the privilege to suffer for Christ's sake (Phil. 1:29).

The last doctrine of the cross to which Peter refers in this great tribute to the cross is the concept that in becoming a human being He was *able* to die. Thus He was "put to death in the flesh, but made alive in the spirit." This is, on the surface, a puzzling statement. The problem in taking "flesh" as the body of Jesus and "spirit" as the human spirit of Jesus is that such a statement seems to deny the bodily resurrection of Christ with a Gnostic idea of survival into the next life as one limited to the human spirit but not to some sort of body. This is precisely why another usage of the words *flesh* and *spirit* is preferred by the majority of commentators: the *sphere* of the flesh and the *sphere* of the spirit.[2] These are in antithesis to one another in this usage. Another way to put it would be the earthly sphere versus the heavenly sphere. Some prefer to capitalize "spirit," because the Holy Spirit is the dominating power in the heavenly sphere. The meaning here, then, is that Jesus was put to death by this evil world but made alive by the heavenly realm, a statement of His triumph. For a similar use of this antithesis of flesh and spirit, see Romans 1:3-4 and 1 Timothy 3:16.

What follows in 3:19-22 is one of the more difficult passages in Scripture. The overall purpose of this section seems to be to show how Christ's suffering on the cross, which led to proclamation to the "spirits now in prison," is a pattern of suffering that leads to proclamation, a follow-up to 3:15, where Christians who suffer are to be "ready to make a defense," although the situations do not correspond exactly.

The first difficulty is the identification of the "spirits in prison." There have been two basic suggestions. One is that they are the disobedient of Noah's day who rejected Noah's preaching, or, as some prefer, Christ's preaching through Noah, if you interpret the words, "in which also He went and made proclamation" as referring to Christ's proclamation "in the Spirit" to the world of Noah's day. The problem with this interpretation is that Christ's suffering on the cross as described in 3:18 would *follow*, not precede, the proclamation made in Noah's day and makes that interpretation implausible.

The other suggestion is that the spirits in prison are fallen angels. Jesus' proclamation to them is the fact of His victory over death and suffering and their ultimate doom. Two problems are connected with this theory. One is that the parallel with our preparedness to give a defense to those whom ask us is not very good, for such an inquiry is not indicated in our text as far as the spirits in prison are concerned. The other is that these spirits in prison are identified as those who were disobedient during the time of Noah, not fallen angels in general, which would make better sense, since such a proclamation would seem logically to be appropriate to all the fallen angels, not a select group.

In answer to this, there is a proposed solution that these spirits in prison were the "sons of God" referred to in Genesis 6:1-4 who cohabited with the "daughters of men." The interpretation is that "sons of God" in the Old Testament are angels. There are at least two problems with this proposal. First, the phrase "sons of God" refers to angels elsewhere in only the poetic literature of the Old Testament, whereas this reference is in a narrative or historical part. Second, the interpretation of the "sons of God" in Genesis 6:1-4 is highly disputed, because there are other alternatives that fit the context better and do not clash with what Jesus taught about angels not having gender and not marrying or having children (Matt. 22:30). My opinion is that Genesis 6:1–4 is connected primarily with Genesis 5, which lists the genealogy of Adam and his descendants; thus, the reference to "sons of God" and "daughters of men" is to Adam's descendants.[3]

Four Views on Who Are the "Sons of God"

- *The "sons of God" and the "daughters of men" refer to Adam's descendants. – Author's View*
- *The "sons of God" denotes angels (Job 1:6; 2:1).*
- *This is the coming of divine, fallen angelic beings. – Unger*
- *The main stress is immortals co-mingling with mortals – Speiser*
- *The co-mingling of the Godly line of Seth with the ungodly line of Cain – Stigers*

Where does that leave us? In our present state of knowledge, no interpretation is without its problems. I have taken the space in this relatively brief commentary to demonstrate a hermeneutical process for the benefit of the readers for whom it is intended, namely, people who are concerned with the expositional values of a passage.

Based on my interpretation of Genesis 6:1–4, I reject the interpretation of "spirits in prison" as angels and understand them to be human beings who were disobedient during the period of Noah's preaching. This accords better with the parallel with 3:15, since our "defense" is to be to human beings. This leaves us with the problem I mentioned above—that if the proclamation takes place *before* Christ's suffering, we do not have a good parallel, for the best parallel has the proclamation *following* the suffering. I suggest that Noah's suffering in being the butt of ridicule during his day may also be in Peter's mind, and that his suffering was also Jesus' suffering in his preincarnate state, since Noah's preaching was really Jesus' preaching through Noah. How do I justify this "quantum leap" hermeneutically? Peter may regard our suffering as Jesus' suffering and our preaching (ideally, at least) as Jesus' preaching to our generation. Thus, another reason why we must "sanctify Christ as Lord in [our] hearts" is that our preaching might be authentically His.

Further justification may be in the fact that the reference to the realm of the spirit—assuming the validity of that interpretation—lends itself well to Jesus' being spiritually present with Noah as He is with us. The "patience of God" (3:20) also lends itself to God's patience in warning sinners over periods of time, and the reference to the construction of the ark that ultimately provided escape for only eight persons alludes to the suffering of Noah as he preached to an implacable generation.

Bear this in mind. Frequently difficult passages like this are difficult because the writer and his original readers had some common facts in their minds that have been lost to the modern reader. There may have been an ongoing discussion during Peter's day of the flood of Noah, especially the meaning of Genesis 6:1–4. This possibility is strengthened by the fact that an apocryphal book, 1 Enoch, does indeed discuss a view that takes the "sons of God" as angelic beings who propagated evil spirits and giants. [4]

Peter's use of this incident also makes sense in light of the fact that whenever such proclamation takes place there are two results—the condemnation of those who refuse the message and the salvation of those who receive it. For further development of the homiletical value of this interpretation,[5] see the concluding homiletical remarks in this chapter.

This fact of two results of proclamation explains the reference to baptism (another difficult part of this passage) in 3:21. Peter sees an analogy of the Flood with Christian baptism. Eight people "were brought safely through *the* water. And corresponding to that, baptism now saves you—not the removal of dirt from the flesh, but an appeal to God for a good conscience—through the resurrection of Jesus Christ" (3:20b–21).

The first matter of exegesis to note is the preposition *through*. Noah and his family were not saved *by* the water but *through* the water. They were saved through the water that was a judgment for the rest of the world. It would appear, therefore, that Peter is making the floodwaters stand for God's judgment, not some saving vehicle. The only sense in which the waters of the Flood were the vehicle of salvation was that the ark remained buoyant through them. That which was a catastrophe for the world was turned into a means of salvation for the eight persons in the ark. Jesus' death was God's judgment on sin, and our faith in His substitution makes His death our death. Nevertheless, the waters of the Flood did not save anyone; only the ark saved those who did not perish in the Flood. The ark would therefore correspond to the sacrifice of Christ, the waters to judgment.

Next, the words "corresponding to" are a translation of the Greek word *antitupon,* from which we get the term *antitype.* The type was the Flood, the antitype, Christian baptism, assuming we have here a bona fide Old Testament type. One of the recognized qualifications of a genuine type is that the New Testament says that it is a type. That seems to be the case here. Therefore, there is no saving efficacy of the waters of baptism. Baptism is a figure for something else that does save, the death of Jesus on the cross.

This fact is further confirmed by Peter's elaboration in 3:21. He clearly disclaims the efficacy of the water itself in the words, "Baptism now saves you— not the removal of dirt from the flesh, but an appeal to God for a good conscience—through the resurrection of Jesus Christ." As through the waters of the Flood eight souls were saved, so through the waters that signify the cross of Christ and His resurrection believers are saved today. The figure itself does not save. Faith in the work on the cross, symbolized by the water, saves. The "answer of a good conscience" refers to the good conscience of sins forgiven through the sacrifice of Christ and therefore constitutes faith.

The early church, incidentally, was accustomed to performing baptism as soon as possible after a person's believing the gospel (see Acts 2:38), and baptism therefore became closely associated with the moment of one's faith. The close juxtaposition of baptism with faith made baptism the act that symbolized salvation. This is why Peter speaks as he does about baptism saving us.

Peter's final word has to do with Christ's exaltation (3:22). The point is that suffering and proclamation of the truth will ultimately lead to the believer's exaltation with Christ. In heaven now, all things, "angels and authorities and powers" have been "subjected to Him." The believer will reign with Christ.

Study Questions

1. How does our good behavior, when we are slandered and reviled, put to shame those who hate us?

2. How did Jesus make proclamation to the spirits now in prison?

3. Why does Peter mention Noah, and those who were brought safely through the floodwaters by the ark?

4. In 3:21 is Peter saying that water baptism itself actually saves?

5. Why does Peter mention the ascension of Christ in 3:22?

6. What seems to be the overall thrust of 3:18–22?

CHAPTER 24

The Attitude of Leaving the Past Behind
1 Peter 4:1–6

Preview:

Christ suffered while walking this earth in the flesh. Although believers are living now in the flesh, they are to live not for lusts of the flesh, but for the will of God. Generally speaking, believers in the Lord have often lived for the desires of the Gentiles, pursuing a course of sensuality. The lost of the world are often surprised that Christians do not continue to run with them in excessive dissipation. The gospel is still preached to them as though they are dead but able to come spiritually alive according to God's will.

The theme for this section is provided by the words of 1 Peter 4:1–2: "Therefore, since Christ has suffered in the flesh, arm yourselves also with the same purpose, because he who has suffered in the flesh has ceased from sin, so as to live the rest of the time in the flesh no longer for the lusts of men, but for the will of God."

Christians are to arm themselves with the realization that as Christ suffered and "died to sin" (Rom. 6:10), therefore leaving the effects of sin behind forever, so should they die to sin as a way of life, leaving the past behind.

Since the word *flesh* appears here without any antithesis being made to "spirit," Peter has in mind the physical sufferings of Christ on the cross. The interpretive question is the meaning of "because he who has suffered in the flesh has ceased from sin." Since Christ's suffering in the flesh involved physical death, the repetition of the words as a generalization in the next clause must, to be consistent, be the same. In other words, Peter is saying that who-ever dies has ceased from sin, a rather obvious reality when applied to human beings. How, then, does this apply to living believers? Believers' identification with Christ in His death, burial, and resurrection is the answer. Because of believers' faith in Christ, God considers believers dead with Christ (Rom. 6:1–11). This cessation from sin does not mean total sinlessness. Remember, believers are being urged to arm themselves with a particular attitude. This attitude entails a determination to live a qualitatively different life that is no longer dominated by sin.

This interpretation is supported by 4:2. Whatever remains of our life "in the flesh" (probably the body here) should not be lived according to the same patterns of the "lusts of men" but instead "for the will of God." Regarding the right attitude for suffering, believers will be far better able to face persecution if their hopes and values are not in this present world, if they have renounced the lusts of men and "ceased from sin."

Peter reinforces this appeal by another form of logic that borders on irony: "For the time already past is sufficient *for you* to have carried out the desire of the Gentiles, having pursued a course of sensuality, lusts, drunken-ness, carousing, drinking parties and abominable idolatries" (4:3). To para-phrase this, "You've already wasted enough time in sin."

A brief look at Peter's catalog of vices will be profitable to clarify what believers leave behind. First, the entire list is placed under the heading of "the desire of the Gentiles," which literally is the "counsel" or "will" of the Gentiles. This language strongly suggests the pressures that the ungodly place on one another to carry out the lusts of the flesh. To resist such pressures will bring the believer into their resentment, something Peter says in 4:4.

The words *sensuality, lusts,* and *carousals* have sexual connotations, while the words *drunkenness* and *drinking parties* involve alcohol, the same ingredi-ents one finds in the modern pagan's idea of a good time. The biggest differ-ence in this list with more modern times is the reference to "abominable idol-atries" that would have occurred in pagan temples. These same temples would, as a further difference, have been the scenes of the drinking and sexu-al activity.

Catalogs of vices were common in Jewish writings, in which the vices were condemned. Although Jews would have been nonparticipants, Peter's readers would have been participants at one time. This fact helps to explain the next verse: "In *all* this, they are surprised that you do not run with *them* into the same excesses of dissipation, and they malign *you*" (4:4). When believers once were a part of such vices, they bonded with those who also participated. The sudden fracture of this bond would lead their pagan friends to wonder what had happened. In Romans 2:14–15 Paul informs us that pagans instinctively know the law and often perform it, but more often they suppress that truth. The mere presence of one who keeps that law pricks the conscience and arouses resentment. In time, this embarrassment may lead to the pagans' salvation as the Holy Spirit works in them and draws them, but the initial reaction will more likely be to "malign" the believer as a form of self-justification.

However, if these pagans do not repent and believe in Jesus, Peter reminds Christians, "they shall give account to Him who is ready to judge the living and the dead" (4:5). The "living" presumably would be those who from Peter's perspective were alive, while the "dead" would pertain to all who had died before that time. Peter makes no reference to those yet to be born perhaps because, like all believers, especially in New Testament times, he was expecting the possibility of the return of Christ within their lifetime.

But the possibility of their ultimate salvation—and thus the justification of the believer's not compromising—is stated in 4:6: "For the gospel has for this purpose been preached even to those who are dead, that though they are judged in the flesh as men, they may live in the spirit according to *the will* of God." The most difficult phrase in this sentence is "even to those who are dead." In context it appears to be the same use of the word *dead* as 4:5, the dead of all ages. The "gospel" as the New Testament describes it is the preaching of the death and resurrection of Christ and a person's response in repentance and faith. The "gospel" or good news prior to that time would have been the message that through the prescribed sacrifices of the sacrificial system and the hope of a coming Messiah, a message that would have varied in content according the progress of revelation at any given time. In Adam's day, for example, the message probably would have included a concept of atonement through a prescribed sacrifice and a vague understanding of the seed message of the gospel given in Genesis 3:15. Later in history that "gospel" would have been augmented by the revelation given to Isaiah in the landmark message of Isaiah 53. With the arrival of Jesus the Messiah and His sacrificial death and resurrection, the gospel had reached its full-orbed form.

Those who believed the gospel among the "dead" would therefore receive the judgment of Genesis 3:19 and be "judged in the flesh as men," namely, physical death, but would "live in the spirit according to *the will of* God." The most difficult part of this verse is contained in the adverb, *even*. The good news was preached *even* to the dead. This means that though the gospel as we know it today was not in existence prior to Jesus' death and resurrection, in essence it was indeed "preached" before that time. It didn't involve going and making disciples of all nations but was communicated through the witness of Israel, the hope of atonement for sin and of a coming Messiah. It was a "come and see" rather than a "go and tell" mission as we have it given in the New Testament by Jesus.[1]

Study Questions

1. With what "same purpose" are believers to arm themselves?

2. Though still existing in the flesh, how are believers in Christ now supposed to live?

3. What do unbelievers do when Christians do not run with them?

4. Why has the gospel been preached?

CHAPTER 25

The Attitude of Urgency
1 Peter 4:7–11

Preview:

Believers are to live knowing that the "end of all things is sure." They are to live with fervency in love and, as good stewards, exercise the gift the Lord has given through the manifold grace of God. Believers are to speak as with the utterances of God and serve so that in all things Christ might be glorified.

First Peter 4:7 establishes the thought of urgency in this passage in the words, "The end of all things is at hand." Two thousand years have passed since Peter wrote these words that convey the biblical concept of imminency. The possibility that Christ could return at any time to rapture the church. Peter locates the reason for urgency specifically in the doctrine of imminency rather than in the expected persecution of believers. But he probably linked the two because persecution will ebb and flow but will nevertheless characterize the present age to its end.

A sense of urgency helps prepare believers for suffering and persecution because it causes them to think more in terms of danger. The routine of life has a dulling effect on us, making us unprepared for things to go wrong. The remedy for this is found, Peter tells us, in being of "sound judgment and sober *spirit* for the purpose of prayer." We must repudiate Pollyanna expectations of this present evil world and face its realities soberly, this usually in prayer.

With these generalities before his readers, Peter focuses on two areas that are surprising in light of the need for a sense of expectation and urgency. One is love for fellow believers (4:8–9), and the other is the practice of spiritual gifts (4:10–11).

Perhaps the most important reason for the command to love fellow believers (implied by the words "one another") is the encouragement and support that this will bring for everyone involved before and during times of trouble. In the Bible, love can be commanded because it is not so much an emotion as it is a decision that leads to action in behalf of its object. This love is to be "fervent," the translation of a term that literally means "strained."[1] Such love in action builds a community of people ready to help one another and therefore serves as a good attitude in regard to suffering. Peter quotes Proverbs 10:12, where "love covers all transgressions," a statement about forgiveness of those who create strife among friends. Thus, in connection with those who persecute, it pertains to forgiveness, not atonement for sin. In addition to the benefits toward fellow believers, then, this love prepares us to forgive and hopefully win those who mistreat us.

In connection with love for fellow believers, Peter adds, "Be hospitable to one another without complaint" (4:9). The word literally means "friendly to strangers." This is an extension of the command to be fervent in love to brethren, because it takes in the stranger. Preparation for difficult times of persecution required willingness on the part of Christians to help strangers, especially in a day when there were few places for travelers to stay. The early Christian mission often relied on believers for accommodations.

The other focus of urgency is Peter's exhortation to exercise one's "special gift" (4:10). The original Greek has no adjective, and the NASB has supplied the word *special* in italics to indicate that these gifts are not mere presents but something special given by God. Peter gives the examples of speaking and serving, and these are found in the lists Paul gives in 1 Corinthians 12:8–10 and Romans 12:6–8. This listing identifies the gifts as "spiritual" gifts, supernatural endowments given to all believers (1 Cor. 12:7). The body of Christ functions on the basis of such gifts, and a functioning body or church is crucial in times of urgency.

The basis for Peter's appeal to exercise our gifts is because we are "stewards of the manifold grace of God." The word *stewards* is the NASB translation of a word that can also be rendered "administrators." It literally means "responsible slave"[2] and is from the same root word as *dispensation*, which means "economy" or "administration" and is the name for the system of hermeneutics on which this commentary series is based. The implication of this is that the household of God, the Church, is intended to be well run and organized, because God is a God of order. At the Judgment Seat of Christ, He will hold each of us accountable for our stewardship. We are stewards of the "manifold grace of God," the word *manifold* meaning that God's grace is manifested in various ways. For example, the Christian life begins with justification by grace through faith. Sanctification is by grace. Christian living is by grace through the Holy Spirit.

This grace underlies the operation of these gifts, two categories of which Peter mentions by way of example. The first is "speaking," a designation that may include several of the gifts Paul lists in 1 Corinthians 12:8–10, such as the word of wisdom, the word of knowledge, prophecy, tongues, and interpretation of tongues. In Romans 12:6–8 the gifts of teaching and exhortation might be included, since they, too, involve some form of speaking. We often refer to evangelism and preaching as gifts, though they are never mentioned as such in any of the New Testament lists, and they also involve speaking.[3]

Speaking is to be done is a prescribed way, and that way makes it clear why grace must be involved. "Whoever speaks, let him speak, as it were, the utterances of God" (4:11). Of the speaking gifts prophecy would have been the most direct utterance of God, because that is true of prophecy in both the Old and New Testaments.

Study Questions

1. Why should Christians live with sound judgment and sober spirit?

2. How should a believer serve the Lord?

3. What is it that Christ deserves to receive? Why?

4. Does speaking with "the utterances of God" mean that these words are "inspired" as the words of the inspired prophets?

CHAPTER 26

The Attitude of Realism
1 Peter 4:12–19

Preview:

Believers are not to be surprised when fiery ordeals come, as though such persecution is strange. As the suffering of Christ is shared by Christians, they are in turn to keep on rejoicing. Christians are not to suffer as evildoers, but they are not to feel ashamed if they suffer for the sake of Christ. If believers in Christ can be judged, how much more so can those who disobey the gospel?

Realism about suffering pervades this section. It begins with the words, "Beloved, do not be surprised at the fiery ordeal among you" (4:12). Then it continues with, "but if *anyone suffers* as a Christian, let him not feel ashamed" (4:16), and finally it concludes with, "Therefore, let those also who suffer according to the will of God entrust their souls to a faithful Creator in doing what is right" (4:19). Christians should nurse no illusions about the true nature of this world. It is a world affected profoundly by the fall of humanity. Unbelievers can be at times friendly and reasonable and at other times beastly. Even in a country where there is officially sanctioned religious liberty, Christians should expect discrimination. I attribute this to two things. The first is our radical lifestyle that in itself serves as a witness but aggravates unbelievers (note 1 Pet. 4:4), and the second is our belief in the exclusiveness of the gospel. In other words, we preach that salvation is only through Christ, and this strikes many as arrogant.

It is realistic to expect trials (4:12). The phrase "fiery ordeal" translates one Greek word *(purosei)* that refers to the refining of metals in furnaces. It came to be a metaphor not unlike the Hebrew word *holocaust,* which referred to the burning of the sacrifice on the altar and eventually in more modern times to the Jewish Holocaust. This kind of trial is similar to the kind James refers to in James 1:2–4 in that it serves as a test. In 1 Peter "fiery ordeal" may be intended to refer to persecution in particular, while the trials in James may be of a great variety including persecution. These "fiery ordeals" are not to be regarded "as though some strange thing were happening to [them]." Such trials are normal.

In enduring these sufferings, Christians share, "to [a] degree," in the sufferings of Christ. For this they should rejoice, so that they "may rejoice with exultation" at Christ's revelation, a reference to Jesus' return. The implication of this encouragement to rejoice in the present when they suffer is that though that rejoicing might be mitigated somewhat by the suffering, it will give them the right as well as the desire to rejoice in a supreme degree ("with exultation") at His coming. The measure of exultation we philosophically determine to have in this world of suffering, when we suffer in a godly way, will be rewarded by a supreme form of that exultation in eternity.

We have an inclination to take rejection as a failure on our part, but realism should inform us that to be "reviled" (4:14) is because of "the name of Christ," not necessarily because of our faults or limitations. Therefore, we should realistically consider ourselves "blessed, because the Spirit of glory and of God" rests on us. Realism tells us, in other words, that this is the natural result of a phenomenon of glory and its effect on those that at that moment, at least, are resistant to God. When the Holy Spirit is making progress in some individuals' lives in drawing them to Christ by slowly breaking down their natural barriers, then this glory is instead attractive to them. Remember the words of Paul in 2 Corinthians 2:15–16: "For we are a fragrance of Christ to God among those who are being saved and among those who are perishing; to the one an aroma from death to death, to the other an aroma from life to life."

But the question is how we can know whether rejection by unbelievers is our fault or due to the glory within us. Peter supplies part of the answer to this question in 4:15. He says, "By no means let any of you suffer as a murderer, or thief, or evildoer, or a troublesome meddler." We make the determination about the cause of rejection by examining ourselves first. Peter lists a few sins that could be the cause. It is a wide-ranging list including some sins we would hope are not to be named among Christians, like murder and theft, and it is not clear whether Peter is contemplating any believer actually committing those sins or is merely giving a list of things not to be known among Christians. However, the references to "evildoer" and "troublesome meddler" might more likely pertain to the Christian who has wandered from a close relationship with Christ. "Evildoer" translates a word that could be understood as any kind of crime or wrongdoing short of the first two, while the last in the list, "busybody," is something more likely to happen among Christians. This is the word's only appearance in the New Testament, but the general idea from the postbiblical appearances in various kinds of Greek literature is of someone who meddles in matters that are none of his or her business.[1]

The better reason for suffering is found in 4:16. If anyone suffers as a Christian, he or she is not to be ashamed but is to "glorify God in this name," that is, the name of Christ bound up in the name "Christian." It takes but little self-examination to determine if one is suffering as a Christian; thus, Peter does not find it necessary to list the corresponding virtues as he did in the previous verse.

The Sufferings and Trials of the Believer

Each member of the body of Christ all suffer together (1 Cor. 12:26).

Most believers endure and suffer many of the same things (2 Cor. 1:6).

Paul suffered tribulations in behalf of those who trust Christ (Eph. 3:13).

Believers are granted to believe in Christ and to suffer for Him (Phil. 1:29).

The Thessalonian Christians received the Word of God with much affliction (1 Thess. 1:6).

Believers are often called upon to suffer and endure tribulations (2 Thess. 1:4).

Believers must bear up under sorrow when suffering unjustly (1 Pet. 2:19).

Believers may suffer for the sake of righteousness (1 Pet. 3:14).

Believers should suffer for doing what is right rather than for doing what is wrong (1 Pet. 3:17).

Believers should not suffer for troublesome, evil sins (1 Pet. 4:15).

Believers, after suffering for a little while, will be matured, confirmed, and strengthened (1 Pet. 5:10).

The apostle John considered himself a fellow partaker with believers in tribulation and trouble (Rev. 1:9).

The final item about which Christians should be realistic is rather unusual—the beginning of judgment with the Church itself (4:17). This verse is often quoted in connection with warnings to believers about their failure to be good witnesses to the world, but here the judgment that begins with the Church has to do with suffering for the cause of Christ. This interpretation is confirmed by the last half of the verse where reference to those who "do not obey the gospel of God," indicates what is the opposite of those who do in the second part of the verse. This is one of the instances in which the word *judgment* occurs in a text but obviously means something slightly different in reference to the two groups described. The "judgment" of the church is disciplinary and formative (implied back in 4:12 with the word *testing*). It involves character formation as in James 1:2–4. The "outcome" of judgment upon those who disobey the gospel is vastly different. Peter never states explicitly what this outcome is, but it takes little imagination, in light of Scripture as a whole, to determine what it will be: condemnation. Peter reinforces this outcome in 4:18: "And if it is with difficulty that the righteous is saved, what will become of the godless man and the sinner?" This quotation comes from Proverbs 11:31 in the Greek Septuagint, hence the difference you encounter if you turn to your Old Testament based on the Hebrew.[2] In the NASB translation of Proverbs 11:31, which follows the Hebrew, the first part of the sentence is, "If the righteous will be rewarded in the earth." "Rewarded" takes the place of judgment understood in the context of this passage in 1 Peter. One can be "rewarded" with God's approval, while another can be "rewarded" in the form of judgment.

The "difficulty" with which the righteous are saved probably refers to the cost of redemption through the sacrifice of Christ. That is the *only* way anyone can be saved, and the question about the godless implies that there is no salvation apart from grace through faith in Jesus' sacrifice.

Peter's conclusion in 4:19 indicates the final aspect of realism toward suffering. When we suffer according to God's will, we entrust our souls to the "faithful Creator." The realism of suffering is that we can only endure in a godly manner by God's grace, and this is accomplished by entrusting ourselves to God, another way of saying that we must depend on God to do His work in us. This procedure, incidentally, applies to anything and everything we do for God.

Study Questions

1. What kind of fiery ordeals could Peter be writing about?

2. Are believers tested to be made to stumble or to be strengthened?

3. In what way can the Spirit of glory and of God rest upon believers?

4. Does 1 Peter 4:19 imply that the Lord is helpless when the Christian suffers? What is the verse trying to tell us?

5. How do verses 12–13 and verse 19 work together in explaining the providence of God in the life of the believer in regard to suffering?

CHAPTER 27

The Attitude of Responsibility Regarding Leaders
1 Peter 5:1-5

Preview:

Peter designates himself as a fellow elder among those to whom he is writing. He urges the leaders who read this letter to shepherd the flock of God over whom they have oversight. Jesus is the Chief Shepherd who will impart a crown of unfading glory to those who are faithful. Younger men are to be subject to the elders, clothing themselves with humility, for God opposes the proud but imparts grace to the humble.

With the "therefore" of 5:1, Peter turns to another subject, addressing the leaders of the church but expanding what he says in connection with the entire congregation. The "therefore" relates this subject back to his discussion of being realistic about suffering and persecution. During such times as these, the role of the elders becomes crucial.

"Elder" translates the Greek *presbuteros*, a word imported from the Jewish synagogue but used appropriately because of its connotations of experience, wisdom, and authority. This term apparently is one of three words used to designate this office: *pastor* (or *shepherd*), *overseer* (or the archaic *bishop*), and of course *elder* itself. Perhaps the term *elder* is the most frequently used of the three in the New Testament. The distinction between this office and that of the deacon is a matter of debate among Christians because of two different arrangements of deacons and elders. In some cases, there were multiple elders in each house church (remember, each city had several house churches) supplemented by deacons, with a division of responsibilities between them. In other cases, there was a single elder in each house church augmented by deacons sharing the same types of responsibilities among them. It is beyond the scope of this commentary to delve into this complicated issue.[1]

Peter, although an apostle, regards himself as a "fellow elder." We can only speculate what this implies. My opinion is that an apostle was normally attached to a local church and was regarded as an elder of that church but served the churches at large in ministry and problem-solving in addition to being a primary source of revelation and teaching. Thus, he would be in over-all authority among the churches. The legacy of the New Testament we have today constitutes the role of divine truth-bearing and authority, but people who know and understand the Scriptures, also serve among churches as medi-ators and trouble-shooters.

One of Peter's qualifications as an apostle was that he was also a "witness of the sufferings of Christ" (see Acts 1:21–22 for this implied qualification). He was a fellow elder but was distinct from most if not all of the elders in the churches throughout the Roman world by being an eyewitness of Jesus' suf-ferings on the cross as well as Jesus' glorious resurrection.

Peter probably includes his fellow elders as "a partaker also of the glory that is to be revealed." It is not clear if he refers to the glory that all believers will share or to a special glory (or reward) to be granted to those who serve as elders. I am inclined to think, since he is addressing and exhorting elders, that he is thinking in terms of an incentive for the exhortation that follows and therefore has in mind that special glory or reward to be given for faithfulness in that office. This interpretation seems to be confirmed by 5:4, where the "crown of glory" is a reference to rewards at the Judgment Seat of Christ.

Peter's charge is to "shepherd the flock of God among you" (5:2). He gives instructions that involve motivation and leadership style (5:2b–3). As to motivation, the elder is to exercise "oversight not under compulsion, but vol-untarily." This passage serves as an example of the other two words for the office of elder, *shepherd* in its imperative form and *oversight*.[2] The term *shepherd* emphasizes the concept of soul care and protection, while *overseer* contains the idea of oversight of the function of the church or management. This lead-ership is not to be done "under compulsion" or for "sordid gain." I might have added for "pride," because people often wrongly place church leaders on a spiritual pedestal, and such adulation feeds the ego. Compulsion involves putting pressure on someone when he or she is reluctant to serve. Indeed, many people who initially shrank from the idea of being a leader eventually became good leaders. But the Holy Spirit brought them to the place where they *became* willing for the right reasons. Money is another reason some desired to become elders. In the modern church, the position of elder typically is not a paid position but voluntary. But in 1 Timothy 5:17 it appears that in the first-century Church some elders were granted "double honor," a reference to financial reimbursement. If today's pastors are to be regarded as elders in the church, one can understand the motivation of "sordid gain." Hence the "eagerness" with which they are to serve must be an eagerness to serve God and His people for totally unselfish reasons. Only if the position of elder is regarded as servant leadership—which is the biblical principle—can motives be pure.

This brings us to another way Peter describes the wrong motivation for the office of elder: the desire to exercise authority for the sake of personal power (4:3). His terminology is "lording it over those allotted to your charge." This is leadership as power rather than servanthood. It involves the manipulation of people rather than leading people for their highest good. In short, it is a worldly model of leadership that Jesus said was forbidden to his disciples:

> Jesus called them to Himself, and said, "You know that the rulers of the Gentiles lord it over them, and their great men exercise authority over them. It is not so among you, but whoever wishes to become great among you shall be your servant, and whoever wishes to be first among you shall be your slave; just as the Son of Man did not come to be served, but to serve, and to give His life a ransom for many." (Matt. 20:25–28)

Peter's use of the expression, "lord it over" is identical to the one Jesus used in Matthew 20:25. Peter must have been recalling Jesus' words from that occasion, and by this time Peter had learned the lesson Jesus was teaching. In Jesus' words, the prepositions *over* and *among* are especially significant. The word *over* suggests hierarchy and the love of position and authority. Contrary to this, the word *among* is appropriate to servanthood, for it connotes no elevation above others.

The elders have those who are "allotted to their charge," an expression that implies a stewardship responsibility in which leaders must be accountable to Christ for how they lead as undershepherds. It further implies that leaders are not acquiring followers on their own. Instead, God is bringing followers to them, for God is building the church, not the leaders, as the leaders do the tasks the Bible lays out for them.

The appearance of Jesus, "the Chief Shepherd." Peter has been dealing with elders, who are shepherds of souls, and such "shepherds" are accountable to the "Chief Shepherd." Both Peter and Paul make references to "crowns" as symbols of rewards. The "crown" was probably a garland or wreath made of leaves or gold in ancient athletic competitions. Such rewards are not payment for human accomplishment but tokens of faithfulness, a faithfulness to let God do His work through the individual.

In 1 Peter 5:5 the other side of the attitude of responsibility toward leadership becomes Peter's focus. The "younger men" are addressed at first, but then the later reference to "all of you" takes in the whole congregation. This side of the responsibility is the submission and obedience aspect—the responsible response to good leadership. This proper response is to "be subject" to the elders and is accomplished by clothing oneself with humility. This makes submission more than an outward respect for authority without the inward acknowledgement of it. The command is based on the general rule quoted from Proverbs 3:34. James puts it this way: "God is opposed to the proud, but gives grace to the humble." The "grace" that is given by God is the ability to lead and the heartfelt ability to obey. Among other things, humility in Scripture is an attitude of need for God to accomplish His will through us.

Study Questions

1. Since Peter describes himself as a fellow elder, could this mean this letter was addressed mainly to a group of church elders?

2. From 1 Peter 5:2-3, list the ways the flock of God is to receive shepherding by the elders.

3. By Peter's injunctions in 5:2-3, is the apostle hinting that it would be easy for the leaders to lord it over the flock?

4. It what way is Christ be the Chief Shepherd?

5. Why does Peter focus on the younger men being subject to their elders?

6. Why does Peter quote Proverbs 3:34 in 5:5 when addressing the problems of younger men?

CHAPTER 28

The Attitude of Submission to God
1 Peter 5:6–11

Preview:

Younger men must learn humility before their elders and before God. When one is humbled, God will "exalt" that child of God at the right time. The devil attempts to destroy believers like a roaring lion on the prowl. Believers are to resist him and stand firm in their faith. When suffering comes, believers must remind themselves that they are ultimately called into the Lord's eternal glory found only in Christ.

First Peter 5:6 is generally linked to the preceding discussion on responsibility toward leadership, but I believe it flows out of that material and constitutes another subject. Having quoted Proverbs 3:34, Peter applies the need for humility and submission to God. If God gives grace to the humble, it behooves believers to humble themselves before God in order to meet the requirement of this much-needed grace. Believers must recognize that trials are permitted by God who is nevertheless still in control.

Peter says that humbling is to take place "under the mighty hand of God." This reference to God's power serves as an incentive as well as a reason for humility. Reliance on oneself takes place apart from a sense of God's sovereignty, and realizing this sovereignty assures him or her that it is safe to be under the mighty hand of God. God can be trusted.

Lenski writes:

"In due season" implies that God will let the lowly remain in their lowly condition here on earth; the time for their exaltation is the last day, the day of the manifestation of Christ; then they shall receive the crown of the glory (v. 4). Who are we to be thus exalted and crowned? The very realization of what is here promised bows us under God's mighty hand in deepest lowliness.[1]

While the apostle Peter is telling the Christians to seek after humility with the result that the Lord might then lift them up, he is not arguing for simply a system of merits. To do this would foster a sense of false humility and pride. The point is that the child of God should humble himself so that God might in a right sense left him up. Peter reminds the believer to be completely and wholly dependent on the heavenly Father and then notes that He at the proper time will lift him up. "(The expression in due time also refers to the return of Christ, as Peter indicates in other passages [1:5; 2:12].) Peter assures the readers that they can fully trust God's word, for he invites them to throw all their cares upon God."[2]

Failure to humble oneself implies the direct opposite: to exalt oneself. To do this is not only foolish but also ill timed. Thus, Peter refers to the "proper time" when the believer is exalted, and it is the time when God exalts the believer, not when the believer exalts himself or herself.

One of the great enemies of humility is self-concern. Anxiety (5:7) occurs when self-exaltation and its accompanying pride appear to us to be threatened. The answer instead is to rid ourselves of anxiety. This cannot happen apart from placing that anxiety in Someone else's hands, Someone we can trust because He is mighty (5:6) and He cares (5:7). The expression, "because He cares for you," is literally, "because to Him your concerns matter to Him."

Here the verb epiripsantes is aorist and means "to throw upon," indicating a decisive act on our part. Peter does not say what the anxiety is; perhaps he had persecution in mind. The application of his exhortation embraces all the difficulty a believer who wants to live godly in a fallen world must face. The "casting" entails an act of the will and would be done prayerfully and in obedience to Jesus' teaching about anxiety (Matt 6:25-34). "He cares for you" means that God is not indifferent to our sufferings.[3]

The other great enemy of humility is the devil, and in 5:8–11 Peter deals with this enemy. This passage is often not seen in its context of dealing with pride. This context has identified pride as a threat to humble submission to

God. Peter identifies the devil as the solicitor of pride, the one who seduces us to yield to our pride and thus replace our dependence on God with it.

Leighton writes:

> While others are turmoiling and wresting, each with his projects and burdens for himself, and are at lengthy crushed and sinking under them, ... the child of God goes free from the pressure of all that concerns him, it being laid over on His God. [With this advantage] he is not racked with musings, Oh! What will become of this and that; but goes on in the strength of his God as he may, offers up poor, but sincere endeavours to God, and is sure of one thing, that all shall be well. He lays his affairs and himself on God, and so hath no pressing care; no care but the care of of love, how to please, how to honour his Lord.[4]

To be sober (5:8) means to be realistic about ourselves and our tendency toward unfounded pride in our abilities or fears about our lack of ability. The correct attitude is realism, as we see in Paul's remark in Romans 12:3: "For through the grace given to me I say to every man among you not to think more highly of himself than he ought to think; but think so as to have sound judgment, as God has allotted to each a measure of faith." True humility is not to portray ourselves as something less than we are but to acknowledge God's gifts and work in us. The words of Paul, "as God has allotted to each a measure of faith," do not mean a certain *quantity* of faith is given to each of us, but instead that each of us has received a *standard* or *measurement* of faith (the meaning of *measure* in this text). One basis for self-evaluation, in other words, is faith in what God has accomplished in us, not what we think of our own accomplishments. The other basis for self-evaluation is the ability that God gives us by His grace.

The devil is on the prowl to seduce us through our pride or our fears and "devour" us. Peter's reference to a "roaring lion" is a metaphor of insatiable hunger. If the Lord is concerned for our welfare, the devil is concerned to devour us. As the old saying goes, "misery loves company." Another important observation here is that the devil is described as our "adversary." Up to this point in 1 Peter, Peter has described the believer's adversaries in the plural. As Paul says in Ephesians 6:12, the real enemies are in the spiritual realm, and here Peter narrows them down to one.

The answer to this threat through pride or fear is to "resist him" (5:9). This is done with firmness of faith that such suffering is universal among Christians. We are not being singled out for persecution. Others are "accomplishing" experiences of suffering. This means that they are successfully enduring by God's grace, and we can count on the same grace to help us during the time of trial.

Peter points these believers to other Christians who are suffering the same ordeal of persecution. He wants to remind them that the same kinds of struggles are coming upon all those who trust Christ. The suffering must have been heavy and painful. In the Greek text Peter actually is saying that they are experiencing the "same kinds of sufferings." The whole body of Christ is affected though not ever believer is under the exact same tribulation. And in fact, some may have escaped these trials and survived the onslaught that was coming against the church in the wider sense. But without a doubt, the body of Christ as a whole was generally hated by the world and the culture of paganism.

Another great encouragement is that suffering is temporary ("for a little while," 5:10). "The God of all grace"—the God who dispenses all ability or power—whose purpose is bound up in his calling us to "His eternal glory in Christ," will eventually bring us to success. This success is described in terms of perfection, confirmation, strengthening, and establishing. *Perfect* pertains to the furthering of our sanctification. *Confirm* means giving us confidence in our salvation. *Strengthen* refers to spiritual power. And *establish* brings us to consistent Christian living.

Peter has encouraged his readers to endure suffering in such a way that the grace of God would be made manifest in their lives. Now in a closing word of benediction he committed them to the God of all grace (cf. 4:10). The benediction briefly summarizes Peter's message of encouragement. Christians' suffering will last only a little while, while their glory in Christ, to which they were called, will be eternal (cf. Rom. 8:17-18; 2 Cor. 4:16-18). ... God Himself would restore them and make them strong.[5]

And Schreiner remarks:

The God who has given such promises also uses exhortations to provoke his people to be faithful until the last day. The exhortations and promises, therefore, should not be played off against each other, as if the exhortations introduce an element of uncertainty to the promises. The exhortations are the very means by which God's promises are secured, and indeed God in his grace grants believers the strength to carry out the exhortations. Still, such grace can never be used to cancel out the need for responding to exhortations.[6]

Peter concludes this section on submission to God with a brief benediction (5:11). It is a statement of the ultimate goal of God in the universe. That goal is "dominion," His acknowledged supremacy. It exists now, but complete human recognition of it is future, as God allows history to play itself out.

Schreiner concludes:

Peter emphasized here the sovereignty and power of God, and hence he used the term kratos [for glory]. The God who permits suffering in the lives of his children, and even allows the devil to rage at them (cf. Job 1—2), is the sovereign God and the God who cares (5:7). The dominion belongs to him—forever. He wields a "mighty hand" (5:6) on behalf of his people. Hence, believers should be full of comfort, knowing that they are on the side of victory and celebration.[7]

Study Questions

1. What is Peter trying to picture when he speaks of being humbled "under the mighty hand of God"?

2. Why is it difficult to cast all our cares upon the Lord?

3. In what ways are believers to be sober and alert for the attack of the devil against them?

4. Is Peter saying that all suffering comes upon us from the hand of the devil?

CHAPTER 29

Final Greetings
1 Peter 5:12–14

Preview:

Silvanus, or Silas, helped Peter write this letter. Peter closes by reminding believers to stand firm in the true grace of God. Both the chosen woman "in Babylon" and Mark send greetings to the readers of this letter. The apostle wishes all those in Christ to find peace.

Peter signs off his letter first with an explanation regarding its composition (5:12). "Through Silvanus, our faithful brother (for so I regard *him*), I have written to you briefly," he begins his final words. Silvanus is a variation of the name Silas, the apostle Paul's companion on his second missionary journey (Acts 15:40). Such references as this more often speak of the individual who might carry the letter to the church or churches, but this statement may imply something else. Some believe that the instrumental use of the preposition *through* (Greek, *dia*) suggests merely secretarial help in taking dictation or carrying the letter to its destination. Others believe it implies a greater role in its composition as Silvanus writes Peter's thoughts in his own vocabulary and style.[1] I believe Silvanus had this larger role in composition due to the difference in style between 1 and 2 Peter (see the introduction).

Next Peter states the purpose for his writing this letted was to exhort and testify of the "true grace of God." With this phrase Peter puts a broad label on his composition and purpose. Indeed, the whole Christian life can be summed up this way, for it consists of the grace of God providing salvation and working that salvation into the believer. I do not, however, as might often be the case in such statements of purpose, regard this reference to grace as the theme of the letter.[2] It seems to me that the idea of suffering is the overriding theme. Grace figures in rather as the means by which suffering can be endured to the glory of God.

What follows next is a farewell greeting. The words are somewhat cryptic: "She who is in Babylon, chosen together with you, sends you greetings, and so does my son, Mark" (5:13). There was a Babylon in Mesopotamia and one in Egypt (where Cairo now stands), but we have no historical evidence that Peter was ever at either of these two places. A name like Babylon has such rich and notorious connotations in the Bible that it could likely have been regarded as a symbolic name—among Christians at least—for Rome. To Jews this would also be possible, for Peter may also be using the name Babylon as symbolic of Christians' exile as Jews recalled their exile in Babylon. Revelation 17 and 18 refer to Babylon as both a great religious organization and economic establishment, but there is dispute among interpreters whether it is a literal city of that name, perhaps rebuilt on the site of the ancient Babylon, or another symbolic reference to Rome.

Another issue is the meaning of the phrase "She who is in Babylon" (5:13). Some have speculated that Peter was referring to his wife, but this seems unlikely since Peter, if he were passing on greetings, probably would mention more than his wife and Mark. It was the custom of the apostle Paul, for example, to refer to many names because of the familiarity among Christians even in the vast expanse of the Roman Empire. Instead, most authorities take this as a reference to the church in that city, the pronoun *she* being appropriate as a designation, since the word for church (Greek, *ekklesia*) is also feminine in gender. Another possible such reference is found in 2 John 1:1, where John passes on greetings from a certain "chosen lady and her children," a designation, some believe, to the church and its members.

There is little doubt that the Mark here is the John Mark of the book of Acts 12:12, 25; 15:36–39; and 2 John 1:1, 13. There is much patristic testimony to the effect that this Mark was a close companion to Peter. Even the Gospel of Mark is attributed to the influence of the apostle Peter. The expression "son" probably indicates "spiritual son," as Peter was Mark's spiritual mentor.

The exhortation to "Greet one another with a kiss of love" is the "holy kiss" of several passages, such as Romans 16:16; 1 Corinthians 16:20; and 1 Thessalonians 5:26. Most commentators believe it involved men with men and women with women, especially given the New Testament moral ethic. Probably the best modern American equivalent is the embrace.

Peter's final words are a wish for peace to "all who are in Christ." In light of the subject of suffering and persecution, this peace would come by God's grace, not pleasant times.

Study Questions

1. Why would Peter need a scribe to help write this letter?

2. Is Babylon here actually the city of Babylon? Or is Peter somehow using the word in a figurative sense? Give the various opinions as well as your own view.

3. From Acts 12:12–25, what do we know about Mark?

4. How is Peter's postscript different from the way Paul closes his letters?

THE BOOK OF SECOND PETER

Effective Knowledge of God

CHAPTER 30

Background of Second Peter

Both 1 and 2 Peter fall into the category of what is known as the General Epistles. First Peter emphasizes suffering, but 2 Peter focuses on false teachers and their deceptive teachings. *Spiritual knowledge* is Peter's answer to overcoming false doctrines. In fact, he uses the word *to know* and its related words sixteen times in the epistle. With six of these references the apostle intensifies the thought by using the words *epignosko* and *epignosis*. These words mean "additional knowledge" and "full or complete knowledge." This knowledge is shared with the believer by the work of the Holy Spirit. "The grace and peace which he invokes upon his readers are to issue in 'the knowledge of God and of Jesus our Lord; seeing that his divine power hath granted unto us all things that pertain unto life and godliness through the knowledge of him'" (1:2–3).[1]

Second Peter could have a similar purpose as 1 Peter, and that is to speak to the Jewish Christian communities scattered throughout the Roman and Greek world. The difference is in the subject matter in Peter that overall appears to be concerned with the invasion of false doctrine into the assemblies. The apostle uses some of the strongest and most emotional language in the New Testament to speak against heresy. R. C. H. Lenski comments: "Second Peter says nothing about impending sufferings; it warns against abominable *libertinists* who scoff at the Parousia of Christ. This letter recalls Paul's warnings as expressed in Acts 20:29–30, 2 Thess. 2:3; 1 Tim. 4:1, etc. 2 Tim. 3:1–9; and John's in 1 John 2:18. These warnings are prophetic, and they begin as early as Acts 20."[2]

Like James, 2 Peter was forwarded to unnamed readers. Some think the audience was the same as 1 Peter, but this cannot be proven. In fact, it may have been sent to a broader readership because of its universal warnings about error. Yet the bulk of the audience probably was Jewish. Only in 2 Peter does the apostle use his full Jewish name, Simon Peter (1:1).

The importance of the book is in the fact that it reveals the imperfection of the early church. It prepares the future church for the truth that error will always raise its ugly head and come against the saints. An incipient Gnosticism had invaded the various assemblies, bringing about an intellectual and antinomian characteristic—*antinomian* meaning that many were tempted to live the "religious" life without moral or doctrinal guidelines or principles. Paul also saw this coming in the errors he addresses in his Colossian letter. There he specifically speaks to the issues among the Colossians while Peter seems to be speaking in broader terms and to a people he may not have met. "Peter did not have an official relation to the people he addresses; he may yet have visited them during the time of Paul's imprisonment at Rome. He, along with others, had made known unto them "the power and coming of our Lord Jesus Christ" (1:1–14). This, then, led to the writing of this Epistle."[3]

The Language of the Book

The Greek of Luke, Acts, 2 Corinthians, Hebrews, and Jude, is more sophisticated and complicated than most other New Testament books. Because this is true also of 2 Peter, many have surmised, the book was not written by Peter but by a forger. Some add to this argument that, because the subject matter is so different from 1 Peter, it certainly could not have been authored by Peter. However, change of subject or a shift in emphasis and word usage is no reason to doubt authenticity.

To counter these claims it has been noted that no forgery of a supposed canonical book has come close to being included as inspired Scripture. The early Church was far more discerning, though certain issues in various books along the way caused some to have doubts, and disputes did occasionally arise in regard to some texts.

Although there is no mention at the end of the book of a scribe or secretary who may have recorded Peter's words, it seems to make sense that this is how the book came about. Again, this certainly does not destroy the idea that Peter was the human author of this epistle. While some critics have focused on the language and word differences between the writings, many scholars also point out that there are a large number of similarities between the two books.

The External and Internal Evidence of Authorship

Some have said that 2 Peter comes with less historical support than any other New Testament book. But this is not necessarily true. There are words and phrases that resemble The Shepherd of Hermas, First Clement, Second Clement, and the *Didache,* all written early between A.D. 90 and A.D. 130. Clement of Alexandria and the churches of Vienne and Lyons seem to have known of its existence. However, Eusebius included it among the questionable works *antilegomena* but not under the books that were actually spurious.

One argument for the slow acceptance of 2 Peter into the canon of New Testament Scripture is the fact that the epistle is so small. It may not have caught on quickly with the Christian public. Also, because the Greek is hard to read, it may not have been very popular for reading or study. Too, often in Church history, silence does not prove that something does not exist or that it is questioned. Many argue that some silence about the book proves that there were no major objections to it being a part of the Word of God.

For certain, scholars have pointed out that there is nothing doctrinally in the book that would raise a flag of doubt, in fact, just the opposite. Second Peter is a marvelous work about the integrity of divine truth and a sound warning for those who turn away from the Lord. In all areas, it relates well to doctrine found throughout both Old and New Testaments. By the fourth century, the book was well accepted. It was included in the canon of the Council of Laodicea (A.D. 363) and in the canon of Athanasius (A.D. 367).

The internal evidence for the authorship of Peter is said to be stronger than the external. Besides the specific name Simon Peter in the introduction (1:1), there are statements and references in the content that point almost exclusively to Peter as author. For example, only Peter, James, and John were at the Lord's transfiguration, and a clear eyewitness account is given to this event in 1:16–18. Too, the writer refers to his impending martyrdom (1:12–15) that the Lord predicted in the Gospel of John (21:18–19). And as in 1 Peter 3:18–20, this second letter refers to Noah and here calls him a preacher of righteousness (2:5).

> Finally, the Christian earnestness, apostolic tone, and autobiographical allusions make it impossible to believe that the epistle is spurious. We, therefore, accept it as a genuine work of the apostle Peter.[4]

Date and Purpose

The book of Jude has many allusions and quotes from 2 Peter. The date of Jude is pretty well established as having been authored around A.D. 75. If 1 Peter was written about A.D. 63, then 2 Peter more than likely followed a few years later, around A.D. 66 or A.D. 67.

Lenski is one of the few scholars who challenges the order of the writing of the two books. He believes 2 Peter was actually the first letter written. He says that if 1 Peter was anticipating near persecution, then the subjects that

Peter brings up in 2 Peter would not have been of burning consequence. The churches would already have been into heavy persecution and suffering, Lenski argues. Therefore, the letters could not have been addressed to the same people. But herein lies the problem with Lenski's argument. Few scholars believe the audiences are exactly the same, though certainly there could have been some overlap of readership, and probably was, because of Peter's statement "this is my second letter" to you. Lenski is almost alone with his theory, and none has followed his line of reasoning and reversed the order of when these books were written.

Peter writes to encourage his readers to grow up in Christian character (1:5–15; 3:18), to encourage a waiting for the Lord's coming (3:1–14), and to warn against "being carried away by the error of unprincipled men" (3:17). The apostle wants the believers to grow up spiritually. He introduces them to grace and to the area of spiritual knowledge and the testimony of the apostles and prophets (1:16, 19–21). The knowledge about Christ shows the right way (2:15) and the "way of righteousness" (2:21). Peter then uses the example of Noah as a preacher of righteousness (2:5) and Lot as "righteous Lot" (2:7). With this Peter makes a contrast with the way of the unrighteous (2:9) and the way of wrongdoing (2:13, 15).

Conclusion

While the predominant audience in 1 Peter was Jewish Christians, this may not have been so in the absolute sense in 2 Peter. In both letters the author frequently uses Old Testament allusions, and in both he sets forth the doctrine of divine inspiration. As with 1 Peter, 2 Peter is applicable to all those in Christ Jesus. While the focus may be toward Jewish Christians, New Testament truth is for all believers in this age of grace. Finally,

> even though the second epistle of Peter is short, the theological emphases are distinct. For example, in the opening verse (1:1), Peter describes Jesus Christ as divine. He writes, "the righteousness of our God and Savior, Jesus Christ." That is, he calls him God and Savior. We observe that Peter does this purposely to stress the divinity of Christ, for in the next verse (1:2) he clearly distinguishes between God and Christ: "the knowledge of God and of Jesus our Lord." For Peter, Jesus is not only divine, but also Lord and Savior (1:11; 2:20; 3:2, 18). Furthermore, Peter encourages the believers to increase their "knowledge of Jesus our Lord" (1:2–3, 8; 2:20; 3:18). And he tells them about the coming of the Lord (1:16) and the day of the Lord (3:10, 12 [God]).[5]

What a rich book to thrill the hearts of all believers today!

Section I

God's Unchanging Truth Changes His Children

2 Peter 1:1–21

CHAPTER 31

Life-Effects of Our Knowledge of God
2 Peter 1:1-11

Preview:

The child of God is granted everything pertaining to life and godliness and, as well, other great promises made to us by the Lord. These truths translate into how believers are to walk with the Lord in godliness and brotherly kindness. These qualities must not be forgotten, or the child of God will have failed to remember his or her divine calling and choosing. These things lead the way into the eternal kingdom.

Peter opens his letter with the customary remarks of first-century correspondence, although this obviously is not a personal letter but a general letter. Unlike the first letter, Peter refers to the name given him by his parents, "Simon" (literally, *Simeon*), as well as that given him by Jesus, "Peter," or "Rock." In addition to his appointment by Jesus as an apostle, he refers to himself as "bondservant." Why he should add these more personal references is not clear. Perhaps an anticipation of his imminent death leads him to these references as he reflects on his position before Christ and mortality. Very subtle emotions can lead a person to say things differently under such circumstances.

In this letter Peter makes no explicit reference to his addressees other than that they possessed "a faith of the same kind as ours." Shortly thereafter he addresses that faith in terms of a precious knowledge of the truth. As I indicated in the introduction, the addressees here are the same group addressed in the first letter, as evidenced by his reference to his previous letter as correspondence with which they were familiar.

Second Peter 1:2 is a somewhat familiar greeting in which Peter asks that "grace and peace be multiplied." The additional reference to the "knowledge of God and of Jesus our Lord" anticipates the theme of the letter with the reference to knowledge. That grace and peace will be channeled through their knowledge of God and Christ. Peter sees knowledge as the fundamental feature of Christianity, but it is distinct in the sense that it is *effective* knowledge, something more than merely a cognitive thing, and furthermore its content is God and Christ.

The first part of the main body of the letter is found in 1:3–11. Peter offers a unique description in this section of how spiritual growth takes place. First, he describes the process as beginning with a divine provision of power (v. 3). Next he indicates that this provision is for the purpose of making us "partakers of the divine nature" as a replacement for the corruption in the world (v. 4). He then informs us that we must be diligent in "supplying" or adding certain virtues to our faith, because faith cannot stand alone (v. 5). There is a supplying or adding of a list of virtues to this faith (vv. 6–7), and in summary (vv. 8–9) he tells us that if these virtues are ours in an increasing way, we will be effective and fruitful in our knowledge of Christ. If this growth does not take place, a person will become blind and shortsighted and likely forget that he or she has been saved in order to be pure from former sins. All this process is intended to make us certain in Christ's calling and election so that we will not stumble (v. 10), and our entrance into heaven will be "abundantly supplied" to us (v. 11).

Let's return to each of these verses and examine them more carefully. Peter says that this "power has granted to us everything pertaining to life and godliness, through the true knowledge of Him who called us by His own glory and excellence" (1:3). The "power" here is the power to change sinners. It's all we need for radical change. Knowledge of Jesus is the foundation of this growth. Such knowledge will be an understanding of Jesus' moral character after which we pattern our lives. Thus, "life" refers to everyday living, and "godliness" qualifies this life as one that pleases God. This is the purpose of our call, a call through two means, His glory and His excellence. "Glory" pertains to the totality of all the divine attributes, attributes such as His love and compassion that desired our salvation to begin with and serve as the goals He has in mind for us. "Excellence" refers to His moral qualities.

These same two, God's glory and excellence, are the means by which God brings about our conversion (1:4). This conversion is described as a granting to us of "precious and magnificent promises," the sum of which Peter assumes his readers already know by virtue of the gospel, but the particular promise here has to do with the change God intends to produce their lives. Certainly the magnificence of all of them is seen in a particular aspect of them related to this change. Peter describes this basis for change in terms of believers' becoming "partakers of *the* divine nature," a striking and profound statement of the nature of the new birth. As children partake of the nature of their parents, so do believers. As the inheritance factors of the parents gradually become manifest in the children, so will the promise of this aspect of the "precious and magnificent promises" gradually become apparent in believers, and the process that Peter is about to describe in 1:5–9 will accomplish it.

Furthermore, the contrasting benefit will be that those who partake of the divine nature will escape "the corruption that is in the world by lust." This corruption will be the basis for the world's judgment. *Sanctification*, another word for what Peter is about to describe, provides the only remedy for corruption by lust. "Lust" here is very strong desire that enslaves a person (as indicated by the prefix to the Greek word for *desire* of the Greek preposition for *upon*, meaning literally "lust upon lust" or overpowering desire). Peter views this lust as the focus of what is wrong in the world. Originally it involves a transfer of desire from God to things God has created (Rom. 1:21), and thus it is worship of things rather than of God. Some form of this idolatry infects the whole human race. Desire itself is not evil; rather, it is the perversion of desire through ungodly means of gratification that the Tempter offers that turns desire into "lust"[1] and thereby into a form of idolatry.

Now let's turn to the positive, salvific aspect of this subject (1:5–9). Peter views the acquisition of these virtues as a process of supplying or adding (see NIV). This supplying implies our desire to let the Holy Spirit work through our faith toward the development of these virtues. Paul refers to the process as "walking by means of the Spirit" in Galatians 5:16. Such "walking" avoids carrying out the lusts or works of the flesh (Gal. 5:19–21) and leads to the "fruit" of the Spirit (Gal. 5:22–23).

Peter begins by telling us to start the process by "applying all diligence" to supply "in your faith . . . moral excellence." The expression "in your faith" along with each of the succeeding virtues (for example, "in your moral excellence," "in your knowledge," in your self-control," etc.) may better be translated "*to* your faith," and so on, making an addition process of it. It probably is not meant to mean a sequential addition, as though one worked on faith first and then went to moral excellence, and so forth, but a simultaneous addition of all the virtues, each arising out of faith. I say this because Paul's listing of virtues in Galatians 5:22–23 refers to them all as singular "fruit," not plural "fruits," which means that they are produced together as the whole of Christian growth.

The first of the qualities, "moral excellence," translates one Greek word that simply means "excellence"—excellence of achievement or mastery of something, in this case, moral goodness, as the context implies.

The next is "knowledge," the thematic word of Peter's whole letter. But here it refers to knowledge of God's will toward a godly life. Mere knowledge apart from godliness is no value.

Following knowledge comes "self-control" (1:6). The Greeks considered this as the heart of their ethical system. In the New Testament it takes on a different twist, because the concept of God's grace permeates Christian behavior, making it something the Holy Spirit does within us and not a mere product of human effort. When we think of self-control, therefore, we need to shift our thinking from personal effort to Paul's metaphor of walking in the Spirit, a figure of dependence on the Spirit. Peter has this in mind because he is talking about all these moral virtues arising out of faith.

After self-control comes "perseverance." This word, by its Greek etymology, implies steadfastness under a threat of something.[2] James sees it as the major accomplishment of the testing of faith (James 1:3–4). Such tests of faith ordinarily occur apart from any sin we may commit, and thus God allows the test but does not directly cause it. Life is full of hazards, and God permits them to become tests that produce perseverance.

To perseverance, the believer adds "godliness." This word has already appeared earlier in verse 3 as one of the goals of our knowledge of Christ. It refers to living that pleases God.

"Brotherly kindness" (1:7) and "love" follow. The term is a translation of one of the three principal words in Greek for love, *philia*, combined with the word for "brother." Ordinarily the three words for love, *eros*, *philia*, and *agape*, are overlapping and close to synonyms in Greek usage. However, when two of them appear together as here, it is safe to assume a slight distinction between them. Therefore, *philia* pertains to love *expressed* among Christians, while *agape* relates more to love that *exists* among the corporate group.

Peter concludes this section in 1:8–11 by promising what the life-effects will be for cultivating these characteristics: "For if these qualities are yours and are increasing, they render you neither useless nor unfruitful in the true knowledge of our Lord Jesus Christ" (1:8). The translators have supplied the word *if*; thus, there is no question that the qualities are possessed through faith. All believers have them. They need to be cultivated,[3] not obtained.

With the cultivation of these qualities, believers are fruitful and "increasing" (or "abounding"). If such growth is lacking (1:9) in someone, that person is "blind *or* shortsighted." The NASB has supplied the "or" in an effort to clarify what is said in the original, although not very successfully: "blind being shortsighted." That would be illogical if understood that way, since one cannot be both at the same time. The thought is that his shortsightedness amounts to blindness, and thus the blindness is self-imposed. Such a person is shortsighted because, as the sentence goes on to say, he has "forgotten *his* purification from his former sins." This is a shortsightedness we might refer to as a temporary loss of memory, something strangely common among believers who are not growing spiritually. Maintaining the memory of original salvation experience is essential, so that we never forget the reason for which we were saved: to pursue the cultivation of these virtues.

With such important issues at stake, Peter exhorts: "Therefore, brethren, be all the more diligent to make certain about His calling and choosing you; for as long as you practice these things, you will never stumble" (1:10). Superficially, this passage sounds like God's calling and choosing of the believer is conditional. The translation "certain" leads to this understanding. It could be better translated "make *firm* his calling and choosing." We are to make our calling and election "firm" in the sense of consistent living. It is not a question here of making our calling and election certain, as though we could lose it, but of making it something that leaves no room for doubt on the part of the pagan world watching us. If we do this, Peter says, we "will never fail." That, of course, is a statement of the ideal, for we all fail to some extent. We simply do not *need* to fail.

The final benefit of this godly living is an abundant "entrance into the eternal kingdom of our Lord and Savior, Jesus Christ" (1:11). It is not a question of entering that kingdom, but in entering abundantly. This pertains, of course, to the Judgment Seat of Christ following the Rapture, a tribunal for scrutiny and reward (or lack of it) for the believer's works (2 Cor. 5:10).

Study Questions

1. By what means has God's divine power been granted to the child of God?

2. List the moral benefits that come when all diligence is applied to the believer.

3. What do these spiritual qualities Peter lists do for the Christian?

4. How can the believer become blind and shortsighted?

5. Does to be diligent to make one's calling certain mean the believer is "working" to keep his or her salvation?

6. As Christians kept out of the kingdom unless they are diligent in their calling?

CHAPTER 32

The Revelatory Source of Our Knowledge of God
2 Peter 1:12–21

Preview:

Peter wants Christians to always be reminded of how they began their spiritual journey and how they have been established in the truth. Believers are not to follow after cleverly devised tales, but are to hold on to the true witness concerning the glory of Christ Jesus. The fact that Christians have the testimony of the apostles gives a more sure prophetic word that is like a lamp shining in a dark place. The prophecy of Scripture was given not by human will, but by men who spoke from God, having been moved by the Holy Spirit.

Having urged his readers to cultivate the various Christian virtues, Peter says that he will always be ready to remind them of these qualities even though he believes them already to know and be established in them (1:12). Peter regards this as his mission as long as he is alive, a condition he figuratively calls his presence in "this *earthly* dwelling" (1:13). The Greek word for "dwelling" is the same word for "tabernacle," the word for the wilderness Tent of Meeting. Peter's readers would easily associate this usage with the place of worship in ancient Israel, especially in terms of its being the dwelling place of God also. To the New Testament Christian there would be the immediate association of the body as the dwelling place of the Holy Spirit (1 Cor. 6:19).

Such is the nature of true ministry to believers, summed up partly in terms of *reminding* Christians of what they already know. Peter stirs up of their memories to encourage them. This is like a military officer going up and down the ranks of soldiers to encourage and coax his troops.

Now in 1:14–15 Peter refers to a premonition of his martyrdom and departure to be with Christ, the passage that informs us of the basic "testament" nature of the entire epistle: to prepare his readers for a difficult future in which he will not be present. When Peter says, "as also our Lord Jesus Christ has made clear to me," he remembers the words of Jesus in John 21:18–19 of the manner of his death: "Truly, truly, I say to you, when you were younger, you used to gird yourself, and walk wherever you wished; but when you grow old, you will stretch out your hands, and someone else will gird you, and bring you where you do not wish to *go*. Now this He said, signifying by what kind of death he would glorify God."

The Knowledge Given to Christians

Believers come to know God when they are saved (Gal. 4:9).

The believer comes to know the love of Christ which surpasses knowledge (Eph. 3:19).

Believers know they have a new dwelling from heaven when they die (2 Cor. 5:1).

Believers need to know how to follow Paul's example (2 Thess. 3:7).

Believers know they are abiding in Christ when they keep His Word (1 John 2:5).

Paul wants the believer to know the hope of his or her calling (Eph. 1:18–19).

Believers need to know how to conduct themselves within the household of God (1 Tim. 3:15).

Because believers love their brothers, they know they have passed from death into life (3:14).

Believers need to know how to respond to everyone with the gospel (Col. 4:6).

Believers know that the Spirit of God is at work when there is confession that Jesus Christ came in the flesh (1 John 4:2).

Believers know the love that God has for them (1 John 4:16).

Believers know for sure the Son of God has come (1 John 5:20).

This leads Peter next to write words that will introduce the main point of this passage (1:15). "And I will also be diligent that at any time after my departure you may be able to call these things to mind." How would this take place? The handing down of Christian tradition at this time would take two principal

forms: training faithful people to propagate the truth (see 2 Tim. 2:2) and putting that same truth into writing. People like Mark would fulfill both of these
methods. Mark was a teacher himself, and according to tradition,[1] he also
inscribed the Gospel of Mark, which is a record of the gospel according to
Peter. Peter's two letters have accomplished this handing down of Christian tradition despite the fact that Peter couldn't have known the extent that his writings would be duplicated—yet he may have expected the same reception for his
own writings as he knew Paul's had already (2 Pet. 3:15–16).

The statement of 1:15 inspires Peter to speak to the subject of the authenticity and reliability of the Bible as a whole in 1:16–21. This passage, especially
1:20–21, is one of two classic definitions of biblical revelation and inspiration; the other is 2 Timothy 3:16–17.

The Bible is unique among the religious writings of the world in that its
message comes through the medium of human events in history, many of
which have been verified, leaving us with good reason to assume that those
that have not been verified historically could be if we but had the time and
financial resources to blanket the biblical world with archaeological excava-
tions. The basis for this historical confirmation is summed up in Peter's significant claim in 1:16–18. What he says here could have been affirmed by all the
biblical characters who were themselves also "eyewitnesses of [Jesus'] majesty"
(1:16). Peter first says that he and the other apostles "did not follow cleverly
devised tales when we made known to you the power and coming of our Lord
Jesus Christ." The Greek word translated "tales" is the same word from which
we get the word *myth,* which here means a "fictional account." In modern
times the historicity of the gospel records of Jesus' life, death, and resurrection
have been challenged in three so-called "quests" or "searches" for the historical Jesus, the first two of which have produced little more than skepticism, the
more recent quest taking a more conservative turn, with the exception of the
extremely radical group called the "Jesus Seminar." Supposedly historical
research criteria have been employed in the more recent quest, but some of
these criteria are questionable, and those who profess to follow the criteria do
not do so consistently.[2] Peter seems to have anticipated such unbelief with the
words we find here, an unbelief that is as old as the gospel itself.

When Peter refers to the "power and coming of our Lord Jesus Christ," he
most likely means the second coming of Christ. I base this conclusion partly
on the basis that the word *coming* (Greek, *parousia*) is one of the three principal words used of the second coming of Christ. The other reason is that Peter's
further explanation of his being an "eyewitness of His majesty" involves his
experience of the transfiguration of Christ. Jesus told His disciples shortly
before that occasion that some of them would see "the kingdom of God after

it has come with power" (Mark 9:1). Six days later Jesus took Peter, James, and John to the mountaintop where Jesus was transformed momentarily from His human to His divine form in all its glory, the same glory that will accompany His second coming.

Jesus' second coming is His coming in glory—not the Rapture—assuming a pretribulation rapture. This event will vindicate both our Lord and us and is the appropriate aspect of the return of Christ for Peter's purpose in this letter, since his purpose is to assure his readers of the foundation and certainty of their knowledge of Christ. Jesus' majesty will be the final convincing proof of who He is, although not all who witness that majesty at that time will welcome it (see Rev. 6:12–17).

Peter next describes in more detail the nature of his certainty of knowledge concerning Christ. He had seen Jesus receive "honor and glory from God the Father." "An utterance . . . was made to Him by the Majestic Glory, 'This is My beloved Son with whom I am well-pleased'—and we ourselves heard this utterance made from heaven when we were with Him on the holy mountain" (1:17–18). This voice from heaven was etched upon Peter's memory, but how would he communicate this memory of majesty to future generations? He answers this question starting with the next verse.

"*So,*" Peter answers, "we have the prophetic word *made* more sure, to which you do well to pay attention as to a lamp shining in a dark place, until the day dawns and the morning star arises in your hearts" (1:19). The "prophetic word" in this sentence refers to the oral form of the prophet's pronouncement—or perhaps the oral form of God's pronouncement in this particular case—a word that needs desperately to be enshrined in the heart by being "made more sure," a Greek word that is used to refer to the certainty or reliability of promises or agreements probably by written confirmation. The result of being "more sure" is that his readers will pay attention to it as they would a lamp (or perhaps a lighthouse?) in a dark place.

Peter offers another intriguing metaphor with the expression of the dawning of the day and the arising of the morning star in believers' hearts. This dawning of the day and rising of the morning star is intended as the terminal point or goal of having confidence in the prophetic word, and it probably refers to the coming of the Lord. The "morning star" in the ancient world usually referred to the planet Venus that would appear just before dawn, so the picture here is probably to the initial appearance of Christ—often referred to in Scripture as a star (Num. 24:17; Rev. 22:16)—followed by the effects of that coming in terms of the arrival of the kingdom.

If there is any doubt up through verse 19 that what Peter had in mind by the expression "prophetic word *made* more sure," verse 20 makes it clear.

It is the inscribed Word, the Scripture. The written Word makes the oral prophecy something lasting, explicit, and memorable. Peter indicates two major significant elements of Scripture—its divine origin and its inspiration by the Holy Spirit.

As to the Word's divine origin, Peter says, "No prophecy of Scripture is a matter of one's own interpretation" (1:20). In the Old Testament the word *prophecy* connotes two things, preaching and prediction. A prophet engaged in both. Preaching to bring people to repentance was his primary work, while prediction, at least so far as the extent of his message was concerned, was incidental. Thus, the word *prophecy* means "divine revelation" and can be applied to the Bible as a whole. That is the way Peter uses it here.

The translation of the Greek word *epiluseos* as "interpretation" is misleading. Literally, it means, "to set free," "to untie," or "to unravel." The NIV and NASB translate it figuratively to mean "to explain" or "interpret." The NIV inserts the word *prophet* in the phrase "one's own interpretation," so that it reads "prophet's own interpretation," which captures the idea of this difficult passage. The best translation would be "perceived," indicating that neither the prophet nor the person receiving the prophecy interprets it out of his or her own perception or understanding. It is Peter's way of saying what Paul says in 2 Timothy 3:16: "All Scripture is inspired by God" (NASB) or "all Scripture is God-breathed" (NIV, the most literal translation of the Greek). Therefore, the verse has nothing to do with hermeneutics and everything to do with its origin from God rather than man.

This interpretation is further confirmed by the next verse (1:21): "For no prophecy was ever made by an act of human will, but men moved by the Holy Spirit spoke from God." The "act of human will" refers back to "one's own interpretation" (NASB). Peter's point is that human beings did not decide to write Scripture. Instead, they were "moved" by the Holy Spirit. The word "moved" (Greek, *pheromenoi*) means "to bear along" and is the graphic word Luke uses in Acts 27:15, 17 to describe his ship being carried by the wind. This implies two things: (1) full awareness or participation by those on board and (2) movement by means of another force than that generated by the boat itself. Applied to the work of the Holy Spirit, this would correspond to the fact that the writers were (1) fully conscious (not in a trance) and using all of their faculties of intellect, emotions, and will (in the sense they also had their individual purposes in writing) and (2) nevertheless were not being motivated solely by those same purposes. The Scriptures are at the same time both human and divine.

This human aspect of divine revelation is further confirmed by Peter's statement that these men "spoke from God." By using their mouths, they showed that they were fully involved. Peter is referring primarily to "prophecy of Scripture." Thus, he means they "spoke" through Scripture, as was the case with the Old Testament prophets who first spoke orally and then in the case of the canonical books "spoke" through Scripture. Although most of the New Testament writings were first written rather than spoken, Peter is including those that had appeared during his day, a probability based on his inclusion of the some of the writings of Paul among "the Scriptures" (3:16).

Study Questions

1. What does Peter mean when he says "the truth . . . is present with you" (2:12)?

2. In 2:14–15, does Peter seem to be saying that his own death was near?

3. What is Peter referring to when he says, "We were eyewitnesses of His majesty" (2:16)?

4. Do the Scriptures come only from the mind of human beings? See 2:20–21.

5. Can believers today speak as if they are inspired prophets like those in the Old Testament?

6. How specifically did God work with His Spirit in inspiring the ancient prophets?

7. What does Peter mean when he says the prophets were "moved" by the Holy Spirit?

Section II

God's Unchanging Truth Challenges His Children

2 Peter 2:1 – 3:18

CHAPTER 33

The Possible Perversion of Our Knowledge of God
2 Peter 2:1-22

Preview:

The apostle reminds his readers that false prophets and teachers will come who teach heresies, even denying the Master who died for them. They will repudiate the truth and exploit believers with false words. But like righteous Lot, the Lord will rescue His own and bring wrath on the ungodly on the Day of Judgment. The false prophets are corrupt, and they speak arrogant words, pretend to know the Lord, and prove who they really are by returning to their own sinful ways.

Peter informs us that Satan will try his best to pervert the precious knowledge of the truth to render it ineffective. *Pure* doctrine is the only truth that will produce converts and spiritual growth. There is hardly an epistle of Paul that does not deal with false doctrine, and Peter is devoting the greater part of his second epistle to the problem as well.

The Old Testament had its counterpart to this problem, Peter reminds us, when he says, "But false prophets also arose among the people, just as there will also be false teachers among you" (2:1). It is significant that Peter makes the distinction between *prophets* of the Old Testament and *teachers* in the New. The gift of prophecy was active in the church of the first century, and there is no reason, in my opinion, to think of prophecy in the New Testament as substantially different from the Old.[1] The difference here is implied by Peter's description of these false teachers as those who "secretly introduce destructive heresies." Prophets in the New Testament were acknowledged possessors of the gift of prophecy. They spoke publicly, and their messages were judged by others (1 Cor. 14:29). There was nothing "secret" about them. The tactic of the Enemy in the New Testament era and the present day is for teachers of false doctrine to infiltrate the church as respectable teachers and gradually introduce their "destructive heresies" once they have gained acceptance.

Peter's use of the future tense ("will secretly introduce") is probably because he is recalling earlier predictions of false teaching such as those by Jesus in Matthew 24:11. I am confident that these people were already active, and Peter is writing to counteract their poison.

Peter calls the false teaching "destructive heresies." The literal rendering is "heresies of destruction," and "destructive" is an eschatological word for the destruction of eternal judgment or eternal loss of fellowship with God.[2] It never suggests total destruction or annihilation, but it serves in Scripture as an antonym for salvation, both states being conscious conditions. Here it refers to the ultimate destiny of the false teachers, and this interpretation is confirmed by the expression that concludes the verse, "bringing swift destruction upon themselves." In this phrase the same word *destruction* appears again. These false teachers teach things that merit destruction, and destruction will indeed come upon them. The word *heresies* in New Testament times was used of divisive opinions. It came to mean teaching that was not orthodox, and that is the way we use it today.

Next follows a remarkable statement of the false teachers. By teaching divisive opinions, they are "denying the Master who bought them." This means one of two possibilities: The first of these is that these teachers are believers that have been redeemed ("bought") and will lose their salvation by denying the faith. This interpretation would assume that such a thing is possible for the individual, based on a concept of the freedom of will to renounce faith once held. This interpretation is usually categorized as Arminian after the theological reaction of James Arminius against Calvinism. The other interpretation is that there is a sense in which redemption, reconciliation, and propitiation, the three principal results of Jesus' death on the cross, are provisional to all humanity but only applicable to those who believe. Therefore, according to this view, those who never truly believe are "bought" in the sense that a provision was made at the cross for them, a provision they reject.[3] This interpretation is held by "moderate" Calvinists, those who reject the stricter Calvinist view that Christ died and paid for the sins of only the elect, a view known as "limited redemption." Thus, this view is referred to as "unlimited" or "universal redemption," a view shared by Arminians and moderate Calvinists. I understand the passage, therefore, as teaching that these false teachers were "bought" or redeemed *provisionally* but that the actual payment is never applied apart from genuine faith.

The following two verses (2:2–3) describe the conduct of these false teachers. First, they are described as acquiring a large following: "Many will *follow* their sensuality" (2:2). The church must recognize that many of its people are not biblically literate, sometimes the fault of a lack of solid biblical and theological preaching and teaching, sometimes simply the fault of the individuals themselves and their pursuit, by way of the church, of interests they perceive in religion, but not truly Christian in nature.

Second, they are *sensual* or licentious. Generally this word (Greek, *aselgeias*) refers to a variety of ways to immorally fulfill bodily desires, especially sexual desires.[4] Cult leaders frequently live immoral lives, and the text says that this sensuality is what many will follow, not so much their teaching. They provide license for immorality in the manner they interpret Scripture. They justify their impure living by emphasizing grace and teaching that God readily forgives sin without expecting repentance and accountability.

This sort of behavior leads, predictably, to the maligning of the way of truth by those outside the church. The fundamental truth of the "way of truth" is grace. Grace is a delicate balance of God's unconditional forgiveness upon the sinner's repentance and a life of purity maintained by the Holy Spirit. Two extremes characterize a lack of balance between these two: (1) legalism, in which the person tries to live the Christian life in his or her own ability, self-righteously adhering to mere rules and regulations, and (2) freedom from purity under the assumption that free grace carries no purpose toward purity. These false teachers promote this latter extreme, and outsiders correctly repudiate it, seeing more clearly than some naïve-professing believers the folly of such an attitude. This is not authentic Christianity.

The third form of conduct of the false teachers is their *greed*. The word translated "greed" here is *pleonexia*, often translated "covetousness," that which is forbidden by the tenth commandment. This characteristic, along with sensuality, indicates the true motivation of these people. They exploit people sexually and financially. This is characteristic of the "health and wealth" gospel, whose teachers emphasize the idea that God wants people to enjoy life and get rich. Their followers give large amounts of money to religious hucksters who promise God's material blessing for doing so. Those in this false form of Christianity have an insatiable appetite for gratification and luxurious living, having discovered that some religious people will follow anyone who seems to offer the good life as a divine benefit.

The outcome for these false teachers is that their exploitation will bring about their judgment with absolute certainty, even though they appear to continue in and enjoy this form of life with impunity. This is the meaning of the words "their judgment from long ago is not idle, and their destruction is not asleep" (2:3). The words of Paul are appropriate at this point: "Do not be deceived, God is not mocked; for whatever a man sows, this he will also reap" (Gal. 6:7).

With this warning of the certainty of judgment of false teachers, Peter launches into an extended warning in 2:4–10a against those who imagine that for some reason (perhaps the belief in grace unaccompanied by accountability) they will escape divine judgment.

Structurally, the whole passage is probably one long sentence[5] with a series of four "if" clauses in 2:4–8 followed by a "then" clause in 2:9–10a.[6] The "if" clauses (called the *protasis*) list several judgments from the past, and the "then" clause (called the *apotasis*) states a conclusion based on the "if" clauses.

The first of the "if" clauses, and the one where the "if" actually occurs in the Greek and lends its pattern to what follows, takes us[7] to the first judgment recorded in Scripture, angels that rebelled with Satan in his fall described in Revelation 12:7–9. Though angels are not mentioned in two Old Testament passages, Isaiah 14:12–17 and Ezekiel 28:11–19, I regard them as also referring to this event.[8] The word translated "hell" by NASB is actually Tartarus, a place similar to Hades where the unsaved that die from Adam's day to the Great White Throne Judgment are assigned where they are "reserved for judgment." After that judgment they are cast into the lake of fire. Tartarus, consequently, is the place where these angels are consigned until they along with Satan are assigned to the lake of fire, the place more properly designated as hell.[9]

The next theoretical "if" clause begins with 2:5, and it pertains to the judgment of the flood of Noah. This is the first reference in this second letter of Peter to the Noahic flood, a subject of which Peter is fond. He spends time discussing this in his first letter (1 Pet. 3:19–20) and will make further reference to it in 3:5–7 in connection with the mockers. The "ancient world" to which Peter makes reference is the world prior to the Flood described in Genesis 6:5–8, so far as the causes for the judgment are concerned. Peter informs us of a fact not found in the Genesis record, although it is implied in 1 Peter: Peter was a "preacher of righteousness." This preaching produced no converts other than the seven members of Noah's own household, but Peter includes it here to indicate the "patience of God" that "kept waiting in the days of Noah, during the construction of the ark" (1 Pet. 3:20). Such patience and its consequent preaching demonstrate the justice of the judgment. We marvel at such preachers as Noah and Jeremiah who faithfully delivered the truth of God without results.

The third "if" clause involves the spectacular judgment of Sodom and Gomorrah (2:6). This form of judgment was by "reducing *them* to ashes," Peter's summary of the words of Genesis 19:24–26, "and He overthrew those cities, and all the valley, and all the inhabitants of the cities, and what grew on the ground." The sin of the cities was homosexuality, and it is interesting that Peter says that God "made them an example to those who would live ungodly thereafter." A special form of judgment came upon those who committed this particularly detestable sin to warn others in the future. The social ramifications of such perversion must be recognized, because it eats like a cancer in society and becomes a catalyst for that society's ultimate demise. There are two aspects of sin in a society where homosexuality begins to be common: its *practice* and its *acceptance*. By "acceptance" I mean the willingness of those who may not practice it but regard it, as we say today, an "alternative lifestyle."

In connection with this judgment, Peter informs us of something else not found in the Genesis record itself that raises questions about the man he mentions in the last "if" clause: Lot (2:7–8). This clause, like the reference to the preservation of Noah and his family during the Flood, provides an aspect of judgment—rescue from judgment—wherein the status of the righteous in societies that abide under the shadow of divine judgment is given us. The rescue of Lot, unlike that of Noah and his family, was really a form of divine discipline, and that explains why it is included as an "if" clause parallel with the other judgment clauses. Lot and his family—at least his two daughters—lost everything they had in this world even though they were rescued from the judgment itself. There is a price to pay for the toleration of evil.

That brings us to the remarkable description that Peter gives of Lot, quite a different picture than what we get from the Genesis narrative where Lot comes across as a weak compromiser, nevertheless one worthy of rescue. Peter amazingly describes Lot as "righteous" and "tormented day after day by *their* lawless deeds." The impression we get of Lot is that, when given the choice by his uncle Abraham (Gen. 13:8–13), he opted for the cities of the plain and lived among godless people for financial gain. The lesson for us is that such a choice results in a living hell ("tormented day after day") and eventually severe discipline.

The "then" clause 2 Peter 2:9 provides us with two contrasting conclusions: (1) "The Lord knows how to rescue the godly from temptation," and (2) the Lord is able "to keep the unrighteous under punishment for the day of judgment." The promise to rescue the godly from temptation provides the alternative for the sorry condition of Lot. He gave in to temptation to compromise for the sake of material gain and paid a price for it. The prospect of judgment, Peter is saying, should lead the godly to avoid that to which Lot succumbed and accept God's "way of escape" from the temptation itself (see 1Cor. 10:13).

As to the unrighteous, they are "kept," or reserved, for judgment. God is not lax. Even though the unrighteous appear to be getting away with their sin, God "keeps" them for judgment. It is like being on death row, except death row offers no such sense of freedom and indulgence that the wicked usually experience.

Verse 10a continues the thought of verses 8 and 9, and it probably should have been made part of verse 9. The words "and especially those who indulge the flesh in *its* corrupt desire and despise authority" (2:10a) indicate a greater degree of sinfulness on the part of some than of others. Thus, the theological view that there will be degrees of punishment in eternal fire is probably correct. The picture in this verse is of unrestrained pursuit of pleasure with no sense of guilt because of the total loss of all conscience toward authority, authority that speaks to whatever conscience the unrighteous may have left but in these extreme cases is totally lost.

Following this frightening warning of certain judgment, Peter turns to the inner character and nature of the false teachers (2:10b–22), whereas in 2:1–3 he spoke of their conduct. The sentence begins with the second part of verse 10, whereas the first part of verse 10 begins with the words "and especially," which conclude verse 9. This is the longest description of its kind in Scripture, exceeding the one found in Jude 1:11–16. It falls into four parts. The first part (2:10b–13a) deals with the pride and arrogance of these teachers, the second (2:13b–16) describes their sensuality, the third (2:17–19) warns of the emptiness and deceit of their teaching, and the fourth (2:20–22) informs us of their apostate nature.

The first characteristic of the false teachers is their pride and arrogance (2:10b–13a). First, Peter describes them as "daring" and "self-willed" (2:10b). Both words are virtual synonyms in the Greek, so that when brought together they mean something like "willfully daring." In light of the general context, I would apply this description to a lack of respect for the things of God, a willingness to intrude into the church and twist the meaning of Scripture to suit their ends. They have no fear of accountability, boldly taking matters into their own hands.

Next, in harmony with this interpretation, they are unafraid to "revile angelic majesties." Angels, including Satan, are powerful beings and should demand our respect, though not our worship. It is likely that evil or fallen angels are in view, as the NASB indicates. But why should the false teachers revile or slander fallen angelic beings, since they are engaged in the very things that would please these demonic beings? Perhaps the reason is that they do so to impress others with their boldness. This would not disturb the evil angelic beings themselves, because they would prefer that people not take them seriously so that they are freer to carry out their deception through the false teachers. We cannot be sure exactly what form this slander took in Peter's day, but any attitude today that does not take them seriously would be dangerous. In spite of the preoccupation TV and movies have with evil spirits today, there is actually a tendency to view it all as entertaining myth. Not to take Satan and his realm of angelic beings seriously could make people vulnerable to their influences.

Angels, on the other hand, "do not bring a reviling judgment against them before the Lord" (2:11). There are two possibilities as to who the "them" are. They may be the "angelic majesties" of the previous verse, so that the meaning is that lesser angels than the "majesties," though they have greater power than the false teachers, never slander their superiors. The other possibility is that the "them" are the false teachers, and the "angelic majesties," though greater in power, do not return the slander against the false teachers.

The question is probably resolved in what appears to be a parallel in Jude, 1:8–10. Jude refers to a specific occasion on which an "angelic majesty," the devil, was not given a "railing judgment" by one of the most powerful of all the elect angels, Michael. Michael instead spoke to the devil in the words, "The Lord rebuke you!"[10] The "them" of 2 Peter are therefore angelic majesties, not the false teachers, if this passage is allowed to contribute to the question.

Peter turns back to the false teachers themselves in 2:12 to continue his description of their arrogant character. They are "like unreasoning animals, born as creatures of instinct to be captured and killed, reviling where they have no knowledge." Arrogance is often borne out of ignorance, but ignorance on the part of the teachers is willful. They make confident assertions about things they know nothing about, and they know nothing because they have deliberately not sought out the truth as good researchers. Animals are creatures of instinct by nature. False teachers are like them only in the sense that they are without moral restraints and have fallen into ungodly moral instincts, following the lusts of their sinful tendencies acquired by birth. We must be careful in this comparison with animals when Peter refers to the destruction of the false teachers. The word used of both is the Greek *phthoran*, a word usually connected with *moral* corruption, which is translated "destroyed" by the NASB and "perish" by the NIV in light of the context where animals are killed and false teachers are brought to eternal accountability. They both will be destroyed but in different ways, animals by extinction, human beings by eternal torment in the lake of fire. Verse 13a continues the thought of verse 12 by adding, "suffering wrong as the wages of doing wrong." This distinguishes the false teachers from the animals to which they have been compared. Animals, in their acts of instinct on one hand, are not blameworthy but merely victims of the imposition of the fall of humanity on them. False teachers, on the other hand, will suffer their destruction because of their "doing wrong," for which they are morally responsible.

In 2:13b–16 Peter describes the false teachers' sensual character. "They count it a pleasure to revel in the daytime. They are stains and blemishes, reveling in their deceptions, as they carouse with you" (2:13b). At first glance, this statement is alarming. They revel in the daytime and "carouse with you," as though other true believers were participating in the same sins. Here again, as in the case of the similarities between Jude and 2 Peter earlier, Jude provides a clue to the meaning of the passage.

Jude 1:12 describes them as "hidden reefs in your love feasts when they feast with you without fear, caring for themselves." The "love feasts" were meals eaten as part of the Christian assembly during which the Lord's Supper was celebrated. In 1 Corinthians 11:21 Paul speaks disapprovingly of the Corinthians' abuse of these suppers, but here Peter is not necessarily saying that true believers were abusing the practice. Rather, it is the false teachers who have appeared "secretly" (2:1) in the congregation who are being castigated. They have turned the meal into a time of carousing, perhaps arousing the suspicions of the believers. They are called "hidden reefs," a reference to underwater reefs that could fatally damage ships that struck them. The love feasts, like smooth waters, could be occasions of deception, because they were times of fellowship when Christians accepted one another on the basis of profession of faith and were not as alert to alien participants.

Peter further describes the false teachers as "stains and blemishes" (2:13). Later, in 3:14, Peter will encourage his readers to be "spotless and blameless," two words built on the same root as these words in 2:13, but exactly the opposite, accomplished in Greek by simply placing the Greek *alpha* at the beginning of the word. In other words, the false teachers are full of spots and unblameless in their character.

Next they have "eyes full of adultery and that never cease from sin" (2:14), which more literally means "eyes filled with adulterous women." In other words, every woman they see, because of these teachers' unbridled lust for sex, is a candidate for sexual sin so far as they are concerned, and their minds rarely depart from such lust.

Furthermore, they entice "unstable souls." The word translated "enticing" was used by fishermen of a lure to catch fish. Although the word could further suggest sexual seduction, in light of the following context, it seems likely that Peter shifts to their teaching and its effects, although sensuality is still in his mind, because the ultimate purpose for their enticement of these unstable souls was some form of physical gratification. This is implied by the phrase "having a heart trained in greed." Ultimately they have it in their minds to become leaders in the church and to be supported by the people they dominate.

To illustrate these teachers, Peter turns to a fascinating character from the Old Testament book of Numbers, Balaam. Instead of the "right way" (2:15), they have gone the way of "Balaam, the *son* of Beor, who loved the wages of unrighteousness." Numbers 22:7 informs us that the leaders of Midian attempted to hire Balaam "with the fees for divination in their hand," and Balaam consulted with the Lord and asked him to curse Israel. Evidently Balaam regarded the Lord as another of his gods with whom he was in league. Balaam was more of a sorcerer, a fact not mitigated by his being called a "prophet," for among the pagan nations at that time "prophet" was a term often assigned to sorcerers who divined the future through their magical arts and consultations with demonic spirits. Balaam was unable to place a curse on Israel, but later, according to Numbers 31:15–16, he counseled the sons of Israel to sin against the Lord by sparing some Midianite women in the defeat of the Midianites at Peor.

Peter has characterized the false teachers as dumb animals (2:12), and this makes his final commentary on Balaam very appropriate. The role of prophet was reversed with a dumb animal, the mute donkey being used by the Lord to prophesy to the prophet and restrain "the madness of the prophet" (2:16).

In 2 Peter 2:17–19 the nature of the false teachers' teaching becomes the subject. The characterization can be analyzed into three categories: (1) it promises satisfaction but is unable to deliver (2:17); (2) it appears to be impressive spiritually but leads into sensuality instead (2:18); and (3) it promises freedom but leads instead into bondage (2:19).

In regards to number 1, the false teachers "are springs without water, and mists driven by a storm" (2:17). The semi-desert area of Canaan had such springs, promising thirsty travelers relief for their thirst. Perhaps they had drunk deeply from the spring on a previous journey, only to find on some desperate occasion that the spring had gone dry. Similarly, those expecting a drought-ending rain promised by dark clouds would be disappointed by a storm that would quickly blow over the parched land leaving only a teasing mist. False teaching perverts the Bible, snatching an idea here and there out of context and building a system of doctrine that appeals to the gratification of the flesh. The so-called "health and wealth" movement fits this perfectly. This teaching promises abundant life without the hardness of life that God uses to strengthen faith and perfect character (James 1). Such teaching is so reprehensible to God that He has reserved "the black darkness" for them, a reference to eternal loss that employs one of the descriptions that Jesus gives for hell: "outer darkness" (Matt. 22:13).

As to number 2, these teachers speak "arrogant *words* of vanity" by which "they entice by fleshly desires" and "sensuality" (2:18). They are like modern "motivational" speakers parading themselves as experts who confidently offer quick and easy solutions to life's problems or how-to-get-rich schemes ridden with flaws when it comes to reality. "Vanity" means "empty" and refers to the fact that when it comes to real life, their theories just don't work. These are impressive speeches, but they "entice by fleshly desires," and before you realize it, they have your money and are long gone. This reminds me, for example, of "spiritual warfare" writers with their new theories on how to deal with sin and live the spiritual life. Their way of dealing with sin may be built around the theory that all sin is caused by demons, and that exorcising the demon of sexual lust will rid you of sexual addiction. Or take some "faith healers" who for a price will promise deliverance from some disease, and when you fail to be healed, tell you that your faith was not strong enough. The people who are targets for these false teachers are interestingly described as "those who barely escape from the ones who live in error," a reference to new converts who have escaped from a godless, immoral lifestyle and are naively susceptible to impressive people whom they believe are true representatives of the Christian faith. False teachers love to prey on these kinds of people, some of whom may be genuine believers and others who have perceived Christianity to be a "quick fix" for all their frustrations.

Finally, number 3, exposes false teachers as those who promise "freedom while they themselves are slaves of corruption" (2:19). False teachers are in bondage to their own cravings, but they promise deliverance from that to which they are enslaved themselves. They are "overcome" and thus enslaved by that which overcomes them.

Peter follows this with an insight about false teachers' bondage (2:20–22). Once they understood the truth that sets free. "They have escaped the defilements of the world by the knowledge of the Lord and Savior Jesus Christ" but have again become "entangled in them and are overcome" (2:20). But how can Peter say that they would be better "not to have known the way of righteousness, than having known it, to turn away from the holy commandment delivered to them" (2:21)? The answer to such a question must entail an answer to whether such knowledge of righteousness included genuine faith and salvation. If these false teachers were once genuine believers, it certainly would be horrible to come so close to ultimate salvation and lose it. Asuming that they had genuine faith at one time, they would have lost that faith somehow in order to carry out their deception convincingly.

However, 2:22 seems to preclude their ever having had genuine faith. Peter concludes his denunciation of false teachers with two proverbs, one from the Bible, the other from a source not known to us today. The false teacher is described as "a dog[11] [that] returns to its own vomit" (Prov. 26:11) and "a sow, after washing, [that] *returns* to wallowing in the mire." Both of these proverbs suggest a return to the past without any fundamental change of character, thus not a very good picture of a true believer who has been regenerated.

One other factor leads me to believe that false teachers were never genuine, committed believers. Peter's words in 2:20, "the last state has become worse for them than the first," seem unmistakably to echo the words of Jesus in Matthew 12:43–45:

> Now when the unclean spirit goes out of a man, it passes through waterless places seeking rest, and does not find it. Then it says, "I will return to my house from which I came"; and when it comes, it finds it unoccupied, swept, and put in order. Then it goes and takes along with it seven other spirits more wicked than itself, and they go in and live there; and the last state of that man becomes worse than the first. That is the way it will also be with this evil generation.

The significant thing to note about Jesus' parable is that the house was "unoccupied," and this, too, is not true by analogy of the genuine believer in whom the Holy Spirit now resides.

Study Questions

1. What was happening historically that caused Peter to dedicate this entire chapter to warning believers of false doctrine and false teachers?

2. According to 2:7, what saved Lot from the judgment that fell on Sodom and Gomorrah?

3. From 2:10–22, list the different ways Peter graphically describes the corrupt and false teachers he is so concerned about.

4. Did these false teachers really know in a personal way the Savior Jesus Christ? See 2:20–21.

5. In 2:21, what does Peter mean when he writes "it would be better for them not to have known the way of righteousness"?

6. What point is Peter trying to make with his rather "earthy" illustrations in 2:22?

7. Were the false prophets Peter describes actually saved?

CHAPTER 34

The Coming Denial of Our Knowledge of God
2 Peter 3:1-7

Preview:

Peter says that he wrote this second letter to stir up the minds of the believers by way of reminder. They should remember also the words of the ancient holy prophets and the commandment of Jesus spoken by the apostles. They must be aware of the mockers who try to deny the promise of the Lord's coming. The mockers argue that judgment has not come and the world is going on as before. But they fail to realize that the heavens and earth are reserved for the judgment that is yet to come!

Peter opens the third chapter of his second letter by saying that he is "stirring up" his readers' minds "by way of reminder" (3:1). Note the similarity of this statement with what is found in 1:12–13 as Peter's statement of purpose there in writing the letter. Thus, what he says here further emphasizes his overall purpose to remind them of the knowledge of God and all it entails. This reminder is concerning the "words spoken beforehand by the holy prophets and the commandment of the Lord and Savior *spoken* by [their] apostles" (3:2). The question is whether "the words" spoken by this array of holy men pertain to the faith in general, the reminder of which would help to equip Peter's readers for the mockers that would challenge the body of truth called Christianity, or whether "the words" pertain to prophecies that such mockers would indeed eventually come.

I am inclined to opt for the former of these two possibilities due largely to the use of the word *commandment,* which specifies a broader range of revelation than mere prediction. Of course, the body of Christian truth would have *included* predictions of the coming of mockers, but Peter's purpose in writing this "second letter," as he calls it, is to reinforce believers' faith in the faith, a divine deposit of knowledge about God and His purposes.

Peter turns to the next aspect of his theme of the knowledge of God with yet another repetition of the key word of the letter, "know" (3:3). "Know this first of all, that in the last days mockers will come with their mocking, following after their own lusts." The connection between this verse and what precedes it is not obvious to the English reader, because what appears to be an imperative ("know") is actually a present active participle ("knowing"). In other words, Peter is saying, "You should remember the words spoken by God's messengers and his very Son, *knowing* that mockers of those words will come." There will come a threat in which that word of truth will be denied. To "remember" to Peter means to hold the truth in the mind so that it is not abandoned as a life principle. It will come under attack, and every effort will be made to discredit it so that the believer might give it up.

Those who attempt this program of ridicule are called "mockers" in the NASB. The KJV and NIV translate it "scoffers," a translation that is a bit superior, because in modern English to mock often means to make fun of someone by acting like them, whereas to scoff means to ridicule, and that, as we shall see, is what Peter goes on to discuss.

These scoffers, Peter informs us, are doing this according to their "lusts" or desires. No specific example is given of what these desires entail. However, the thing that Peter says they scoff at provides a sufficient clue: the return of Jesus Christ. What they do not like is the idea of divine intervention into history for calling the human race into accountability. The desire behind such an objection as this would be the desire for independence of any accountability to God. This is, in fact, the basic sin from which all other sins flow. This happens in the "last days," a phrase that generally pertains to the messianic age introduced at Jesus' first advent and culminated in His second advent to establish His universal kingdom on earth, the Davidic kingdom. The characteristics of the last days intensify as the age progresses, so we can expect this kind of sin to intensify the closer we get to Jesus' return.

The ridicule of the scoffers has to do with what they perceive as a lack of any indicators of Christ's return (3:4). The word used is "coming" (Greek, *parousia*), a word that can refer to either Christ's return to translate living believers and resurrect dead believers (1 Thess. 4:13–18), or His return to establish His millennial kingdom (1 Thess. 3:13). Since this coming constitutes judgment and accountability of the scoffers by implication of their scoffing at it, it is safe to say that Peter has in mind Christ's second coming to judge the Gentiles and establish His kingdom (see Matt. 25).

The appeal the scoffers make is to their perception that "since the fathers fell asleep, all continues just as it was from the beginning of creation." They claim that since creation there has been no intervention by God, that things simply go on in a naturalistic, predictable way. All catastrophes are the random results of purely natural causes, not divine judgment. Why should things start being different now than they were in the past? The "fathers" to whom they make reference are likely to be the patriarchs of Israel. It is highly unlikely that Christian "fathers" would be involved. This would be an unlikely way to refer either to Jesus or the apostles. This interpretation is supported by Peter's reference to the flood of Noah in 3:5–6, which takes us back into the beginnings of biblical history.

Now the scoffers, Peter maintains, are overlooking the greatest divine intervention in history during which the entire world was judged: the flood of Noah (3:5–6). Peter connects this event first with the creation of Genesis 1 in which "by the word of God the heavens existed long ago and the earth was formed out of water and by water, through which the world at that time was destroyed, being flooded with water." Waters were separated so that dry land could contain the biological creation in Genesis 1, and waters were caused to overrun their boundaries so that most biological life could be destroyed in Genesis 6.

The scoffers' neglect of this great fact of earth history is in a statement that is translated by the NASB, "it escapes their notice," but the Greek is difficult so far as *syntax* is concerned and has yielded several translations by each of the major versions. The NIV translates it, "But they deliberately forget," and the KJV renders it, "For this they are willingly ignorant of."[1] The presence in the sentence of the word for "wishing" or "willing" seems to point in the direction of the NIV and KJV as the correct translations.

Whoever these scoffers were at the time Peter wrote is not clear to us now, but modern scientists with their purely naturalistic, uniformitarian view of earth history fit the description perfectly. They willfully ignore the fact of creation, here interestingly connected with the Flood in Peter's description, as well as the fact of the Flood. It is typical for many less-than-literal and less-than-biblical interpreters to disregard the Flood as either universal or significant as they project the earth's age into the millions of years. They see no reason to be concerned by any divine judgment, because to them there is no Creator-God to judge. This is a deliberate, prejudiced interpretation of the actual facts that could point them to the Creation and the Flood and inform them of the correct view of divine intervention. In other words, they are willfully ignorant of the facts.[2]

Peter concludes his description of the denial of our knowledge of God by describing the future judgment the scoffers deny (3:7). This future judgment will be radically different, not involving water this time, but fire. The ungodly scoffers will be destroyed by the very judgment at which they scoff.

Study Questions

1. Could it be in 3:1 that Peter knew his readers were getting lax in their diligence, and that they were beginning to listen to certain false teachings?

2. What are the sources of Peter's "reminders" in 3:2?

3. From 3:3, what is at the heart of the mockers' doubts about the Lord's return?

4. On what basis do the mockers argue that the promise of the Lord's return is delayed?

CHAPTER 35

The Coming Vindication of Our Knowledge of God
2 Peter 3:8–13

Preview:
God does not count time as human beings do; He is certain to keep His word. The Lord delays judgment in order to offer repentance to all, wishing that none would perish. When the final Day of the Lord comes, there will be no warning. The physical elements will be consumed, and the arrival of new heavens and a new earth will follow.

In spite of the denials by scoffers, God's sovereign plan and timetable will be carried out. The delay of the coming of the Lord, since the Flood, for example, has lasted several millennia, but this should not concern us, because delay does not imply any change in plans to a God whose relation to time is vastly different from ours. Peter tells us that we should "not let this one *fact* escape [our] notice . . . that with the Lord one day is as a thousand years, and a thousand years as one day" (3:8). The point of this statement is not something that should be taken literally as a basis for calculating the age of the earth or some broad time scheme in which references to "day" other than a calendar day should be assumed to be a thousand years in length. Rather, the point is that God is not affected by time, so that His essential nature changes or His plans change. The statement is associated with God's immutability.

Such an interpretation is confirmed by the next verse with the words, "The Lord is not slow about His promise" (3:9). The scoffers have demanded evidence of the "promise" of His coming by arguing from the apparent naturalistic uninterrupted nature of things as they know them. Peter is offering comfort to believers by pointing out that the "slowness" of the Lord in fulfilling the promise of His coming should not be viewed "as some count slowness." Instead, the slowness or delay is really part of His patience toward those whom He calls "you."

We should understand the following clause, "not wishing for any to perish but for all to come to repentance," by the "you" that precedes it. The "you" pertains to Peter's readers, identified in 1:1 as "those who have received a faith of the same kind as ours," that is, believers. The process of the salvation of the elect, in other words, prolongs the age. Whatever the truth of the matter may be—whether God does not want *anyone* to fail to come to repentance or whether He only wants *those chosen* to come to repentance—is not the issue here at all. Instead, the meaning is that God's patience in this text is toward those who have already repented and those who have not yet come to repentance, an interpretation governed by who his readers are.

The reassuring statement, "But the day of the Lord will come like a thief" (3:10), emphasizes the certainty of the event in a way not obvious to the English reader. The words "will come" stand at the *beginning* of the sentence in the Greek, the way the Greeks would show emphasis. To capture this idea the translators italicized the words for emphasis where they appear in good English order, so as to read, "But the day of the Lord *will surely come* like a thief."

The phrase "like a thief" means *unexpectedly*, at least to the scoffers and others without any such hope. The idea that Jesus comes secretly to "steal" believers out of the world in a so-called "secret rapture" is not the idea here. The expression "day of the Lord" does not refer to the Rapture anyway. Old Testament usage[1] of the expression points, instead, to a time of judgment upon the whole world, involved with the Seventieth Week of Daniel 9 and what many refer to as the "Tribulation period." Judgment is Peter's general subject throughout this letter.

A description of the Day of the Lord follows as a time during which "the heavens will pass away with a roar and the elements will be destroyed with intense heat, and the earth and its works will be burned up." Although it might be tempting to identify this description with the dissolution that leads to the new heaven and earth of Revelation 21:1, I am inclined to see it as an apt summary of the events of the Tribulation period in Revelation 6–16. Cataclysmic events that drastically alter the surface of the planet and affect the heavens themselves take place not only as judgment on the people on the earth but as preparation for the coming Millennium, which is described in such passages as Isaiah 30:1–10 as considerably different from life as we know it today. More common than this interpretation is another one held by perhaps a majority of premillennial commentators. This interpretation sees the destruction described in 3:10 as the same as found in 3:12, referred to there as the "day of God" and clearly called "new heaven and a new earth," more clearly identifying it with Revelation 21:1. I would agree that overall, the "day of the Lord" encompasses the period of the Tribulation as well as the Millennium, but I take the reference to "day of God" as the eternal state and distinct from the "day of the Lord." "Day of God" may be a more appropriate term for the eternal state following the Millennium in light of 1 Corinthians 15:24–28 where, at the end of the kingdom age or Millennium, the Son offers up the kingdom to the "One who subjected all things to Him, that God may be all in all."

The Old Testament and the Day of the Lord

The Lord will be exalted in that day (Isa. 2:11).

The day of the Lord is a day of reckoning (Isa. 2:12).

The day of the Lord will come with fury and anger (Isa. 13:9).

A day of distress will fall on Jacob and the nations on that day (Jer. 30:8).

Israel will not stand in the battle on the day of the Lord (Ezek. 13:5).

The day of the Lord is a time of doom for the nations (Ezek. 30:3).

The day of the Lord is destruction from the Almighty (Joel 1:15).

The day of the Lord is sure to come (Joel 2:1).

No one can endure the day of the Lord (Joel 2:11).

The sun and the moon will be darkened on the awesome day of the Lord (Joel 2:31).

Multitudes will come to the valley of decision on the day of the Lord (Joel 3:14).

The day of the Lord will be a day of darkness (Amos 5:18, 20).

The day of the Lord will fall on all of the nations (Obad. 1:15).

The great day of the Lord will be a day of wrath and distress (Zeph. 1:14-18).

God will gather the nations against Jerusalem on the day of the Lord (Zech. 14:1-4).

Peter declares:

Since all these things are to be destroyed in this way, what sort of people ought you to be in holy conduct and godliness, looking for and hastening the coming of the day of God, on account of which the heavens will be destroyed by burning, and the elements will melt with intense heat! But according to His promise we are looking for new heavens and a new earth, in which righteousness dwells (3:11–13).

Peter's point is that the world as we know it is not one with which we are to become closely linked in terms of lifestyle or values, because it is under God's judgment and therefore is temporary. The fact that we should not only be "looking for" this day but also "hastening" its coming is an arresting statement. How can we "hasten" that day, one that is fixed in the eternal plan of God? My answer to that question is influenced by the nature of the delay and God's unwillingness that any of the elect should perish (3:9). We are instruments of God's patience during this age, and we "hasten" it by being efficient instruments of bringing the elect to repentance. The coming of the Lord may be a fixed date in the eternal counsels of God, but we are the means to its end.

A final point to observe in this section is the fact that "righteousness dwells" in the new heavens and earth. This expression implies the permanency and pervasiveness of righteousness, something to look forward to indeed.

Study Questions

1. Since the destruction of the Day of the Lord is certain to happen, how should believers live?

2. And what should children of God be looking for as they live out their life in a troubled world?

3. What is the basis of the promise of new heavens and a new earth?

4. According to Peter, what will most characterize the new heavens and the new earth?

5. What could Peter have meant by "the elements will be destroyed with intense heat"?

6. In this section Peter ties Christian conduct to the fact of this coming final earthly judgment. He says twice that believers should be anticipating this happening by "looking for . . ." In what way could children of God be longing for the new heavens and new earth?

CHAPTER 36

Final Appeal to Be Faithful to Our Knowledge of God
2 Peter 3:14–18

Preview:

The promises Peter refers to in the preceding verses should cause the believer in Christ to be living a peaceful, spotless, and blameless life. Paul is an example of God's patience toward one who needed the salvation offered by Christ. Though Paul writes deep things in his letters, and some who are untaught and unstable distort them, nevertheless his letters are comparable to "the rest of Scripture." Believers are urged to further grow in the grace and knowledge of the Lord and Savior Jesus Christ.

With a final transition word—"therefore," a Greek conjunction used only in 1:10 and 1:12 besides here—Peter concludes his letter with an appeal for his readers "to be found by Him in peace, spotless and blameless" (3:14). The use of the verb "be found" suggests the idea that upon Jesus' appearance at the Resurrection and translation (1 Thess. 4:13–18), Jesus will find them in this condition. "Spotless and blameless" are the opposites of two corresponding words used earlier of the false teachers (2:13). They are also two words used of Christ in 1 Peter 1:19. "Spotless" is morally pure, and "blameless" is free from any rebuke at the Judgment Seat of Christ. Inasmuch as sin is likely for all of us, I would view this appeal as something to aim for, though none of us will achieve perfection.

Peter asks his readers to "regard the patience of our Lord *to be* salvation" (3:15). In light of the previous discussion of the patience of the Lord in not desiring that any fail to come to repentance—the explanation for the two-thousand-year delay in the coming of the Lord—I would say that to "regard the patience of the Lord as salvation" is to be willing to wait patiently for the Lord, realizing that He is using this delay to bring salvation to those who remain unrepentant.

To support this advice, Peter invokes the words of Paul, whom he refers to as "our beloved brother." This way of speaking of Paul goes contrary to many modern theories that Paul and Peter were at odds with one another, a viewpoint that arises at least partly out of the scene Paul describes in Galatians 2:11–14. However, Paul claims that all the Jerusalem apostles agreed with his gospel in the same letter (2:7–10). Godly men can disagree, but godly men will not bear grudges.

Since Peter makes only a general reference to the writings of Paul, we cannot be certain of precisely what writing of Paul he has in mind.[1] Since there is no extensive passage in the Pauline corpus on the patience of God, especially as it pertains to the delay of the Lord's coming, Peter probably had in mind the general topic of "salvation," which would embrace a large body of Pauline writings. Furthermore, since the subject is covered "in all his letters," it must be a broad one, and salvation is certainly a subject throughout Paul's letters. Such a statement as this would indicate the solidarity between Peter and Paul, a fact that needed to be publicized for the benefit of the church at large.

Peter acknowledges also that Paul's letters speak "of these things, in which are some things hard to understand" (3:16). Whether this has to do with Paul's style or content is also difficult to say. By "style" I mean the difficulty in determining in the brevity of Paul's expressions where a sentence ends as well as in understanding some of his statements in their context. By "content" I mean the profundity and complexity of Paul's thought. Either of these or a combination of them would qualify for Peter's description.

Understanding Paul is one thing, but distortion is another, and those who distort his writing are "untaught and unstable." As an example, I think of the way, some time later in history, a man like Marcion, regarded as a heretic by the church as a whole, totally misunderstood Paul's concept of the "flesh" in its several ramifications. As a Gnostic, Marcion taught that Paul was talking about the literal body as something essentially sinful rather than the tendency of sin that lies within every human being. Gnostics viewed everything material as basically sinful, something to be rigidly denied and ultimately escaped from. This Peter adds, is done "to their own destruction," an ominous pronouncement that refers both to the effects of false teaching on the perpetrators themselves as well as their eventual destiny in hell.

The most significant statement that Peter makes about Paul's writings, however, is extremely valuable in reconstructing just how the New Testament's twenty-seven books became recognized as authoritative or inspired. Peter classifies Paul's writings as "Scripture" in the statement, "the rest of the Scriptures" to which he compares them. I have suggested already that possibly all of Paul's writings had been written by this time, and this allows us to include writings of the New Testament in both Paul's teaching about Scripture in 2 Timothy 3:16–17 as well as that of Peter in this letter (2 Pet. 1:20–21). This means that when a writing of the New Testament was first received, it was recognized as inspired at that time, not after years of indoctrination and the influence of leaders of the church at ecumenical councils.

In view of "untaught and unstable" people who distort the Scriptures, Peter's final admonition appears in 3:17–18. "Knowing this beforehand"—that is, knowing this danger of the distortion of the Word of God—Peter warns, "Be on your guard so that you are not carried away by the error of unprincipled men and fall from your own steadfastness, but grow in the grace and knowledge of our Lord and Savior Jesus Christ." Christians need to become alert and discerning every time they listen to teaching or a sermon. They need to grow in grace—God's power to understand, live, and serve—as well as in the knowledge of Christ to avoid being victimized by men who have no qualms about distorting and perverting the truth of Scripture. The hazard is that they may fall from their steadfastness—note that he does not say, "fall from their faith." Sound doctrine promotes sound and stable living. False doctrine produces instability for believers, a state of confusion, and frustrated living.

The latter part of verse 18 turns into a benediction: "To Him *be* the glory, both now and to the day of eternity. Amen." All biblical admonitions imply the work of the indwelling Holy Spirit, so that godly living and growth are to the glory of God, not to our own glory.

Study Questions

1. Do you believe most Christians today really long for and look for the consummation of the world and eternity with Christ Jesus?

2. What would cause Christians today to forget about His return?

3. What should believers guard against?

4. How does the child of God grow in grace and in the knowledge of the Lord?

5. How can Christ *now* receive glory?

Bibliography

Adamson, J. B. *The Epistle of James.* New International Commentary on the New Testament. Grand Rapids: Eerdmans, 1976.

Barbieri, Louis A. *First and Second Peter.* 2D ed. Chicago: Moody Press, 1980.

Barclay, William. *The Letters of James and Peter.* The Daily Study Bible. 2D ed. Philadelphia: Westminster, 1960.

Bauckham, Richard. *Jude, 2 Peter.* Word Bible Commentary. Waco, Tex.: Word, 1983.

Bear, F. W. *The First Epistle of Peter.* Oxford: Blackwell, 1947.

Best, E. *1 Peter.* New Century Bible. London: Oliphants, 1971.

Blum, Edwin A. *2 Peter.* Expositor's Bible Commentary. Vol. 12. Edited by Frank Gaebelein. Grand Rapids: Zondervan, 1981.

Burdick, D. W. *James.* Expositor's Bible Commentary. Vol. 12. Edited by F. E. Gaebelein. Grand Rapids: Zondervan, 1981.

Calvin, John. *The Epistle of Paul the Apostle to the Hebrews and the First and Second Epistle of St. Peter.* Grand Rapids: Eerdmans, 1963.

Cranfield, C. E. B. *The First Epistle of Peter.* London: SCM, 1950.

Davids, Peter. *Commentary on the Epistle of James.* New International Greek Testament Commentary. Grand Rapids: Eerdmans, 1982.

Davids, Peter H. *The First Epistle of Peter*. New International Commentary on the New Testament. Grand Rapids: Eerdmans, 1990.

Green, Michael. *The Second Epistle General of Peter and the General Epistle of Jude.* Tyndale New Testament Commentary. Grand Rapids: Eerdmans, 1968.

Grudem, Wayne. *The First Epistle of Peter.* Tyndale New Testament Commentary. Grand Rapids: Eerdmans, 1988.

Hiebert, D. E. *The Epistle of James: Tests of a Living Faith.* Chicago: Moody Press, 1979.

———. *First Peter: An Expositional Commentary.* Chicago: Moody Press, 1984.

Hillyer, Norman. *1 and 2 Peter, Jude.* New International Bible Commentary. Peabody, Mass.: Hendrickson, 1992.

Hort, F. J. A. *The Epistle of St. James: The Greek Text with Introduction, Commentary as far as Chapter IV Verse, and Additional Notes.* London: Macmillan, 1909.

Hubbard, D. A. *The Book of James: Wisdom That Works.* Waco, TX: Word, 1980.

Kelly, J. N. D. *A Commentary on the Epistles of Peter and of Jude.* Harper's New Testament Commentaries. New York: Harper & Row, 1969.

Kistemaker, S. J. *The New Testament Commentary: Exposition of the Epistle of James and the Epistles of John.* Grand Rapids: Baker, 1986.

Lloyd-Jones, D. M. *Expository Sermons on 2 Peter.* London: Banner of Truth, 1983.

Martin, Ralph A. *James.* Word Biblical Commentary. Vol. 48. Waco, TX: Word, 1988.

Mayor, J. B. *The Epistle of St. James. The Greek Text with Introduction, Notes and Comments.* 1897 reprint. Grand Rapids: Zondervan, 1954.

Mayor, Joseph B. *The Epistle of St. Jude and the Second Epistle of St. Peter: Greek Text with Introduction.* Grand Rapids: Baker, 1979.

Michaels, J. Ramsey. *1 Peter.* Word Biblical Commentary. Waco, TX: Word, 1988.

Moo, Douglas. *James.* Tyndale New Testament Commentary. Rev. ed. Grand Rapids: Eerdmans, 1987.

Motyer, J. A. *The Message of James.* The Bible Speaks Today. Downers Grove, IL: InterVarsity Press, 1985.

Mounce, Robert H. *A Living Hope: A Commentary on 1 and 2 Peter.* Grand Rapids: Eerdmans, 1982.

Plummer, Alfred. *The General Epistles of St. James and St. Jude.* New York: A. C. Armstrong, 1903.

Ropes, J. H. *A Critical and Exegetical Commentary on the Epistle of St. James.* International Critical Commentary. Edited by C. A. Briggs, S. R. Driver, and A. Plummer. Edinburgh: T. & T. Clark, 1916.

Selwyn, E. G. *The First Epistle of St. Peter.* London: Macmillan, 1949.

NOTES

Chapter 1—Background of James

1. Henry Clarence Thiessen, *Introduction to the New Testament* (Grand Rapids: Eerdmans, 1958), 272.

2. Ibid., 274.

3. Everett F. Harrison, *Introduction to the New Testament* (Grand Rapids: Eerdmans, 1974), 383–84.

4. John MacArthur, *James* (Chicago: Moody Press, 1998), 1–2.

5. R. C. H. Lenski, *The Interpretation of the Epistle to the Hebrews and the Epistle of James* (Minneapolis: Augsburg, 1966), 578.

Chapter 2—Faith Tested by Trials

1. E. Beyreuther and G. Finkenrath, *"chairo,"* in *Dictionary of New Testament Theology,* ed. Colin Brown (Grand Rapids: Zondervan, 1977), 2:359.

2. *Heart* in the Old Testament is the most comprehensive term for the inner person and seems to include mind, emotions, and decisions of the will. See Andrew Bowling, "heart" in *Theological Wordbook of the Old Testament,* ed. Gleason Archer and Bruce Waltke (Chicago: Moody Press, 1980), 1:466–67.

3. This transition particle (Greek, *de*) is not translated in the NIV, and this may reflect the view of those translators as well as a number of commentators that a new subject begins here. This, in my opinion, is not good exegesis or faithfulness to the original text.

Chapter 3—Faith Tested by Temptation

1. The Greek word here is used generally in the New Testament in the case of very serious theological error. See W. Gunther, *"planao,"* in *Dictionary of New Testament Theology,* ed. Colin Brown (Grand Rapids: Zondervan, 1976), 2:457–61.

2. This is true even for those who have the gift of celibacy. The God-ordained celibate simply has the gift to control that drive and thus remain single.

3. In Jewish thought, something that permeates the letter of James, light is always associated with good, while darkness and shadows are associated with evil.

Chapter 4—Faith Authenticated by Obedience

1. Many manuscripts actually have a different word here, the Greek *hoste,* which means "thus." The KJV follows this reading. Many other manuscripts have the word *iste,* which means, "you know," the reading followed by NASB, NIV, and most other modern versions. They reason that since the two Greek words differ in merely one letter of the alphabet, it would be very easy for a copyist to change it and that the more likely word in the original would have been "you know" rather than "thus." See Bruce Metzger, *A Textual Commentary on the New Testament* (Stuttgart: United Bible Societies, 1975), 680.

2. Here is a word of wisdom from one who is a perennial offender in the matter. Men need to listen to their wives the way James is recommending.

3. Greek, *threskia.*

Chapter 5—Faith Authenticated by Brotherly Love

1. The italics are in the NASB and reflect the translators' policy of showing when they are supplying words that are not in the Greek text but are implied and necessary to make good sense.

2. The NASB is quite literal, while the NIV offers a more "dynamic equivalent" at this point and translates "do not hold your faith" with the words, "as believers."

3. Greek *prosopolamxiais,* a compound of "face" and "to receive."

4. The unusual word James uses for "assembly" is the Greek *suna-goge*, from which English derives its word *synagogue*. Though the word is a synonym for the Greek *ekklesia* or English *church*, *suna-goge* is never used in the rest of the New Testament to designate the Church. As indicated in the introduction, the use of the word here in James attests to James's early composition.

5. Note that in his instructions to Timothy for dealing with the rich among the Ephesians (1 Tim. 6:17–19), Paul does not condemn wealth as such, merely the danger of covetousness.

6. I am using the word *Law* in the more narrow sense of the Law of Moses (hence I have capitalized it), although the principle here would be applicable to any kind of law system.

Chapter 6—Faith Authenticated by Works

1. The word *Shema* is the Hebrew for "Hear" in "Hear, O Israel!"

2. For the various meanings of "to justify" (Greek, *dikaioō*), see W. F. Arndt and F. W. Gingrich, *A Greek-English Lexicon of the New Testament and Other Early Christian Literature* (Cambridge: Cambridge University Press, 1967), 196.

3. The word is *eteleiothe*, the aorist passive of *teleioō*, "to make perfect" or "complete" or "reach a goal."

4. The Hebrew word thus translated can also be rendered "innkeeper," but prostitution and innkeeping often went together in the ancient world.

Chapter 7—Faith Demonstrated by Controlling the Tongue

1. This assumes a scientific creationist position in which dinosaurs are believed to have been contemporary with humankind from creation to the flood of Noah and beyond, a position I prefer because it allows a literal interpretation of the Creation account of Genesis.

Chapter 9—Faith Demonstrated by Hostility to the World

1. There is no explicit passage in Scripture or known noncanonical books precisely like this. Therefore, James is probably expressing a general teaching from Old Testament Scripture of God's jealousy for his people.

2. The NIV reads, "Or do you think Scripture says without reason that the spirit he caused to live in us envies intensely?" If NIV is correct, of course, then there is no reference in James to the Holy Spirit.

Chapter 10—Faith Demonstrated by Submission to God's Will

1. In spite of the scholarly opinion against it, I take a position with many of the Church fathers in the view that this passage in Isaiah as well as the other in Ezekiel 28:12–15 pertain ultimately to Satan. Most modern scholarship interprets these two passages as "oriental boasting" on the ruler's part or sarcasm on the prophet's part, but I believe they are to be understood literally, and that makes it impossible to see the earthly rulers as the subject throughout. Satan lies behind evil earthly rulers, and we get a glimpse of him as the revelation penetrates behind the earthly to the cosmic ruler that incites their deeds.

Chapter 12—Faith Demonstrated by Patience in Trials

1. Those who make no such dispensational distinction between the assembly in the air and the return to earth find the generic nature of the word *parousia* and its applicability to either rapture or return an argument that they are part of the same event with no distinction between them. The distinction, therefore, cannot be sustained on grounds of the meaning of the word *parousia* but must be done so on other hermeneutical grounds, and this is a fact accepted by all dispensationalists.

2. Even Douglas Moo, a posttribulationalist who does not believe in the imminency of the Rapture as I have defined it, regards this as a statement of imminency (*James*, Tyndale New Testament Commentaries (Grand Rapids: InterVarsity Press, 1985), 170.

3. The word *rain* is not in the Greek text but is supplied by the translators. The expression "early and latter" always signified rain to people in Palestine.

4. This text therefore would serve as evidence of the time of this judgment to be following the Rapture, since 1 Corinthians 3 and 2 Corinthians 5 give no hint about time.

Chapter 13–Faith Demonstrated by Powerful Prayer

1. W. F. Arndt and F. W. Gingrich, *A Greek-English Lexicon of the New Testament and Other Early Christian Literature* (Cambridge: Cambridge University Press, 1967), 115.

2. The appearances of this term in the letter of James proves that this office existed very early in the Church, contrary to the opinions of some who think church organization to any extent did not exist until the second century.

3. Arndt and Gingrich, *Greek-English Lexicon*, 34.

4. It is interesting to note that further substantiation of a ceremonial purpose is found in the Roman Catholic sacrament of extreme unction, or last rites, which is based partly on this text. Of course, that sacrament is not for healing as this text clearly states, but the religious nature of the anointing is seen as a very ancient understanding of the text, and that is important.

5. A literal word-for-word order in English illustrates the difficulty: "very is strong a prayer of a righteous man being made effective."

Chapter 14–Faith Demonstrated by Restoring the Erring

1. Interpreting equivocal salvation passages in light of unequivocal salvation passages can be explained as follows: One unequivocal passage is Romans 8:28–39, where Paul discusses unconditional justification. If justification is indeed unconditional, then true believers cannot lose their salvation. An equivocal salvation passage is Hebrews 6:4–8, wherein one interpretation would yield the possibility of believers losing their salvation. The principle to which I refer is to interpret Hebrews 6:4–8 in light of Romans 8:28–39, in other words, to prefer an interpretation that maintains the believer's ultimate perseverance in salvation. To do this preserves the principle of noncontradiction. If the believer's justification is unconditional, we should look for an interpretation of Hebrews 6:4–8 that will not contradict that principle.

Chapter 15–Background of First Peter

1. Martin Luther, *Commentary on Peter and Jude* (Grand Rapids: Kregel, 1990), 10.

2. Simon J. Kistemaker, *Peter and Jude* (Grand Rapids: Baker, 1993), 17.

3. Ibid., 20.

Chapter 16—The Resource of Salvation

1. I am aware of the "problem" of this view. According to this view, people are saved only by the plan and predetermined will of God. No reason is given why God does not elect all. Perhaps we should ask instead, Why does He elect any? He has no obligation to save anyone, yet in grace He elects some.

2. I need to point out, however, that such unconditional election follows logically from a belief in the total depravity of humankind. God, in other words, could never "foreknow" anyone being saved if all are totally depraved; that is, their wills are totally in bondage to sin with no inclination to seek for God or respond with faith from within them. One's view of depravity will either result in a view of unconditional election or election conditioned on foreseen faith. If you allow for humanity's ability to exercise faith apart from effectual grace, the alternative to total depravity that might be described merely as "depravity," then foreknowledge of faith can be the basis for election. If you view passages like Romans 3:11 as teaching total depravity—the will is totally contrary to God—then you have to acknowledge that effectual grace is necessary for anyone to come to faith.

3. It is my opinion that Jesus became the Son at the time of the Incarnation. Among orthodox theologians the dominant view is that Jesus was eternally the Son, a view largely based on Psalm 2:7. Probably the majority of the Church fathers who said anything about this issue took the view that Christ's sonship was eternal. I believe Jesus is the eternal Second Person of the Godhead and that His sonship was eternal in the mind of God, so such an opinion does not deny His deity. I prefer to refer to Jesus prior to the Incarnation as the eternal Word, the concept provided by the prologue of the fourth Gospel. I take Psalm 2:7 as prophetic, not necessarily a statement of eternal sonship.

4. See Marvin R. Vincent, *Word Studies in the New Testament* (Grand Rapids: Eerdmans, 1965), 4:431.

5. I prefer the term *perseverance,* the "P" of the acronym TULIP, or five points of Calvinism. The common Western expression "security of the believer" sounds a bit passive to me, and believers are everything but passive in the maintenance of their salvation, even though their ultimate salvation is totally in the hands of God.

6. I use the term *mystery* in a less technical sense than the biblical use of the word. The biblical usage throughout both New and Old Testaments means "something not revealed before this revelation." In my use it means something not fully understood, as I explain in the text that follows.

7. The pronoun translated "what person" is probably neuter, not masculine, thus "what time."

Chapter 17—The Resource of Godly Behavior

1. One of the first principles of biblical interpretation is to ignore the man-made chapter and verse divisions. The original Hebrew and Greek contained no chapter, verse, or word divisions. Everything was run together in a continuous, unbroken line, conforming to the practice in ancient literature.

Chapter 18—Relationships toward Those Who Reject the Believer

1. When I refer to "this chapter," I refer to the section that constitutes a "subject," in this case, 2:4–12. Each of the chapters in this commentary, therefore, begins a new subject. Scriptural divisions like the chapter are man-made and subject to question, as are mine. The next smaller unit is the paragraph that constitutes an "idea." The smallest unit is the sentence that constitutes a "thought." The largest division—when a book has an overall theme—is the entire book or letter itself.

2. Reprobation is the election of some to be eternally lost and serves as the corollary in the strict Calvinistic system to election to salvation. The alternative to this in the moderate Calvinistic system is "preterition," the act by which God allows the nonelect to carry out their depraved will, leading ultimately to eternal punishment.

3. Those who advocate "replacement theology" are usually amillennial or postmillennial in their views of Revelation 20 and inter-

pretation of the thousand-year kingdom. Their emphasis is on *continuity* between the Old and New Testaments, whereas dispensationalists like myself see more in terms of *discontinuity*. In addition to this, there is a tendency to take a nonliteral hermeneutic when it comes to eschatology and matters concerning the relationship between Israel and the Church. This approach to a nonliteral hermeneutic is not necessarily arbitrary on their part. They make a case for the idea that Israel's rejection by God and loss of the national kingdom promises and the transfer of the kingdom promises to the Church that includes believing Jews, so that God's ancient promises to Israel in the Old Testament will nevertheless be spiritually fulfilled to those Jews who believe during the present age.

Chapter 19—Relationships toward Worldly Authorities

1. None of these terms—"free men," "all men," "brotherhood"— are gender-specific in the Greek. Perhaps better translations in light of the modern gender-specific controversy should be "free people," "all people," and "brethren," although the word *brethren* may seem archaic to some.

Chapter 20—Relationships toward Worldly Masters

1. This involves a principle of hermeneutics that recognizes progress in the Bible's way of dealing with cultural issues. It could be called "redemptive movement," in which the biblical reaction to current culture is always an improvement ("redemptive") to some degree and changes over time in harmony with progressive revelation. Sometimes the ideal ethic is established by creation order in Genesis, as is the case with the issue of the role of women, but becomes less than ideal due to the Fall, and finally is restored as in the case of the New Testament's view. In my hermeneutical system, the New Testament contains, at least in seed, the final redemptive form of the ethic. William J. Webb suggests the terminology "redemptive movement" in his book *Slaves, Women and Homosexuals: Exploring the Hermeneutics of Cultural Analysis* (Downers Grove, IL: InterVarsity Press, 2001). I take issue with Webb's theory that redemptive movement goes beyond the New Testament and improves on it. This creates the problem of

where one places limits on what the future ethic should be. It goes beyond interpretation of the Bible and moves into speculation as to what is "redemptive." Instead, I believe the New Testament contains the final ideal ethic.

2. In modern translation philosophy, there are two competing schemes. One is called "formal equivalence," a more-or-less literal word-for-word translation whereby a word may often be translated the same throughout the Bible. Translations that follow this philosophy include the KJV and the NASB. The other is called "dynamic equivalence," an attempt to translate a biblical word or phrase with its closest modern idiomatic equivalence. The New Living Translation is an example of this. This latter approach is not exactly a paraphrase but comes close to that in some places. The NIV is something of a mixture of the above two philosophies with a leaning toward dynamic equivalence.

Chapter 21—Relationship with One's Spouse

1. The egalitarian (evangelical feminist) objection that "head" means "source," not "authority over," as has been traditionally understood, is asinine, even if there are a few cases of this usage outside the Bible. Here as well as in the Ephesian passage, Paul is talking about authority, not some sort of respect due to the husband based on the fact that Eve had her "source" in Adam.

2. J. Ramsey Michaels, *1 Peter* in *Word Biblical Commentary* (Waco, TX: Word, 1981), 157, cites D. L. Balch, *"Let Wives Be Submissive . . .": The Origin, Form, and Apologetic Function of the Household Duty Code* (Haustafel) *in 1 Peter.*

Chapter 22—Relationships in Summary

1. Albert Barnes, *Notes on the New Testament*, 14 Vols. (Grand Rapids: Baker, 1983), 13:165.

2. Simon J. Kistemaker, *Peter and Jude* (Grand Rapids: Baker, 1993), 130.

3. Robert Leighton, *Commentary on First Peter* (Grand Rapids: Kregel, 1972), 310–11.

Chapter 28—The Attitude of Submission to God

1. R. C. H. Lenski, *The Interpretation of I and II Epistles of Peter, the three Epistles of John, and the Epistle of Jude* (Minneapolis, MN: Augsburg, 1966), 224.

2. Simon J. Kistemaker, *Peter and Jude* (Grand Rapids: Baker, 1993), 198.

3. Frank E. Gaebelein, gen. ed., *The Expositor's Bible Commentary*, 12 Vols. (Grand Rapids: Zondervan, 1981), 12:250.

4. Robert Leighton, *Commentary on First Peter* (Grand Rapids: Kregel, 1972), 486

5. John F. Walvoord, Roy B. Zuck, eds. *The Bible Knowledge Commentary, New Testament* (Wheaton, IL: Victor Books, 1983), 856-57.

6. Thomas R. Schreiner, The New American Commentary, 38 Vols. *1, 2 Peter, Jude* (Nashville: Broadman & Holman, 2003), 245-46.

7. Ibid, 246.

Chapter 30—Background of Second Peter

1. Henry Clarence Thiessen, *Introduction to the New Testament* (Grand Rapids: Eerdmans, 1958), 287.

2. R. C. H. Lenski, *The Interpretation of I and II Epistles of Peter* (Minneapolis: Augsburg, 1966), 237.

3. Thiessen, *Introduction to the New Testament*, 290.

4. Ibid., 289.

5. Simon J. Kistemaker, *Peter and Jude* (Grand Rapids: Baker, 1993), 226.

Chapter 31—Life-Effects of Our Knowledge of God

1. Greek has no separate word for "lust" as English does for evil desire. The context always determines whether the Greek *epithumia*, "strong desire," is evil or good.

2. Greek *hupomone*, literally "the abiding under something."

3. A literal translation would be: "For these things being in you and abounding makes you not barren nor unfruitful in the Lord Jesus Christ."

Chapter 32—The Revelatory Source of Our Knowledge of God

1. This widely accepted tradition comes from one of the early Church fathers, Papias, who is quoted by the early Church historian Eusebius in *Eusebius: Ecclesiastical History*, Loeb's Classical Library, vol. 1, trans. Kirsopp Lake (Cambridge: Harvard University Press, 1926), 3.39.15. The quote reads, "Mark became Peter's interpreter and wrote accurately all that he remembered, not indeed, in order, of the things said or done by the Lord."

2. See Michael J. Wilkins and J. P. Moreland, eds., *Jesus Under Fire: Modern Scholarship Reinvents the Historical Jesus* (Grand Rapids: Zondervan, 1995), for an evaluation of the methods of the Jesus Seminar.

Chapter 33—The Possible Perversion of Our Knowledge of God

1. It is beyond the scope of this commentary to deal at length with this issue or to discuss the question of whether the gift of prophecy is for today or not. Wayne Grudem, *The Gift of Prophecy in the New Testament and Today* (Westchester, IL: Crossway, 1988), should be consulted as a presentation of the view that a kind of prophecy is active today but is not the same phenomenon as in the Old Testament. I myself hold to the "cessationist" view that some gifts like prophecy are no longer active, a view based on my interpretation of 1 Corinthians 13:8–10.

2. The Greek is *opoleias*, "destruction" in the genitive case and *apopleian* in the accusative case. See H. C. Hahn, "destroy," *The New International Dictionary of New Testament Theology* (Grand Rapids: Zondervan, 1975), 1:464.

3. It is my view as a "moderate" Calvinist that this statement about the false teachers and their ultimate destruction supports the view that in some sense Christ died for them, contrary to the stricter Calvinist view that Christ died only for the elect, those who are destined for salvation.

4. A. C. Bauer, W. F. Arndt and F. W. Gingrich, *A Greek-English Lexicon of the New Testament and Other Early Christian Literature* (Chicago: University of Chicago Press, 1957), 114.

5. The original Greek manuscript, judging by early copies that have been preserved, was not punctuated by commas, periods, and

semi-colons, nor by capitalized first words in the sentences. Early writing was one long, extended series of words unbroken by word divisions, verses, or chapters. Thus, a decision like this, agreed upon by most experts, is, though based on their judgment, probably valid.

6. The NASB upon which this commentary is based provides some of these "ifs" for us, although only verse 4 has an "if" in the original Greek. They are found, as you can see, in verses 6 and 7 but perhaps should have been inserted in verse 5 as well. Then in the beginning of verse 9, the "then" is inserted where interpreters believe it is implied, though the Greek does not contain it.

7. Some commentators assign this reference to the angels that fell to Genesis 6:2 with its mention of the sons of God and daughters of men that cohabited and produced a race of giants. My interpretation is determined by the fact that I connect Genesis 6:1–4 with the previous chapter as a summary of the genealogy involving the descendants of Seth, thus having nothing to do with angels.

8. The interpretation of the Isaiah and Ezekiel passages is not widely held anymore by most interpreters, but I attribute this shift away from an opinion held by some of the early fathers of the church as a hermeneutical shift away from literal or normal interpretation. Most modern interpretations are nonliteral, a tendency that makes dispensationalists like myself a vanishing breed.

9. Since evil spirits or demons in the world today are believed to be among the angels that fell with Satan, apparently not all the fallen angels are presently consigned to Tartarus.

10. This story of a dispute over the body of Moses by Michael and the devil is found in an apocryphal book, *The Assumption of Moses*, concerning which we have only fragments. This is reported by several Church fathers, Clement of Alexandria, Origen, and Didymus of Alexandria. Since the story does not appear in Deuteronomy or Joshua where we would expect, its authenticity is suspect. However, Jude is perhaps merely using it as an illustration without vouching for its historicity. My opinion, since Jude seems to be reporting it as a fact, is that it represents a true but extrabiblical tradition.

11. Peter does not have our modern domesticated pet in mind. In the Middle East at this time in history, dogs were generally wild and vicious, thus making them a good metaphor for false teachers.

Chapter 34—The Coming Denial of Our Knowledge of God

1. A literal translation could be, "For this is willfully concealed to them," and put into more idiomatic English, "They wish it to be so."

2. The classic work on this subject, of course, is John C. Whitcomb and Henry M. Morris, *The Genesis Flood: The Biblical Record and Its Scientific Implications* (Philadelphia: Presbyterian and Reformed, 1965).

Chapter 35—The Coming Vindication of Our Knowledge of God

1. See such passages as Isaiah 13:9–10; Ezekiel 30:1–3; Amos 5:20; Zephaniah 1:14; and Zechariah 14:1–7.

Chapter 36—Final Appeal to Be Faithful to Our Knowledge of God

1. Which writing or writings of Paul may be referred to here is complicated by the fact that we do not know precisely to whom Peter was writing. If Peter is writing, as I have suggested in the introduction, to Christians in a large geographical area like the Roman Empire during the middle 60s of the first century, most of Paul's writings had appeared, but we still would not know which one or ones these readers were aware of.

About the Author

William H. Baker is adjunct professor of theology and hermeneutics at The Moody Graduate School. He has taught Bible and theology at John Brown University, Philadelphia College of Bible, and for more than twenty-five years at the Moody Bible Institute. His other publications include *On Capital Punishment, In the Image of God,* and *Sanctification.* In addition, he is the author of several courses for the Moody Bible Institute External Studies Department and of numerous articles for *Moody Magazine, Decision,* and *Fundamentalist Journal.* Dr. Baker received his B.D. and Th.M. from Talbot School of Theology and his Th.D. from Dallas Theological Seminary. He is also currently the pastor of Grace Bible Church in Westfield, Wisconsin.

About the General Editors

Mal Couch is founder and president of Tyndale Theological Seminary and Biblical Institute in Fort Worth, Texas. He previously taught at Philadelphia College of the Bible, Moody Bible Institute, and Dallas Theological Seminary. His other publications include *The Hope of Christ's Return: A Premillennial Commentary on 1 and 2 Thessalonians, A Bible Handbook to Revelation,* and *Dictionary of Premillennial Theology.*

Edward Hindson is professor of religion, dean of the Institute of Biblical Studies, and assistant to the chancellor at Liberty University in Lynchburg, Virginia. He has authored more than twenty books, served as coeditor of several Bible projects, and was one of the translators for the New King James Version of the Bible. Dr. Hindson has served as a visiting lecturer at both Oxford University and Harvard Divinity School as well as numerous evangelical seminaries. He has taught more than fifty thousand students in the past twenty-five years.